The Modularity
of Emotions

The Modularity
of Emotions

Edited by
Luc Faucher and Christine Tappolet

© 2006 Canadian Journal of Philosophy

University of Calgary Press
Calgary, Alberta, Canada

ISSN 0229-7051   ISBN 978-0-919491-32-8

University of Calgary Press
2500 University Drive NW
Calgary, Alberta
Canada T2N 1N4
www.uofcpress.com

Library and Archives Canada Cataloguing in Publication

The modularity of emotions / edited by Luc Faucher and Christine Tappolet.

(Canadian journal of philosophy. Supplementary volume 0229-7051 ; 32)
Includes bibliographical references and index.
ISBN 978-0-919491-32-8

1. Emotions (Philosophy). I. Faucher, Luc, 1963- II. Tappolet, Christine III. Series.

B105.E46M64 2007   128'.37   C2007-906760-3

Cover photo courtesy of David Moll.
Cover design by Melina Cusano.

Printed and bound in Canada.

∞ This book is printed on acid-free paper.

Table of Contents

4. The Modularity of Particular Emotion Types

CANADIAN JOURNAL OF PHILOSOPHY
Supplementary Volume 32

Introduction: Modularity and the Nature of Emotions[1]

LUC FAUCHER AND CHRISTINE TAPPOLET

Are our experiences of fear, disgust, anger, joy, pride or compassion, for instance, more akin to states such as feelings or sensations, which are often thought to lack cognitive content, or are they more like perceptions or else like judgments? If emotions are informational or cognitive states, should we take emotions to be perceptions of a certain kind or else propositional states with a fully conceptual content? Are emotions passive states or are they at least to a certain extent subject to the will? Are some or all emotions basic, in the sense of being universally shared and innate or are they cultural constructions? Do some, or all, emotions threaten theoretical or practical rationality or are they, to the contrary, essential preconditions of rational thought and action? These are some of the many questions that emotion theorists have tried to answer.

Since the publication of Jerry Fodor's *The Modularity of Mind* (1983), a new set of questions, answers to which provide at least partial replies to the questions just mentioned, has emerged in the philosophy of emotions. Are emotions, or at least some of them, modular? This would mean, minimally, that emotions are cognitive capacities that can be explained in terms of mental components that are functionally dissociable from other parts of the mind. This is what is suggested by the often noticed conflicts between emotions and thought.

---

1 Our thanks to Frédéric Bouchard, John King, Mohan Matthen and Pierre Poirier for helpful comments.

For instance, Hume asks us to consider "the case of a man, who being hung out from a high tower in a cage of iron cannot forbear trembling, when he surveys the precipice below him, tho' he knows himself to be perfectly secure from falling, by his experience of the solidity of the iron, which supports him."[2] The emotion of fear this man experiences is characterized by recalcitrance with respect to thought. Since this is taken to be one of the hallmarks of modularity, one might be tempted to conclude that emotions, or at least some types of emotions, are modular (especially if you think that modules are natural kinds, because then the presence of one characteristic of modularity would be a reliable basis to infer the presence of the others).

Several authors have argued that emotional phenomena exhibit some of the properties Fodor attributes to modules (Charland 1995; Griffiths 1997; Öhman and Mineka 2001; Prinz 2004). Obviously, the answer to the question whether emotions are modular depends on what modularity is taken to be. The concept of modularity in which most recent discussions about the modularity of emotions have been framed is the one put forward by Fodor himself. However, different concepts of modularity, corresponding to different kinds of modular systems, have been proposed in the literature. In this introduction, we shall give a brief overview of the main concepts of modularity that have been offered in recent literature. After this, we turn to a summary of the papers collected in this volume. Our primary aim will be to explain how the modularity of emotion question relates to traditional debates in emotion theory.

1. Varieties of modularity concepts

As has been pointed out by Richard Samuels (2000), the term 'module' usually refers to functionally specific mental structures supposed to underlie particular cognitive capacities. But this general idea has been spelled out very differently, the term having been used to refer to quite different things. Though Samuels distinguishes between three kinds of modules, we think it useful instead to consider six kinds of modules.[3]

---

2 Hume (1739–40), Book 1, Part III, Section XIII. For a strikingly similar case, see Montaigne (1588), book II, chap. 12.

3 For a more complete list than Samuels,' see Segal (1996).

We do not hereafter propose a typology of modularity, but try instead of identify some of the ways in which the term is used. Thus, it should not come as a surprise that some uses of the term are compatible with or even encompass other uses.

(1). The first kind of modules are what could be called *boxological modules*. For instance, they are the boxes that cognitive scientists posit to explain a capacity when they proceed to a functional decomposition.[4] According to Fodor (2000), this form of modularity is a pretty diluted and non-contentious one. Almost everybody accepts the idea that cognitive capacities will have to be explained by invoking functionally individuated mechanisms (which Fodor prefers not to call "modules," 2000, 58). This form of modularity is also pretty neutral as to the properties of these mechanisms, so much of the work in cognitive science will consist in trying to discover what these are. In some cases, scientists will attribute to them properties that make them "modules" in a stronger (and more contentious) sense, sometimes not.

Given this, the emotional system itself, as well as the systems responsible for particular emotions, can be considered boxologically modular. But saying that is pretty uninformative as to what the properties of the emotion modules are. It might be considered only a heuristic step in the direction of a more thorough description of them.

(2). A more substantial form of module is one that Samuels calls *Chomskian modules* (see also Fodor 2000). They consist in domain-specific bodies of information (databases) or mental representations that account for a cognitive capacity. In order to distinguish such a body of information from a mere collection of beliefs about a particular domain, such as hockey, it is best to consider that Chomskian modules are both innate and inaccessible to consciousness. This is in any case how Chomsky himself conceived of the structures underlying our linguistic competence. According to Chomsky, our linguistic competence is based on an innate and consciously inaccessible system of mental states encoding the grammar of natural languages (1988).

---

4 Functional decomposition is an explanatory strategy in cognitive science according to which to explain a general capacity like vision or language, what one has to do is to identify component tasks that need to be performed in the system in order to produce the overall capacity.

Transposed to the case of emotions, the claim would be that our emotional reactions are: a) based on a body of information, which is b) innate and consciously inaccessible. What kind of information could that be? One quite natural possibility is to claim that the information in question concerns evaluative features of the world. Fear would depend on information concerning what is dangerous, grief on information concerning what constitutes a loss.[5] One important question is whether such information is innate (or 'prepared,' as it is often put in the literature; Öhman and Mineka 2001). It is clear that even if there are some things, such as spiders or loud sounds, that we are innately predisposed to fear, we are able to learn to fear other things.

(3). In his *The Modularity of Mind*, Jerry Fodor proposed the model of the architecture of the mind that is probably the most discussed in the literature on emotions. According to him, the mind is made up of three elements: sensory transducers (whose function is to convert physical stimulation into neural signals), input and output modules (whose function is to process the information coming from the sensory transducers or to prepare it for motor effectors), and a central system (in charge of analogical thinking, reasoning, and abduction). Modules in this model are essentially "processing devices" (a sentence parser would be a good example of such a device) that take representations specifiable in syntactic terms as input and produce representations as output according to a function (also specifiable in syntactic terms).[6]

Fodorian modules are mechanisms of cognitive processing characterized by the following properties[7] (see Fodor 1983; 1990):

---

5   This suggestion would seem to fit well with some versions of the so-called appraisal theory of emotions (Arnold 1960; Lazarus 1991; Scherer et al. 2001).

6   Chomskian modules and Fodorian modules are not incompatible; quite the contrary. More often than not, the innate databases are processed by an encapsulated cognitive mechanism. As Coltheart puts it: "processing modules will generally incorporate knowledge modules [a kind of Chomskian module] – the syntactic processor will have, as part of its internal structure, a body of knowledge about syntax" (1999, p. 118; see also Segal 1996, 144).

7   There is some question as to whether these characteristics are definitional or necessary conditions for the application of the term or if they are just properties that some paradigmatic cases of modules have (or tend to have as members of

1. *Domain-specificity*: A device is domain specific if its responses are restricted to a specific class of stimuli (Fodor has suggested recently that this is not enough for domain-specificity. According to him, 'domain specificity' "applies neither to information nor to processes, but rather to the way that the two of them interact"; 2000, 61). For instance, the visual system processes only visual inputs, whereas the auditory system is dedicated to auditory inputs.

2. *Mandatoriness*: The actions of the modules are automatic; they cannot be completely turned off voluntarily (you cannot directly control whether or not a module will process a given input). For instance, you cannot but process a sentence in English upon hearing it.

3. *Limited central access to the mental representations that modules compute*: As a rule, one can say that only the "final consequences of input processing are fully and freely available to the cognitive processes that eventuate in the voluntary determination of overt behavior" (Fodor 1983, 56). Therefore, the intermediate representations (for instance, in Marr's theory of visual perception, the representations forming the 2 ½ sketch) as well as the computational processes necessary to elaborate a representation of the distal cause of a proximal stimulation are in principle inaccessible to consciousness.

4. *Informational encapsulation*: Not all characteristics of modularity are of equal importance. For Fodor, informational encapsulation is the "heart of modularity" (2000, 63).[8] A module is informationally encapsulated if, in the processing of information, its access to beliefs, desires, and utilities is restricted (or, to put it differently, if it is limited to information that is in its database).[9] This character-

---

a natural kind). If such were the case, it would then be an empirical question to know if a particular module had all or some of these properties; see the fourth sense of modularity below for such a view. A related question is whether the characteristics admit of degrees or not. Fodor has explicitly stated his preference for the former (1983, 37).

8 Again, the fact that encapsulation is a central property of modules is shown in Fodor's definition of modules: "A module is, inter alia, an informationally encapsulated system – an inference-making mechanism whose access to background information is constrained by general features of cognitive architecture, hence relatively rigidly and relatively permanently constrained." (Fodor 1985 / 1990, 201)

9 "To a first approximation, nothing affects the course of computations of an encapsulated processor except what gets inside the capsule; and the more the

istic is also known as "cognitive impenetrability" and is meant to describe the fact that the modules are insensitive to what a person presumes, expects, or desires. As Coltheart (1999) remarks, being encapsulated is not incompatible with top-down processing, as long as the background information used in the top-down processing is restricted inside the module (the example being phoneme restoration, where phoneme identification has access to the lexical inventory of a subject language).

5. *Fast processing*: Because modules do not have to consult all the information available in the system, but only a restricted class of it (so they do not fall prey to the infamous 'frame problem'; Dennett 1987), they are able to compute faster.

6. *Shallowness of output*: Because of information encapsulation, the output of the modules has to be representations of basic categories. To put it differently, the representations produced by the modules cannot include background knowledge (or they would not be produced by modules); therefore, they have to be conceptually simpler (more basic) than representations produced with background knowledge. This is sometimes taken to mean that the output is non-conceptual in the sense that the modules generate information but not thoughts or beliefs (Carruthers 2006; also see Ogien *this volume*). However, it might just mean that the concepts involved in the production of the output are restricted to what is in the proprietary database of the module (see Charland *this volume*).[10]

7. *Fixed neural architecture*: From the neural implementation point of view, modules are often associated with a fixed neural architecture. Though modules don't have to be, there is reason to think that it

---

processor is encapsulated, the less information that is. The extreme case is, I supposed, the reflex; it's encapsulated with respect to all information except what's in the current input" (2000, 64).

10 Or again differently: "Since input systems are, by assumption, informationally encapsulated ... the categorizations such systems effect must be comprehensively determined by properties that the visual transducers can detect: shape, color, local motion, or whatever. Input systems ... are confined ... to categorizations which can be inferred, with reasonable accuracy, from such 'purely visual' properties of the stimulus." (Fodor 1983, 97)

might be advantageous for them to be localized in restricted brain regions.[11]

8. *Characteristic and specific breakdown patterns*: Given the fact that modules are functionally independent from each other (and that they might be localized in restricted brain regions), one should expect characteristic and specific breakdown patterns, where (after a lesion, for instance) one module would stop working while the working of others is left untouched. Cases like visual agnosia (inability to recognize familiar objects or faces) or language aphasia (difficulty in producing and comprehending language) are examples of the kind of very circumscribed breakdown that one should expect from a modular architecture.

9. *Characteristic pace and sequencing of ontogeny*: Work from developmental psychologists shows that modular competences have specific developmental patterns. For instance, children go more or less through the same stages while developing their theory of mind (for a review, see Saxe et al. 2004), stages that have nothing to do with the stages they go through while learning language or recognizing faces (*pace* Piaget). Moreover, it seems that the learning is robust, not easily perturbed by deprivation (or degradation) of environmental information. Both these characteristics suggest that development of modules is endogenously driven (i.e., they are innate) and that, therefore, environment acts at most as a trigger.

At first blush, emotions seem to have all the characteristics of modularity. If emotions are modules, then the question of the relation between emotions and beliefs or thoughts becomes clear. Recalcitrance, the fact that emotions are sometimes not affected by what we consciously believe or think about a situation, is explained by the modular nature of emotions (Griffiths 1990). And so the fact that some imaginary representations of situations trigger emotional reactions is to be expected if these representations are of the sort that usually trigger or initiate the effect or part of emotional modules, also known as the "affect program."

---

11 This is sometimes called "anatomical modularity." To restate what we just said, though some people have suggested it does, cognitive modularity does not imply anatomical modularity. (For a discussion on this issue, see Bergeron and Matthen, *this volume*, as well as Bergeron 2007.)

(4). A fourth kind of module is what might be called a *Darwinian module*. It is the kind of module favoured by evolutionary psychologists, such as Cosmides and Tooby (1995) and Pinker (1997). (See also Sperber 1994; 2002). The view of evolutionary psychologists is similar to the first notion of modularity (boxological modularity) we presented, except that they see modules as products of natural selection, that is, as solutions to adaptive problems that plagued the human species for eons. Since there were many different kinds of adaptive problems that humans faced in their environment, and, according to evolutionary psychologists these problems could not be solved adequately by a general problem solver, the solution that Mother Nature had to hit upon was to produce an architecture of the mind replete with specialists (modules). Evolutionary psychologists have thus been known for advocating a "massively modular view of the mind"; that is, a view of the architecture of the mind with "hundreds and thousands" of modules, where these are not limited to the periphery of the mind (as they are for Fodor), but also comprise some central capacities of the mind, like reasoning.

For evolutionary psychologists, modularity refers first of all to "functional specializations" or "evolved specializations" of the mind (Barrett 2006; Barrett and Kurzban 2006),[12] the properties of which cannot be specified in advance. It is therefore empirical research that should decide, for each module or specialization, what properties it has (some might be innate, some might be learned[13]; some might be fast, others slow[14]; some might be like Chomskian modules, some

---

12   "We have also used the term modularity to mean the tendency of biological systems to evolve functional specializations and the term module to refer to an evolved specialization, regardless of the degree to which it exists in a heavily policed informational quarantine or operates on information available to other procedures in the architecture. In this usage, we did not mean to invoke Fodor's particular and narrow concept of modularity, which appears to make information encapsulation a defining feature rather than (in our view) an occasional concomitant" (Tooby et al. 2005, 309).

13   For examples of the latter, see Karmiloff-Smith 1992.

14   "For example, being fast and automatic might be properties expected of a snake detection device, but not for those responsible for mate choice, decision making under uncertainty, or making inferences about social exchanges" (Machery and Barrett 2006, 16).

like Fodorian modules, others different from them both; for a similar point, see Coltheart 1999). In a way, evolutionary psychologists adopt a bottom-up approach, starting with a very minimal definition of modularity and venturing out to discover how modularity is realized in each case.

As a consequence of the view that modularity refers to "functional specializations" of the mind shaped by natural selection, it is expected that modules will be domain-specific[15] ("boxological modularity" is not in principle committed to that). The idea is that, because modules are designed to process information in a specialized way, they will also have specific "input criteria"; they will process only certain types or formats of information. For instance, a system specialized in recognizing faces will only accept visual information with certain configurational characteristics (so, in principle, it has access to all visual information, but only processes some of it; for a distinction between *access specificity* and *process specificity*, see Barrett 2005).

Finally, a Darwinian perspective on modularity allows one to distinguish between the proper and the actual domain of a module. The proper domain of a module is the domain that the module has been selected to deal with, for instance, face recognition. The actual domain is the domain with which the module is dealing now, despite not having necessarily been selected for it. For instance, it is said that the module in charge of face recognition is also used for car recognition by car experts (Gauthier et al. 2005). Many have argued (for instance, Duchaine et al. 2006) that car recognition cannot be the "proper domain" of the module, i.e., that it has not (cannot have been) selected because it was doing that.[16]

Cosmides and Tooby (2000) have suggested that emotions are Darwinian modules; that is, they are solutions to adaptive problems encountered by our hunter-gatherer ancestors.[17] The role of emotions,

---

15 Barrett and Kurzban (2006) see it as a *necessary consequence* of functional specialization (630).

16 Others have argued that car recognition depends on some more general ability that is applied to both faces and cars (see Bergeron and Matthen, *this volume*; and for a slightly different version of the same argument, Faucher et al., in press).

17 "Each functionally distinct emotion state – fear of predators, guilt, sexual jealousy, rage, grief, and so on – will correspond to an integrated mode of operation that

according to them, is to coordinate independent programs (programs governing perception, memory, learning, goal choice, etc.) to produce adaptive responses to certain classes of stimuli that are associated with reliable cues signalling their presence in the environment (bitter taste for poison or unknown faces looking straight at you for predators, for instance).

Thinking about emotions as Darwinian modules has also been instrumental in bringing to the fore what might be taken to consist in the rationality of emotions (like fear or anger) that look *prima facie* irrational or that appear to motivate irrational behaviour (Ketelaar and Au 2003; Cosmides and Tooby 2004; Haselton and Ketelaar, in press; see Jones, *this volume* and de Sousa, *this volume*).

(5). A fifth kind of module is what Segal (1996) calls a *diachronic module*. Some psychologists think that the mind has modules the function of which is to take input from the developmental environment and to build (as output) the modules we end up with as adults. Chomsky's "language acquisition mechanism" (LAM) would be such a diachronic module. In recent versions of his theory, the LAM is constituted by parameters that can be switched on or off, depending on the linguistic environment a child grows in. Diachronic modules in this model can thus produce limited variation in the 'synchronic modules,' depending of the developmental environment they are in (for instance, a French generative grammar if the child develops in a French environment).[18]

Many people have talked about emotional development, but their positions on the subject diverge. Some argue in favour of the innateness (and by this they mean the presence at birth) of the basic emotions, 'development' being characterized by the enlargement of the set of stimuli that can trigger the emotion and by the greater control

---

functions as a solution designed to take advantage of the particular structure of the recurrent situation or triggering condition to which that emotion corresponds" (Cosmides and Tooby 2000, 101).

18 Now, the end product of diachronic modules can be Chomskian modules or Fodorian modules or other sorts of modules evolutionary psychologists suspect might be out there. It can also be parametrized as suggested by Chomsky or by a more Fodorian computational algorithm or even by something entirely different, as long as it takes 'developmental inputs' and produces reliably adult modules as an output.

one can exercised on one's reactions (Ackerman et al. 1998). In this model, basic emotions do not develop (in this sense, there is no developmental module as such); they have to wait for the maturation of other mechanisms to get their adult form. As we mentioned earlier, some think that the 'appraisal mechanisms' can be set the same way grammars are thought to be set. If such is the case, you would get for each emotion a mechanism similar to the LAM, for instance, a Fear Acquisition Mechanism, a Disgust Acquisition Mechanism, etc. (for suggestions in this direction, see Öhman and Mineka 2001 for fear and Knapp 2003 for disgust). Finally, others see the development of emotions more as a contingent reconstruction depending on certain (physical, social and cultural) aspects of the environment as well as on more endogenous factors such as genes (see, for instance, Campos et al. 1996; for a review of the positions, see Faucher and Tappolet, in press). In this case, development would not be programmed the same way Chomsky claims language is, but it would still be modular in the sense that, if the environment is normal, the end result of development will be a particular static module. (Development would start with biases that direct development in a particular direction; see Faucher et al., in press.)

It is when talking about the appraisal mechanism of emotions that people are the closest to the kind of acquisition mechanism Chomsky was proposing for language. Indeed, some think that it would be advisable to posit a "fear-" or a "disgust-acquisition mechanism"; that is, mechanisms which would constrain the class of stimuli that could elicit the emotion (for instance, no one is disgusted by rocks and, likewise, people can more easily learn to fear snakes than flowers).

(6). The last kind of module we would like to describe can be called a *biological module*[19]: Talk about modules is not confined to psychology; it also takes place in biology. In this discipline, the term refers to the fact that organisms are composed of "quasi-independent parts that

---

19 We are aware that the term "biological" might be a bit confusing after using the term "Darwinian module." We used the term "Darwinian module," following Richard Samuels (2000), to designate the functionally specialized computational mechanisms posited by the evolutionary psychologists. These are a subclass of the biological modules we are talking about here. Of course, Chomskian and Fodorian modules can be biological modules as well.

are tightly integrated within themselves ... but develop or operate to a certain degree independently of each other" (Schlosser and Wagner 2004a, 1–2).[20] Modules are thus aspects of organisms on which natural selection can act,[21] as well as building blocks that can be used for construction of new traits (see Marcus 2006). For that reason, they are sometimes also called "evolution modules" (see Schlosser, 2004, for a review).

Biological modules can be characterized either as structures or as processes. Characterized as structures, modules are units the components of which have more intimate connections between themselves than with their surroundings (Schlosser and Wagner 2004b, 4). Cell types or organs (such as insects' segments or limb buds) are structural modules. Characterized as processes, modules are units that interact with each other in an integrated fashion, but that "behave relatively invariantly in different contexts" (Schlosser and Wagner 2004a, 4). Examples of such modules are gene regulatory networks and signalling cascades (like Hedgehog or Notch; for discussion of these and others, see chapters in Schlosser and Wagner 2004b). For instance, Notch pathway is thought to promote cell fate decisions, in early neurogenesis but also in "epidermal derivatives, various parts of the central nervous system, ... lymphocytes, gut, lung, and pancreas"

---

20 See also Griffiths (2007): "The fundamental notion of modularity in evolutionary developmental biology is that of a region of strong interaction in an interaction matrix. A metazoan embryo is modularized to the extent that, at some specific stage in development, it consists of a number of spatial regions that are developing relatively independently of one another.... Developmental modules are typically organized hierarchically, so that modules exist on a smaller physical scale within individual, larger scale modules. The individual cell represents one prominent level of this spatial hierarchy. At a lower level than the cell are particular gene control networks." (201)

21 In a recent paper, Arthur refers to these modules as "developmental cassettes," suggesting that they are "evolution modules" (units on which natural selection acts): "The concept of an interaction pathway – and the group of genes that encode its components – as comprising a sort of developmental cassette that can be treated as a unit of evolutionary change is an attractive one. Different kinds of evolutionary process involving such units can be considered, including their divergence in separate lineages after speciation and their co-option for a new developmental purpose within a lineage, possibly coincident with the appearance of new morphological structures such as limbs" (Arthur 2002, 762).

(Schlosser 2004, 532). In most of these different domains, it fulfils a similar function; that is, it mediates cell fate decisions among adjacent cells (though the fates are different depending on the domain).

Because it only recently became fashionable to talk about biological "modules" (see, for instance, the collections of Callebaut and Rasskin-Gutman, 2005, and Schlosser and Wagner 2004b),[22] not many philosophers or psychologists have been thinking of emotions explicitly in terms of biological modules. The exception is Paul Griffiths (in press; but see also Dumouchel, *this volume*, for a different way to think about emotions along the lines of biological modules), who, in a recent paper, argues that thinking in terms of biological (developmental) modules (that is, in terms of quasi-independent parts that are tightly integrated within themselves and that can operate independently of each other) might be a step forward in the direction of a sounder evolutionary psychology. In such a psychology, much emphasis would be put on homological traits (and descent with modification) instead of on analogical traits (as is the case with evolutionary psychology at the moment).[23] According to him, homological traits have more 'causal depth' than analogical traits. To illustrate, he uses emotion as an example:

> [S]uppose that two animals have psychological traits that are homologous – the basic emotion of fear in humans and fear in chimpanzees.... We can predict that, even if the function of fear has been subtly altered by the different meaning of 'danger' for humans and for chimps, the computation methods used to process danger-related information will be very similar and the neural structures that implement them will be very similar indeed.... [S]imilarities due to homology (shared ancestry) are notoriously deep – even when function has been transformed, the deeper you dig the more similarity there is in mechanisms. Threat displays in chimps look very different from anger in humans, but the more you understand about the facial musculature, the more similar they appear. The same is almost certainly true of the neural mechanisms that control them. (Griffiths, in press)

22　This is not to say that the idea of modularity has not been around for a while; see, for instance, Simon (1966) and Gould and Lewontin (1979).

23　For a very similar argument, see Matthen (1998).

*

There is a great variety of structures that have been called "modules." The six kinds of modules we have described here are not the only ones distinguished in the literature (see, for instance, Hurley 1998, as well as Sneddon, *this volume*, for a distinction between horizontal and vertical modules), but they are the main ones in the recent debate. As should now be obvious, the question whether emotions (the emotional system or else the systems responsible for particular emotional kinds) are modules thus splits into at least six sub-questions. The questions addressed by the contributions to this volume are: a) whether emotions are modules of this or that kind, and b) what this entails with respect to our understanding of emotional phenomena in general. We have thus divided the different chapters along the lines of three traditional questions in the philosophy of emotions, i.e., the rationality of emotions question, the question whether there are basic emotions, and the question whether emotions are perceptions. Finally, the last part of this volume puts together contributions that focus on the modularity of particular emotional phenomena, such as shame.

2. Emotion theory and the modularity question

The rationality of emotions. A question which is as old as emotion theory is that of the relationship between emotions and reason. Although emotions have traditionally been criticized because of what was considered their opposition to reason, the renewal of interest in the emotions in the last twenty years has come with a marked revalorization of emotion (de Sousa 1987; Lazarus 1991; Damasio 1994; Nussbaum 2001). Emotions have been claimed either different from, but necessary for, theoretical and practical reason, or else part and parcel of rational thought. This question of the rationality of emotions is taken up here by Karen Jones and Ronald de Sousa.[24] As Jones underlines, the claim that emotions are rational is far from obviously compatible with the view that emotions are modular in the Fodorian or Darwinian senses.

Karen Jones takes a critical, but sympathetic, look at what she calls the "new pro-emotion consensus." She starts with a detailed account of the different ways emotions are claimed to contribute to rationality,

---

24 Also see Lance and Tanesini (2004).

such as by improving our access to reason or by facilitating appropriate action. The question is how these feats are possible if emotions are encapsulated and mandatory. She claims that Tooby and Cosmides' evolutionary account of emotions fails to show how emotions contribute to practical rationality in the contemporary world and argues that, while Jesse Prinz's theory of recalibration might do so, this would be at the cost of having to abandon the claim that emotions are modular in the way vision is. She concludes that what is in fact needed to vindicate the pro-emotion consensus is more empirical work concerning the plasticity of emotions (on this, see Faucher and Tappolet, in press).

Ronald de Sousa encourages us to take what he calls "a political stance" with respect to the emotions. Though there is evidence that our emotions are modular in some ways, there might be reasons to resist this putative fact and even to seek to change it. Discussing the merit of the view that emotions are modular, de Sousa distinguishes between Fodorian modules and Darwinian modules, the latter being the kind of module that advocates of so-called basic emotions favour. He claims that, although some emotions, i.e., "basic emotions," are governed by Darwinian modules, this kind of modularity does not make them currently adaptive. But neither does it make them socially or individually useful, since such modules belong to what he calls the "first track" mind, which is largely encapsulated from reasoning. This is why de Sousa suggests that, instead of following either the biological evidence or our predictive and explanatory needs, our conception of the emotions should get its inspiration from art, something which would allow for a life of greater emotional richness.

Basic emotions. The idea that some emotions are more basic than others, the latter being constructed out of basic building-blocks, goes back at least to Descartes. Though following the work of psychologists, such as Paul Ekman (2007), and philosophers, such as Griffiths (1997), the thesis that some emotions, such as fear or disgust, are basic is often presented as a fact, it is still very controversial. This debate opposes psychologists with a biological bent (Ekman 1972; Friesen 1972; Tooby and Cosmides 1990), who claim that (at least some) emotions are pan-culturally and universally shared as well as innate, to social constructionists (Averill 1980; Armon-Jones 1986; Harré 1986), according to whom emotions are socio-cultural constructions that vary from one socio-cultural context to another (for some proposals as to how both approach could indeed be compatible, see Faucher 1999 and Mallon and Stich 2000). The claim that emotions, or at least certain of them are basic, is often associated with the view that these states are modular. The question whether there are basic emotions is central to the essays of James Russell, Robyn Bluhm and also Paul Dumouchel. It is noteworthy that all three contributors take issue with so-called basic emotion theorists.

In his contribution, psychologist James Russell launches an attack on basic emotion theory. He argues that this program is not well supported by empirical evidence. According to basic emotion theory, emotions are complex adaptive responses that provided solutions to problems our ancestors encountered. Given that one tenet of basic emotion theory is that emotions are modular – they are, mainly, fast, innate, mandatory, encapsulated responses – doubts pertaining to basic emotion theory also threaten the modularity thesis. Russell argues that emotions are in fact composed of separate component processes, such as what he calls "core affect," which is a neurophysiological state that is accessible through conscience and which is exemplified by the experience of feeling good or bad. The modularity question, he claims, is best asked with respect to each of these components. Core affect, in particular, is characterized by a certain amount of modularity. It is has a unique output; it is fast and innate; it is subject to an evolutionary explanation; it is produced by a dedicated neural processor; it is mandatory, i.e., automatic and involuntary; and it is largely, but not completely, encapsulated.

In her paper, Robyn Bluhm explores the idea that, contrary to what advocates of the basic emotions thesis suppose, there are discontinuities between emotions in animals and humans. These discontinuities, she claims, have important consequences for the extent to which we can consider human emotions as modules. Using work by developmental psychologists like Allan Schore as well as Stanley Greenspan and Stuart Shanker (on the role of social interaction in the development of emotional regulation) and by specialists of human brain evolution like Deacon, she argues that human emotions do not have most of the characteristics attributed to modules by Fodor – that is, they are not encapsulated, nor mandatory, nor are they subserved by a distinct neural basis, and finally, their development is not endogenous but depends on social interactions. Such a view, going strongly against the claim of phylogenic continuity central to the basic emotion theory, might open the door to a view quite similar to Russell's, a form of psychological constructionism, or even to a form of social constructionism.

Anne Jacobson is interested in showing that, despite the fact that some instances of certain emotions (like fear) are not "informationally encapsulated," some are. After considering phenomena like *emotional contagion* and what she calls "primitive emotions" (those emotions shared with other animals), she argues that these can be explained using a type of non-propositional (and non-conceptual) representation. Though they do not have all the properties traditionally attributed by philosophers to representations (i.e., intentionality), they play an important role in the explanation of the emotional phenomena just mentioned. Indeed, because they are exclusively explained by their causal properties, they are the right kind of representations to play a role in those emotional phenomena that are modular.

As we said earlier, Paul Dumouchel is exploring a radically different way of thinking about emotions. After explaining how biologists use the notion of modularity (see our sixth sense of modularity above, more specifically the view of modules as processes), he proposes that emotions could profitably be thought of as biological modules. He is particularly drawn by the fact that biological modules are often invoked to explain population-level phenomena (coordination), bypassing the level of the individual. He claims the same is true for emotions. According to him, there are sub-personal affective modules the function of which is the coordination of individuals. Dumouchel then explores how this way of thinking about emotions helps to resolve two difficulties that more traditional views of basic emotions cannot solve: the "sincerity problem" and the "indeterminacy problem."

Emotions as perceptions. The many analogies between emotions and perceptual experiences have led some emotion theorists to the view that emotions are a kind of perception (de Sousa 1987; Goldie 2000; Tappolet 2000; Prinz 2004). A striking fact is that both perceptual experiences and emotions allow for cases of conflict with higher cognition. In cases of perceptual illusion, as in the Müller-Lyer illusion, what we perceive conflicts with what we believe or know to be the case. The same kind of phenomena is present in emotions. As Hume noted, we often experience fear while we believe or even know that what we fear is neither dangerous nor fearsome. Thus, both perceptual experiences and emotions, or at least some of them, seem to share at least one important modularity characteristic: informational encapsulation. For the same reason, the evaluative content of emotions has been considered to be non-conceptual (Tappolet 2000; see also Tye 2006). Of the four contributions that address the question whether emotions are perceptions of a kind, three are favourable to a perceptual account of emotions, while the last one, that of Louis Charland, favours a more cognitivist model of emotions.

As he did before in his *Gut Reactions* (2004), Jesse Prinz defends a perceptual account of emotions in the tradition of James and Lange. In cognitive science, most people working on perception take it that it is to some degree modular. It is thus a small step to argue that, emotions being some kind of perception, they might also be modular. This is exactly what Prinz claims (more precisely, he suggests that emotions are perception of 'concerns' and they do so by registering the state of the body, that is, through introception). As he suggests, there is no big difference between getting mad and seeing red. But contrary to his 2004 book, Prinz changes his view on modularity and instead of adopting the Fodorian view on modularity, proposed his own, what he calls "quasi-modularity" (which drops the "informational encapsulation" characteristic of modules and replaces it by the notion of "stimulus dependency").

Andrew Sneddon's aim in his chapter is to compare two ways of thinking of emotional perceptions. The central difference between these models, which are grounded in fundamentally different views of the mind, concerns the notion of modularity. One model uses classic, Fodorian, modules, which are characterized by Susan Hurley as "vertical" and are contrasted with so-called "horizontal" modules (Hurley 1998). The other model uses these "horizontal" modules, which are modular in virtue of being content- and task-specific, but which are such that processing closer to the outputs of the systems can have feedback effects on processes closer to the inputs. Suggesting that these models can be applied to emotions, Sneddon discusses some empirical tests that might adjudicate between these two models of emotional perception.

In "Assembling the Emotions," Vincent Bergeron and Mohan Matthen argue that there is an important analogy between visual experience and the emotions. The first part of their paper consists in a general discussion on the best way to characterize modularity. After distinguishing between cognitive and anatomical modules, they argue that the identification of the functional contribution of anatomical modules to cognitive performance ought to be finer grained. This is because, they argue, the cognitive performances identified by psychologists as the product of cognitive modules are often carried out by multiple anatomical components cooperating to produce outputs. For instance, as they suggest, our visual experience consists of two different kinds of components, a representational component *plus* a "feeling of presence" that marks the experience as relating to a real object. In the same way, emotions would consist of a purely cognitive evaluative component *plus* what they call "a state of moral deixis," which locates the agent in his own world of values and makes an evaluation motivationally relevant. In support of this conception, they discuss evidence from frontal lobe lesions and their impact on emotional response and social cognition. They claim that the dissociations of emotional response and social cognition fail to show that emotion is separate from cognition and argue instead that the manner of entertaining value-content is separate from cognition itself and is located in a separate area of the brain.

In his piece, Louis Charland takes issue with the usual association of the modularity thesis and the perceptual conception of emotions. According to him, there are good reasons to consider the possibility that there may also be cognitive modular factors operating in emotion, especially in emotional pathologies like depression. Charland argues that what is lacking in contemporary discussions is an appreciation of the symbol-processing computational character of Fodorian modularity and a proper understanding of the import of the distinction between modularity and transduction. On the basis of Aaron Beck's cognitive theory of depression (Beck 1976), Charland argues that depression is a cognitive module.

Types of emotions. Consider the disgust you feel at the sight of a putrefied corpse, the fear you feel when watching a horror movie, the pride you experience after having made it to the end of a difficult hike or the love you feel for a close friend. Obviously, emotions are a varied lot.[25] This is why the modularity question (or more exactly the modularity questions, given that plurality of modularity concepts) should in fact be asked of each emotion type. It might well turn out that some emotions, such as fear and disgust, are modular in one sense of the word, while others, such as pride or love, are not. Two of our contributions focus of particular emotional phenomena.

Ruwen Ogien concentrates on an emotion that is more cognitively loaded, i.e., shame. To be ashamed of your big ears, for instance, you need to believe that you have big ears. According to many, you also need to believe that the size of your ears somehow speaks against you – maybe you consider that they violate some aesthetic canon, for instance. The question Ogien considers is whether the fact that shame necessarily involves such beliefs, as well as the fact that shame behaviour does not automatically result in typical behaviour, means that shame lacks modularity. He argues on the basis of a discussion of the cheater-detection module postulated by Cosmides and Tooby, that shame, as well as other cognitively loaded emotions such as pride or guilt, are so-called "conceptual modules." Such mechanisms lack strict encapsulation since they take complex social information as input. Ogien argues however that the modularity claim of emotions such as shame can be upheld even in the absence of automatic and predictable behavioural output. The reason for this is that the explanation of actions that such emotions provide are what Elster (1999) calls "explanations by mechanism"; that is, causal explanations which do not allow for predictions. Thus, we are not forced to give up the causal model that is essential to modularity.

In his contribution, Timothy Schroeder focuses on pleasure. In his view, pleasure and surprise are closely related, in the sense that pleasure (and displeasure) depends on a modular system the outputs of which are expectations. He argues that there is a modular system that forms what he calls "gut-level" expectations, which he distinguishes from beliefs about what is likely. This modular system would be responsible for an interesting portion of cases in which it seems to us

---

25 Things get even more complicated if moods, such as elation or depression, are added to the picture. See de Sousa's contribution for the modularity of moods.

that our feelings of pleasure and displeasure are not appropriate to our circumstances, and this in turn would provide the explanation for some of the phenomena that have led people to call the emotions "modular."

Bibliography

Ackerman, B. P., J.A.A. Abe, and C. E. Izard. 1998. Differential emotions theory and emotional development. In *What Develops in Emotional Development?*, eds. M. F. Mascolo and S. Griffin, 85–106. New York: Plenum Press.

Armon-Jones, C. 1986. The thesis of constructionism. In *The Social Construction of Emotions*, ed. R. Harré, 2–56. Oxford: Blackwell.

Arnold, M. B. 1960. *Emotion and Personality*. New York: Columbia University Press.

Arthur, W. 2002. The emerging conceptual framework of evolutionary developmental biology. *Nature* 415: 757–64.

Averill, J. R. 1980. A constructivist view of emotions. In *Emotion: Theory, Research and Experience*, Vol. I. *Theories of Emotion*, ed. R. Plutchnik and H. Kellerman, 305–339. New York: Academic Press.

Barrett, H. C. 2005. Enzymatic computation and cognitive modularity. *Mind and Language* 20: 259–87.

Barrett, H. C. 2006. Modularity and Design Reincarnation. In *The Innate Mind: Culture and Cognition*, ed. P. Carruthers, S. Laurence and S. Stich, 199-217. Oxford: Oxford University Press.

Barrett, H. C., and R. Kurzban. 2006. Modularity in cognition: Framing the debate. *Psychological Review* 113(3): 628–47.

Beck, A. T. 1976. *Cognitive Theory and the Emotional Disorders*. New York: Meridian.

Bergeron, V. 2007. Anatomical and functional modularity in cognitive science: Shifting the focus. *Philosophical Psychology* 20: 175–95.

Callebaut, W., and D. Rasskin-Gutman. 2005. *Modularity: Understanding the Development and Evolution of Natural Complex Systems*. Cambridge (Mass.): MIT Press.

Campos, J. J., R. Kermoian, and D. Witherington. 1996. An epigenetic perspective on emotional development. In *Emotion: Interdisciplinary Perspectives*, ed. R. Kavanaugh, B. Zimmerberg, and S. Fein, 119–38. Mahwah, NJ: Lawrence Erlbaum Associates.

Carruthers, P. 2006. The case for massively modular models of mind. In *Comtemporary Debates in Cognitive Sciences*, ed. Rob Stainton, 3–21. Oxford: Blackwell.

Charland, L. C. 1995. Feeling and representing: Computational theory and the modularity of affect. *Synthese* 105: 273–301.

Chomsky, N. 1988. *Language and Problems of Knowledge*. Cambridge (Mass.): MIT Press.

Coltheart, M. 1999. Modularity and cognition. *Trends in Cognitive Sciences* 3(3): 115–20.

Cosmides, L., and J. Tooby. 1995. From function to structure: The role of evolutionary biology and computational theories in cognitive neuroscience. In *The cognitive neurosciences*, ed. M. Gazzaniga, 1199-1210. Cambridge (Mass.): MIT Press.

———. 2000. Evolutionary psychology and the emotions. In *Handbook of Emotions* (2nd ed.), ed. M. Lewis and J. M. Haviland-Jones, 91–115. New York: Guilford.

———. 2004. Knowing thyself: The evolutionary psychology of moral reasoning and moral sentiments. In *Business, Science, and Ethics*. The Ruffin Series No. 4, ed. R. E. Freeman and P. Werhane, 93–128. Charlottesville, VA: Society for Business Ethics.

Damasio, A. 1994. *Descartes' Error: Emotion, Reason and the Human Brain*. New York: Gossett/Putnam.

Dennett, D. C. 1987. Cognitive wheels: The frame problem in AI. In *The Robots Dilemma: The Frame Problem and Other Problems of Holism in Artificial Intelligence*, ed. Z. Pylyshyn, 41-64. Norwood, NJ: Ablex Publishing.

de Sousa, R. 1987. *The Rationality of Emotion*. Cambridge (Mass.): MIT Press.

Duchaine, B. C., G. Yovel, E. J. Butterworth, and K. Nakayama. 2006. Prosopagnosia as an impairment to face-specific mechanisms: Elimination of the alternative hypotheses in developmental case. *Cognitive Neuropsychology* 23(5): 714–47.

Ekman, P. 1972. Universal and cultural differences in facial expressions of emotion. In *Nebraska Symposium on Motivation*, vol. 9, ed. J. Cole, 207–82. Lincoln: University of Nebraska Press, 1971.

———. 2007. *Emotions Revealed: Recognizing Faces and Feelings to Improve Communication and Emotional Life* (2nd ed.). New York: Henry Holt.

Elster, J. 1999. *Alchemies of the Mind*. Cambridge: Cambridge University Press.

Faucher, L. 1999. Émotions fortes, constructionnisme faible et élimination. *Philosophiques* 26(1): 13–35.

Faucher, L., and C. Tappolet. In press. Facts and values in emotional plasticity. In *Fact and Value in Emotion. Consciouness and Emotion series*, ed. L. Charland and P. Zachar. Amsterdam: John Benjamins

Faucher, L., P. Poirier, and J. Lachapelle. In press. The concept of innateness and the destiny of evolutionary psychology. *Mind and Behavior*.

Fodor, J. 1983. *The Modularity of Mind*. Cambridge (Mass.): MIT Press.

Fodor, J. 1985/1990. Précis of *The Modularity of Mind*. *Behavioral and Brain Sciences* 8: 1–42; reprinted in J. Fodor, *A Theory of Content and Other Essays*. Cambridge (Mass.): MIT Press, 195–206.

Fodor, J. 2000. *The Mind Doesn't Work that Way*. Cambridge (Mass.): MIT Press.

Friesen, W. V. 1972. Cultural differences in facial expressions in a social situation: An experimental test of the concept of display rules. Doctoral dissertation, University of California, San Francisco.

Gauthier, I., K. M. Curby, and R. Epstein. 2005. Activity of spatial frequency channels in the fusiform face-selective area relates to expertise in car recognition. *Affective Behavioral Neuroscience* 5(2): 222–34.

Goldie, P. 2000. *The Emotions: A Philosophical Exploration*. Oxford: Oxford University Press.

Gould, S. J., and R. Lewontin. 1979. The spandrels of San Marco and the Panglossian paradigm: A critique of the adaptationist programme. *Proceedings of the Royal Society*, London, B, 205: 581–98.

Griffiths, P. E. 1990. Modularity and the psychoevolutionary theory of emotion. *Biology and Philosophy* 5: 175–96.

———. 1997. *What Emotions Really Are*. Chicago: University of Chicago Press.

———. 2007. Evo-Devo meets the mind: Towards a developmental evolutionary psychology. In *Integrating Development and Evolution*, ed. R. Sanson and R. N. Brandon, 195-226. Cambridge: Cambridge University Press.

Harré, R. 1986. An outline of the social constructivist viewpoint. In *The Social Construction of Emotions*, ed. R. Harré, 2-14. Oxford: Blackwell.

Haselton, M., and T. Ketelaar. In press. Irrational emotions or emotional wisdom? The evolutionary psychology of affect and behavior. In *Hearts and Minds: Affective Influences on Social Cognition and Behavior*, ed. J. Forgas,. 8th Sydney Symposium of Social Psychology. New York: Psychology Press.

Hume, D., 1739–40/1973. *A Treatise of Human Nature*, ed. L. A. Selby-Biggy and P. H. Nidditch. Oxford: Clarendon Press.

Hurley, S. L. 1998. *Consciousness in Action*. Cambridge (Mass.): Harvard University Press.

Karmiloff-Smith, A. 1992. *Beyond Modularity: A Developmental Perspective in Cognitive Science*. Cambrdige (Mass.): MIT Press.

Ketelaar, T., and W. T. Au. 2003. The effects of guilty feelings on the behavior of uncooperative individuals in repeated social bargaining games: An affect-as-information interpretation of the role of emotion in social interaction. *Cognition and Emotion* 17: 429–53.

Knapp, C. 2003. Moralizing disgustingness. *Philosophy and Phenomenological Research* 66(2): 253–78.

Lance, M., and A. Tanesini. 2004. Emotion and rationality. In *New Essays in the Philosophy of Language and Mind, Canadian Journal of Philosophy*, suppl. vol. 30, ed. M. Ezcurdia, R. Stainton, and C. Viger, 275–95. Calgary: University of Calgary Press.

Lazarus, R. S. 1991. *Emotion and Adaptation*. New York: Oxford University Press.

Machery, E., and C. Barrett. 2006. Debunking *Adapting Minds*. *Philosophy of Science* 72: 232–46.

Mallon, R., and S. P. Stich. 2000. The odd couple: The compatibility of social construction and evolutionary psychology. *Philosophy of Science* 67(1): 133–54.

Marcus, G. F. 2006. Cognitive architecture and descent with modification. *Cognition* 101: 443–65.

Matthen, M. 1998. Biological universals and the nature of fear. *Journal of Philosophy* 95: 105–132.

Montaigne, M. de. 1588/1962. *Essais*, vol. I. Paris: Garnier-Flammarion.

Nussbaum, M. C. 2001. *Upheavals of Thought: The Intelligence of Emotions*. Cambridge: Cambridge University Press.

Öhman, A., and S. Mineka. 2001. Fear, phobias and preparedness: Toward an evolved module of fear and fear learning. *Psychological Review* 108: 483–522.

Pinker, S. 1997. *How the Mind Works*. London: Allen Lane.

Prinz, J. J. 2004. *Gut Reactions: A Perceptual Theory of Emotion*. New York: Oxford University Press.

Samuels, R. 2000. Massively modular minds: Evolutionary psychology and cognitive architecture. In *Evolution and the Human Mind: Modularity, Language and Meta-Cognition*, ed. P. Carruthers and A. Chamberlain, 13–46. Cambridge: Cambridge University Press.

Saxe, R., S. Carey, and N. Kanwisher. 2004. Understanding other minds: Linking developmental psychology and functional neuroimaging. *Annual Review of Psychology* 55: 87–124.

Scherer, K. R., A. Schorr, and T. Johnstone, eds. 2001. *Appraisal Processes in Emotion: Theory, Methods, Research*. Oxford: Oxford University Press.

Schlosser, G. 2004. The role of modules in development and evolution. In *Modularity in Development and Evolution*, ed. G. Schlosser and G. P. Wagner, 519–82. Chicago: University of Chicago Press.

Schlosser, G., and G. P. Wagner. 2004a. Introduction: The modularity concept in developmental and evolutionary biology. In *Modularity in Development and Evolution*, ed. G. Schlosser and G. P. Wagner, 1–11. Chicago: University of Chicago Press.

―――, eds. 2004b. *Modularity in Development and Evolution*. Chicago: University of Chicago Press.

Segal, G. 1996. The modularity of theory of mind. In *Theories of the Theories of the Mind*, ed. P. Carruthers and K. Smith, 141–57. Cambridge: Cambridge University Press.

Simon, H. 1966. *The Sciences of the Artificial* (3rd ed.). Cambridge (Mass.): MIT Press.

Sperber, D. 1994. The modularity of thought and the epidemiology of representations. In *Mapping the Mind: Domain Specificity in Cognition and Culture*, eds. L.A. Hirschfeld and S.A. Gelman, 39-67. New York: Cambridge University Press.

―――. 2002. In defense of massive modularity. In *Language, Brain and Cognitive Development: Essays in Honor of Jacques Melher*, ed. E. Dupoux, 47–57. Cambridge: Cambridge University Press.

Tappolet, C. 2000. *Émotions et Valeurs*. Paris: Presses Universitaires de France.

Tye, M. 2006. The thesis of nonconceptual content. In *The Structure of Nonconceptual Content, European Review of Philosophy*, vol. 6, eds. C. van Geen and F. de Vignemont, Stanford: CSLI Publications, 8–30.

Tooby, J., and L. Cosmides. 1990. The past explains the present: Emotional adaptations and the structure of ancestral environments. *Ethology and Sociobiology* 11: 375–424.

Tooby, J., L. Cosmides, and H. C. Barrett. 2005. Resolving the debate on innate ideas: Learnability constraints and the evolved interpenetration of motivational and conceptual functions. In *The Innate Mind: Structure and Content*, eds. P. Carruthers, S. Laurence, and S. Stich, 305–337. New York: Oxford University Press.

1. Modularity and the Rationality of Emotions

CANADIAN JOURNAL OF PHILOSOPHY
Supplementary Volume 32

Quick and Smart? Modularity and the Pro-Emotion Consensus

KAREN JONES

I. Introduction

Within both philosophy and psychology, a new pro-emotion consensus is replacing the old dogmas that emotions disrupt practical rationality, that they are at best arational, if not outright irrational, and that we can understand what is really central to human cognition without studying them. Emotions are now commonly viewed as evolved capacities that are integral to our practical rationality. An infinite mind, unencumbered by a body, might get along just fine without emotions; but we finite embodied creatures need them if we are to be capable of responding appropriately to our reasons and navigating in a risky world with poor information, limited attention, and restricted computational power.[1] Emotions are clever design solutions to the problem of making fast decisions in response to significant practical problems posed by the natural and social worlds: we perceive a danger and fear immediately primes us to take protective action. On this view, the theory of emotions is an essential part of a theory of

---

1 For discussions of functional (and some dysfunctional) emotions see Chapter Three of Ekman and Davidson (1994). Damasio (1994) has been instrumental in forging the emerging pro-emotion consensus, as has de Sousa (1987). Tooby and Cosmides (1990) and Cosmides and Tooby (2000), to be discussed in section IV, argue that emotions are adaptations, selected for the speed with which they enable responses to fitness-relevant situations. On the other side, Elster (1999) offers a sustained challenge to the claim that emotions contribute positively to rationality, while Ekman (2003) delivers a mixed verdict recognizing both the enabling and the disruptive potential of emotion.

ecologically situated and constrained rationality – that is to say, of *human* rationality (Samuels et al. 1999; Gigerenzer 2000). Pro-emotion theorists also think that their position has revisionary implications, perhaps even radical ones. There is a tendency within philosophical and commonsense thinking to disparage the emotions and to suppose that wise deliberation and objective inquiry are dispassionate. But if emotions contribute positively to ecologically situated rationality, then commonsense and philosophical norms of rationality that embed false assumptions about their disruptiveness may need to be revised (Damasio 1994; Jones 2003a).

In this article, I explore the presuppositions of the emerging consensus that emotions contribute positively to human practical rationality and that, as a result, our norms of rationality need revision. I argue that a pro-emotion position presupposes that emotions are capable of coming to be directed towards new objects in virtue of a cognitively modifiable range of triggering properties. Put another way, it presupposes that emotions can, with experience and regulation, become reason-tracking mechanisms that enable an agent reliably to track the way her concerns are implicated in concrete choice situations.

This is a substantive and controversial assumption, which is in prima facie tension with the claim that emotions are modular. I explore this tension in the light of two quite influential theories of the emotions, an evolutionary psychology account defended by Tooby and Cosmides (Tooby and Cosmides 1990; Cosmides and Tooby 2000) and Prinz's embodied appraisal account (Prinz 2004). Both accounts are put forward as modular accounts. I argue that the first account does not support a positive connection between emotion and practical rationality and that, while the second account *might*, there is a real question as to whether it preserves the property of cognitive encapsulation typically taken to be the hallmark of modularity. Once we are clear about the presuppositions of the pro-emotion consensus, it becomes apparent that we need more empirical research exploring the scope of strategies for effective emotional regulation, transformation, and control and that the new consensus will be entrenched or lost on the basis of such work. Despite its current vogue, there can be no easy lip service given to the pro-emotion position.

II. Presuppositions of the Pro-emotion Consensus

Two distinct questions drive the emerging pro-emotion consensus: How do emotions contribute to human rationality? What norms of rationality apply to us in virtue of our being intelligent creatures equipped with both judgment and emotion? The relationship between these questions is complex and, as we will see, it is possible to maintain that emotions make an important contribution to human rationality while yet maintaining a conservative stance with respect to norms of rationality.

II.i. How do Emotions Contribute to Human Rationality?

A pro-emotion theorist might assert any one of, or any combination of, four different claims regarding the positive contribution of emotions to human rationality:

(a) *Improving access to our reasons:* Emotions contain information that is potentially useful to deliberation. They carry information about how a situation has been evaluated (Clore 1994, 105); they signal events that are relevant to our values and concerns (Frijda 1994, 113). They also affect salience and memory and shape interpretation (de Sousa 1987; Ekman 2003). They make us interpret considerations as reasons where otherwise we might not have (e.g., the curt remark – was it really curt? – becomes seen as a reason for return rudeness). It is because of the control that emotions exert over perception, interpretation, and memory that they can "run away" with us: we see only the evidence that would confirm our emotion because we see the evidence through the lens of that emotion.

It is uncontroversial that emotions are associated with such shifts in practical perception. (Though it is disputed whether they should be seen as partly constituted by such interpretive schemata or whether they merely typically set them in train: for our purposes this dispute does not matter.) What is more controversial is whether such shifts can enhance our access to our reasons often enough for their influence on deliberation and choice to be positive, on the whole. If we are responding to a situation by bringing to it an emotional framing that does not belong there, as happens with emotional "spill over," projection, and phobia, then we will interpret the situation incorrectly. We will think we have reason to act when we do not. Similarly, repeated mental replaying of past emotionally laden episodes, as often happens when "working through" powerful emotional experiences, especially negative ones, will prevent our responding appropriately to the choices we currently face. An advocate of a pro-emotions position is committed to saying that emotions can, reliably enough, often enough, enable us to latch onto our reasons (Jones 2003c). Often enough they enable us to track the way our concerns are implicated in concrete choice situations. Their ratio of reliable to unreliable information is not such as to make them a liability.

(b) *Facilitating planning agency:* It is widely recognized that emotions have a role to play in organizing goals and sub-goals into planning hierarchies. Persons with affective impairment display significant impairment in their planning agency (Damasio 1994, 37 and 193).

(c) *Supplementing decision-theoretic reasoning and remedying its deficiencies:* Damasio argues that somatic markers simplify deliberation by attaching positive or negative valence to possible courses of action. Possible actions that are negatively marked are quickly eliminated from consideration, thereby reducing the number of action options that need to be considered to a field that can be managed by, for example, traditional decision-theoretic methods (Damasio 1994, 173). De Sousa likewise argues that emotions reduce deliberative complexity by setting in train interpretive schemata that control salience and restrict the background information that the agent accesses in deliberation (de Sousa 1987, 195).[2] Further, they have a role to play in cases of indeterminacy between two choice options, such as can arise with equipoise (equal reason for either option) or incommensurability (de Sousa 1987, 194).

---

2 Elster argues that both Damasio and de Sousa construct a strawman account of rational choice theory. Rational choice theory does not demand that we survey all possible action options – there are infinitely many such options (Elster 1999, 290). Elster is right that both Damasio and de Sousa attribute to decision theory an irrational "addiction to reason." But that does not undercut the pro-emotion camp's chief claim, rephrased as the claim that rational choice methods need supplementing and emotions are one of the mechanisms we use to supplement them. In particular, they are one of the mechanisms that determine the salience of action options. (There are others, including habit and environmental prompt.)

(d) *Facilitating appropriate action:* Folk psychology and experimental psychology alike recognize that emotion is intimately connected with action. There is a range of possible views regarding the strength of this connection. At one end is the view that emotions are, perhaps *inter alia,* dispositions to action, so that to be afraid is to be disposed to flee. Somewhat less extreme is the hypothesis, forwarded by Oatley and Jenkins, that "emotions make ready a small suite of plans, already assembled either in evolution or individually, that can be called upon when time or other resources are scarce" (Oatley 1992, 176). A still looser connection between emotion and action is posited by Clore (1994, 110) and Prinz (2004) who argue that, rather than priming the agent to undertake specific actions, or to enact one of a narrow range of stereotyped action plans, emotions facilitate action in a general way.

Emotions can facilitate action through their effects on the body and on motivation. In "cold" or non-emotional deliberation, there is the potential for a gap between a decision about where the weight of reasons lies and motivation to pursue the option judged best, a gap that opens up the possibility for weakness of the will. Thus, for example, the dangers of cigarette smoking, though known, can fail to engage the agent's motivational set, either at all, because she does not vividly represent them to herself, or sufficiently to overcome her craving for nicotine. In emotionally laden deliberation, the agent's motivation is already engaged and so she is prepared to embrace the selected action option – provided that it accords with the emotion that is driving deliberation.

Emotions are either partly constituted by, are perceptions of, or typically set in train (for our purposes it does not matter which) patterns of bodily changes. These changes prime the body for action. It might be thought that it is a mistake to consider such physical priming a potentially positive contribution to practical rationality, even though it can contribute to the likely success of action. After all, the objection presses, the success of our actions depends on luck and so is not up to us, while the criticism or praise implicit in rationality assessment is appropriate only concerning things that are up to us. Thus, practical rationality stops with decision and motivation to act on decision.

I think it is a mistake to argue for such hard and fast borders to the domain of practical rationality. The rationality of a decision depends on the prospects for success of the chosen course of action. Emotions have *coordinated* effects on salience and on the body: they prime the body for those highly general categories of action that their effect on the perception of reasons tends to make salient. By so priming the body they also increase the prospect of success for actions of that highly general kind. Emotions coordinate body and mind in ways that potentially enhance our ability to act as we have reason to do; through this coordination they have the potential to contribute positively to our practical rationality.

To argue that emotions facilitate action by motivational and physical priming is not yet to argue that emotions facilitate *appropriate* action. Indeed theorists as hostile to the emotions as the Stoics can agree that these connections hold – *that*, they may argue, is precisely the problem with emotions. They prepare us to embrace motivationally actions we should shun and leave us in physical turmoil when we would be better served by calm. The kind of motivational and physical priming emotions set in train will be helpful only if the emotion is itself an appropriate response to the situation. If it is not, we will be primed in all the wrong ways. Thus a pro-emotion theorist who argues that emotions facilitate appropriate action must also be committed to the claim that emotions can improve our access to our reasons; that is being committed to (d), commits you to (a). However, the reverse commitment does not hold. One can think that emotions' positive role is limited to their capacity reliably to inform us about how our concerns are implicated in concrete situations and that their relation to action is either neutral or something of a liability that requires careful management.

The pro-emotion position regarding the contribution of emotions to action is on strongest ground on the assumption that emotions prime action in a general way while leaving considerable latitude for the actions so primed to be tailored to the particular context. It is on next strongest ground on the assumption that emotion-types are individuated in a more fine-grained way than folk psychology presupposes (Cosmides and Tooby 2000, 93). For example, if fear is subdivided into fear of predators, fear of being stalked and so on, and each has its own associated action (flight and freezing, say), there is more chance that the primed action will be an appropriate response to the situation. Going more fine-grained allows for actions to be more precisely tailored to the specific situation. However, given choice situations can present more than one significant concern, positing a fine-grained but tight connection is less likely to support the claim that emotions facilitate appropriate action than is positing a weaker, more general action-priming effect. The pro-emotion position is on weakest ground if emotions are classified into broad kinds and the connection between them and action is hypothesized to be very tight. If emotions dispose the agent to just one relatively specific kind of action (fear to flight, anger to retaliation, say), they are unlikely to facilitate appropriate action. Similarly, if emotions set in train one of a small suite of stereotyped action plans, they are unlikely to promote the kind of flexible action responses rationality requires.

II.ii. What Norms of Rationality Apply to Us?

The radical pro-emotion theorist claims that proper appreciation of the positive contribution emotions make to human practical rationality has implications for the norms of rationality that should govern human agents. Some of the norms at issue might specifically mention the emotions, such as commonsense norms enjoining deliberators to keep a cool head. Other norms might make no explicit mention of the emotions but their cogency rests on assumptions about the likely usefulness or otherwise of emotions in enabling wise decision-making. For example, norms prohibiting akrasia may presuppose that only judgment enables an agent non-accidentally to act as she has most reason to do, a claim that is false if you accept that emotions enable us to register and respond to our reasons even when those reasons are not accessible to judgment (Bennett 1974; Arpaly 2000; Jones 2003a). Into the category of norms of rationality also belong images, metaphors, and ideals of the good deliberator, such as lists of the virtues they have, that are looser than norms and that may resist codification in rules or heuristics but that are nonetheless supposed to exert normative pressure over agents. These have been the target of feminist exploration and critique (Lloyd 1984; for a review see Jones 2003b).

It might be thought that a revisionary pro-emotion position with respect to norms of rationality follows simply from accepting that emotions make a positive contribution to human rationality and, hence, that a pro-emotion answer to the question of how emotions contribute to human practical rationality automatically grounds a revisionary normative project. Damasio (1994), for example, supposes that commonsense and philosophical disparagement of the emotions should give way before evidence that affective impairment brings with it impairment in practical rationality and that normal emotional functioning is important for normal practical reasoning ability. Further, if emotion can be shown to be ubiquitous, flavouring even small day-to-day choices, as is the case on the somatic marker hypothesis, norms such as those proposed by the Stoics that urge that emotional responses be eliminated would be shown to be impossible (Long and Sedley 1987, 410–23). The Stoic position is thus refuted by application of the principle that "ought-implies-can." Positions weaker than Stoic extirpation that nonetheless call for rigorous containment and control of the emotions are likewise vulnerable to empirical findings that such levels of control are impossible to achieve.

A revisionary pro-emotion position is not so simply secured, however. Both arguments presuppose that the point of a norm is to specify a target ideal. Target ideals are rebutted by showing that they are unachievable or by showing that achieving them would not be a good thing. Thus if a norm presupposes a level of control it is impossible to achieve, then it is to be rejected on the grounds that it is senseless criticizing someone for failing to achieve the unachievable (Flanagan 1991). Likewise, it seems downright perverse to criticize someone for failing to achieve something that if achieved would be disastrous.

However, not all norms specify target ideals. Many – perhaps most – specify *regulative* ideals. A regulative ideal is supposed to exert normative guidance over the practices (whether cognitive or other) of those who fall under its jurisdiction. A norm or ideal of rationality can serve a regulative function and thus be a good norm or ideal without being attainable: the point of striving for the stars is not reaching them, but rather doing better than one would have had one had a more modest target in view. This matters, because only if we assume that norms of rationality regarding the emotions specify target ideals rather than regulative ideals is the question of what norms to endorse answered by showing that affectless deliberation is impossible for human deliberators, or that the affectless would be practically impaired: it might yet be that we should strive to be as little influenced by emotion as we can, knowing that our natures will prevent us from achieving this end.[3] Perhaps striving for low emotion is the best way to have the benefits of affect without the burdens. Thus we do not get a position with revisionary pro-emotion norms merely from the observation that those with emotional deficits also have deficits in practical rationality. Even if those with fully cool heads would be practically stupid, the advice contained in the old adage to keep a cool head may yet be sound.

Revisionary pro-emotion norms of rationality such as norms enjoining us to cultivate rather than suppress the emotions embed substantive and controversial assumptions about the possibilities for successful emotional cultivation. They presuppose that we can do better by trying to think with the whole mind, using the resources of both intellect and emotion, than by relying on intellect alone. As such they presuppose that emotions reliably convey information about how our concerns are implicated in concrete choice situations and that, by and large, they facilitate appropriate rather than inappropriate action in response to those concerns. These are non-trivial assumptions, and the evidence for them is far from unambiguous. Indeed, these assumptions are in at least prima facie tension with the claim that emotions (or some emotions) are modular.

III. Modularity and a Prima Facie Tension with Pro-emotion Presuppositions

The notion of modular mental processes was first introduced by Fodor (1983), who positioned them between simple reflex responses (such as the eye-blink response) and complex information-processing systems that are arbitrarily sensitive to the organism's beliefs and desires. Like reflexes, cognitive modules are encapsulated: they do not have access to information contained elsewhere in the organism's information-processing systems (in that sense they are dumb); but unlike reflexes, cognitive modules carry out informationally complex tasks (and in that sense are smart). Modules can be thought of as special-purpose mini-computers equipped with their own proprietary database and charged with undertaking information processing regarding a single domain, such as constructing representations of three-dimensional objects from properties of surface reflectancies.

---

3   For a parallel argument concerning norms of objectivity, see Antony (1993).

Fodor (1983) proposed nine hallmarks of modularity: modular systems are informationally encapsulated, fast, opaque (higher cognitive processes lack access to the representations contained within the module), domain specific, mandatory, deliver shallow outputs, have relatively localized neutral architecture, suffer patterned breakdown, and are ontogenetically determined, unfolding in patterned sequences. This list of hallmarks is not taken to be definitive of the notion of modularity by those, such as Carruthers, who accept the massive modularity thesis, according to which the mind consists of multiple modules (Carruthers 2003). Carruthers charges the list with being "cooked" to describe input systems (this seems especially true of "delivers shallow outputs") and thus with being potentially hostile to the thesis that the mind consists of multiple modules (Carruthers 2003). The items of the list can come apart, so that we can have fast, opaque, domain-specific processes that are the result of general learning – driving a car, for example (Woodward and Cowie 2003). Thus the presence of some items on this list should not be taken as indicative of the presence of the others. Moreover, each of the characteristics admits of degrees, so rather than classifying cognitive processes as modular or not modular, we should think of them as relatively more or relatively less modular. Indeed, "modularity" is currently used so loosely that some charge it with surreptitiously grounding invalid inferences, as when, for example, arguments for one characteristic on the list are taken to ground conclusions regarding the presence of the others (Woodward and Cowie 2003).

Not all the features on Fodor's original list are potentially problematic from the perspective of pro-emotion positions and so, though of empirical interest, can be set aside for our purposes. For example, it counts neither for nor against the possibility that emotions should be reliable signals of how the agent's concerns are implicated in concrete choice situations whether they have relatively localized or relatively distributed architecture or whether or not they are subject to patterned breakdowns. Informational encapsulation and mandatoriness are, however, clear prima facie threats to the pro-emotion camp. Modular processing takes processing decisions out of the hands of conscious decision-making: the module does its job whether we will it to or not, and does it without benefit of knowledge stored elsewhere in the system.[4] This enables modules to purchase speed, though at the cost of the rigidity that follows from mandatory activation and from not being able to bring to bear all that is potentially relevant to its processing.

Modular processing can generate veridical outputs only when, within a domain, the environment makes available relatively stable cues that the module can exploit by using processing that embeds presuppositions concerning those environmental regularities. Such embedded presuppositions reduce the search space, enabling quick processing that is nevertheless accurate to the extent that the embedded presuppositions hold (Sterelny 2003, 186–87). Modules can be "tricked" into delivering erroneous outputs when the environment is manipulated so that the embedded presuppositions are false. Illusions arise when features internal to the module are exploited in this way. The encapsulation of modules means that the output is impervious to the subject's knowledge that it is erroneous: no matter that you know that the Muller-Lyer lines are the same length, no matter that you understand fully how the illusion works, you will still see them as different lengths. The most judgment can do is intervene in the space between perceptual experience and belief to insulate the visual experience from giving rise to belief in the normal way.

Modular mechanisms would be unlikely to deliver veridical solutions to decision problems that are "informationally open" (Sterelny 2003, 188) and that depend, for adequate solution, on complex situation-specific cues. Such problems lack the predictable cue structure that modules need to exploit in their fast processing. There is reason to believe that most practical problems are of this open-textured kind, for two reasons: first, the cues that signal a concern is implicated in a concrete choice situation are often various and recognizing them can take considerable experience and judgment. (Recognizing the signs of infidelity provides a simple example [Sterelny 2003, 189].) Second, choice situations are rarely single-track and typically implicate more than one of the agent's values. An adequate response to such situations thus requires integrating information derived from a variety of

---

4 For an overview of the arguments regarding whether we should expect evolution to favour a modular architecture for reasons of computational tractability and further references, see Sterelny and Griffiths (1999, 326–32).

cues. Practical judgment serves that integrative role. However, insofar as emotions set in train interpretative schemata and thus shape and colour an agent's interpretation of a situation, they can readily derail judgment's integrative project and lead to a single-stranded interpretation of a complex choice problem. If emotional processing is automatically engaged and escapes the brakes of judgment once engaged – as is the case on the assumption that emotions are modular – then, prima facie, emotions will tend to hinder rather than assist the agent in responding well to the choice situations she faces. The traditional view of the emotions as disrupters of practical rationality is more likely true than false.

Proponents of modularity who want to position themselves in the pro-emotion camp can make one of two responses to this prima facie tension: they can accept that the tension is real and pursue a splitting strategy, claiming that some – the basic emotions – are modular, others are not, and limiting their claim of positive contribution to non-modular emotions.[5] Typical lists of modular emotions include surprise, fear, anger, disgust, sadness, and joy. [6] Other emotions that are important tools for practical navigation in the social world and that are of special significance for ethics, such as guilt, shame, compassion, and indignation, do not figure on most standard lists of basic emotions. Perhaps a pro-emotion stance can yet be taken towards them. An alternative response is to deny that the tension is real. Perhaps modular accounts have the resources to explain the kind of flexible appreciation of the practical significance of choice situations that the pro-emotion position presupposes. No charge of incompatibility made merely in the abstract can be convincing; we have to look at actual accounts and see how they fare. It is to that task that I now turn.

---

5 Griffiths (1997) pursues a splitting strategy arguing that the category of emotion does not form a natural kind and is best split into three distinct categories.

6 For a revised longer list of basic emotions including amusement, anger, contempt, contentment, disgust, embarrassment, excitement, fear, guilt, pride, relief, sadness, satisfaction, sensory pleasure and shame, see Ekman (1999).

IV. Evolutionary Psychology and the Emotions

Recall that evolutionary psychology aims to understand the mental mechanisms that underlie and explain our behaviour; in this respect, it differs from its predecessor, sociobiology, which inherited behaviourism's hostility to mental mechanisms. Like sociobiology, evolutionary psychology is committed to adaptationism (the view that most features of organisms are adaptations and hence that the overwhelming force in evolution is natural selection).[7] This commitment is indicated by its use of "adaptive thinking" as a heuristic. Adaptive thinking sets out to infer the design solution from a characterization of the problem. Adaptive thinking arguments concerning mental mechanisms have four stages: first, identify an adaptive problem faced in the Environment of Evolutionary Adaptation; second, identify the environmental cues available to help solve that problem; third, construct an information-processing design that could solve the problem, using the available cues; fourth, test to see if the mental mechanisms so posited exist. Tooby and Cosmides apply this adaptationist strategy to their investigation of the emotions.

Tooby and Cosmides (1990) hypothesize that emotions are modules that serve to modify, in a coordinated fashion, the functioning of a suite of further processes, including cognitive, behavioural, and physiological processes, thereby enabling the organism to respond appropriately to fitness challenges repeatedly encountered in the EEA. They can be thought of as "superordinate programs" (Cosmides and Tooby 2000, 92) that function to coordinate an organized response to the situation by setting in train a characteristic set of fitness-enhancing changes in other processes including goal setting, motivation, cognitive interpretation, attention, and physiology (Tooby and Cosmides list seventeen classes of such processes). These coordinated responses better enable the organism to deal with the fitness challenge posed by the environment:

> [E]ach emotion state – fear of predators, guilt, rage, grief, and so on – will correspond to an integrated mode of operation that functions

---

7 This gloss is something of a simplification, but not significantly distorting for our purposes. For a discussion of different adaptationist theses and problems with the adaptationist program, see Sterelny and Griffiths (1999, 224–50).

as a solution designed to take advantage of the particular structure of the recurrent situations these emotions correspond to. (Tooby and Cosmides 1990, 410)

Emotions register environmental cues that signal, in the EEA, some fitness-relevant situation. It is the presence of these cues and their stability in the EEA that enabled a modular solution to the decision problem. Positing such cues amounts to the assumption that the problems to which the emotions are evolved solutions are informationally bounded (Sterelny 2003, 188). Cosmides and Tooby offer the following as examples of these cues and the fitness-relevant situations they signal:

> Low blood sugar signals a depleted nutritional state, the looming approach of a large fanged animal signals the presence of a predator, seeing your mate having sex with another signals sexual infidelity; finding yourself alone or avoided by others signals that you have few friends (Tooby and Cosmides 1990, 411)

Hunger, fear (or perhaps fear of predators), sexual jealousy, and sadness, respectively, are evolved responses to these situations made possible by the reliable occurrence of environmental cues to which the emotions become keyed.

It might be thought that it follows from evolutionary psychology's (hereafter "EP") claim that emotions are adaptations (i.e., that they have a natural-selection story to call their own) that they will contribute positively to practical rationality in some, if not all, of the ways outlined in answer to the second question regarding the relation between emotions and rationality: they help us focus on our reasons; increase the efficiency of deliberation, sometimes indeed letting us cut straight to the right action without further thought; and they facilitate appropriate action, preparing both body and motivation to take an action option within the range demarcated by the emotion.[8] And from

---

8 In fact there might be a problem here: Cosmides and Tooby are not clear about how tight the connection between emotion and behaviour is. Their reference to "highly stereotyped behavior" and "specific acts" becoming "more available as responses" may indicate that they mean to posit a relatively tight connection

this it might be inferred that our norms of rationality should not portray emotions as dysfunctional disruptions that should be subject to heavy cognitive regulation.

Tooby and Cosmides are, however, at pains to argue against this interpretation of their evolutionary "just-so" story. If a trait is an adaptation, it follows by definition that it conferred a fitness benefit in the EEA; but *nothing* follows from that about the trait's current adaptiveness. Only if present conditions resemble EEA conditions in relevant ways, so that the environmental cues the system was selected to track continue to indicate fitness-relevant situations and the output of the system continues to interact with other systems in the right way to generate the right kind of behaviour, will an adaptation be adaptive outside the EEA. If emotions were stimulus-response mechanisms, we'd need only the assumption – it is still a big one – that the cues continued to signal fitness relevant situations. But since they are, by hypothesis, mechanisms that interact with and regulate other mechanisms, mechanisms that are themselves subject to further interaction and constraint, the odds are massively against the whole package of input and interaction working out in the way it would need to to continue to be adaptive under conditions as different from the EEA as are our current conditions.

Cosmides and Tooby are explicit that nothing follows regarding the current adaptiveness of emotions:

> Emotion programs, for example, have a front end that is designed to detect evolutionarily reliable cues that a situation exists (*whether or not these cues reliably signal the presence of that situation in the modern world*).... Far from being internal free agents, these programs have unchanging structure *regardless of the needs of the individual or her circumstances,* because they were designed to create states that worked well in ancestral situations, regardless of their consequences in the present. (Cosmides and Tooby 2000, 93; emphasis added)

(2000, 106–7). Recall from section II.i that the tighter the connection the less likely it will be that emotions enable appropriate behaviour, though the more emotions are classified into fine-grained types, the tighter the connection that can be posited.

Karen Jones

Things are worse yet: on no plausible account of practical rationality will a cognitive system that maximizes (or even satisfices) fitness contribute significantly to the practical rationality of any but the oddest of human agents, since only the very strange (if not the downright creepy) have among their goals increasing their relative reproductive success. Natural selection doesn't care about the goals of individuals only the success of lineages. We should thus be sceptical of grounding a pro-emotion position on the basis of EP, for two reasons: traits that are adaptive under EEA need not (indeed often will not) be adaptive now, and adaptiveness hasn't got much to do with rationality, anyway. If you accept *this* story of the emotions, then you should take the attitude towards them that Peter Singer (2005) does. Singer accepts an EP story and so thinks emotions are nothing but disruptions. They have nothing to teach us about our reasons for action, since they're keyed to outmoded fitness cues; they lead us to make significant mistakes in our moral epistemology; and they actively prevent us from acting according to our reasons by priming motivation and behaviour in opposition to a rational understanding of our best reasons. In current conditions they are downright dangerous even to the point of threatening our species' survival. Our best hope lies in their control and in insulating practical judgment from them.

None of this means, of course, that a story – EP or otherwise – that posited evolved emotional modules could not be combined with a pro-emotion position, only that Tooby and Cosmides' version cannot be so combined. It is easy enough to see the problem: they claim emotions are keyed to specific cues set up as triggers in the EEA, "large hairy fanged thing" and so on. That is, they suppose emotions "embody knowledge of the evolutionary past" (Griffiths 1997, 116); in virtue of embodying that knowledge, they remain enmeshed in that past. There is empirical evidence that emotions do not work like this: only sudden loud noises and loss of physical support are universal fear triggers and there is no in principle limit to the things that can be feared from radiation poisoning, to kittens, to the erosion of civil liberties. If emotions are to be capable of contributing positively to practical rationality they need to be able to come to be attached to new cues, to things that mark, here and now, not fitness-relevant properties, but properties that answer to concerns the agent has, or should have. That is, we need a theory of emotional calibration that will permit the kind of affective learning that gives considerable flexibility to the

18

things that can serve as emotional triggers and that, at least over time, allows reflective judgment a role in shaping the contours of emotional responses. Jesse Prinz develops just such a theory *and* he claims his account meets the criteria for being an account of the emotions as modular, which makes his the theory to turn to next.

V. The Embodied Appraisal Account

Like Cosmides and Tooby, Prinz seeks a unified account of the emotions which draws no fundamental distinction between the so-called basic and higher cognitive emotions. His proposal is neo-Jamesian. Recall that James thinks emotions are nothing but first-personal phenomenological perceptions of changes in bodily state: they are *feelings* of bodily changes. Perception of an eliciting object (a snake on a path, say) triggers bodily changes and these are perceived through feelings; that feeling just is the emotion. As James notes, this changes the usual explanatorily order: we do not tremble because we are afraid, we are afraid because we tremble (James 1884).

Prinz makes two additions to this Jamesian core. From Damasio, he allows that bodily changes can be perceived without being felt so that emotions need not be conscious (Prinz 2004, 201–5). From Dretske, he borrows the resources to add the crucial element to his theory: emotions do not merely register bodily changes; they are also appraisals and, though simple, have representational properties. They represent not by virtue of having constitutive thoughts with semantic properties, or by virtue of resemblance, but by virtue of *tracking*. Emotions represent the core-relational themes that covary with the patterns in bodily changes that they register.

According to Dretske a mental state represents what it is "set up to be set off by"; that is, a state represents that which it has the function of reliably detecting (Prinz 2004, 54). Natural selection favoured registering patterns in bodily changes because those states covaried with "core relational themes" such as irrevocable loss, or demeaning offence.[9] Emotions represent such core relational themes through registering patterns of bodily changes.

---

9 In explicating these core relational themes, Prinz makes use of the analyses offered by appraisal theorists, especially Lazarus (1991).

This gives us a representational element to emotions without having to tack it on as a belief or thought accompanying the perception of patterned bodily changes. But so far we have not made any advance on Cosmides and Tooby's account because we haven't yet got a story about how emotions can come to be triggered by all sorts of things, most of which were not found in the EEA and so cannot have been the cues for situations presenting core relational themes under conditions of selection. This is where Prinz introduces the notion of calibration files and of recalibration. Representational states can be recalibrated; that is, they can come, through learning, to be set off by things other than, or additional to, that which they were initially set up to track (Prinz 2004, 99). Prinz posits calibration files as the mental mechanism that links emotional response to trigger: they are structures in long-term memory that link judgments, thoughts, imaginings, or perceptual cues to the patterns of bodily changes that constitute embodied appraisals. In this way, he claims, we can build on our natural endowment and come to have complex, cognitively mediated emotions. Natural selection may have put some triggers in our calibration files, more likely it gave us learning programs that tell us how to fill these files. For example, infants look to care-givers for cues as to how to approach unfamiliar objects, and emotional contagion teaches children what to fear, what to hate, and what to be disgusted by well before they are capable of grasping what it is in virtue of which the things are supposed to merit the response. Explicit learning and experience can add others and so we can come to be afraid of electric shocks and of the erosion of civil liberties under anti-terror laws. Non-basic emotions, such as jealousy, emerge when new calibration files are set in place that recruit existing embodied appraisals to serve the purpose of tracking new core relational themes (Prinz 2004, 101). (Prinz suggests that jealousy may recruit anger, or possibly a blend of anger, sadness, and disgust, and recalibrate it to judgment and other markers of infidelity.)

If this story works, Prinz will have solved the learning problem that, unsolved, prevented EP from being able to support the emerging pro-emotion consensus. If we have the capacity to engage in good calibration file housekeeping (a question that is far from resolved), emotions can come to track core relational themes in their full richness, with all their variety of signals, whether perceptual cue or judgment. Emotions will be able to provide us with information about the presence of dangers, losses, and so forth. Further, if emotions have the cognitive, desiderative, and physiological sequelae assumed by the pro-emotion position, then they will be able to facilitate practical rationality in the ways listed in section II.i above.

Prinz is aware that once he allows emotions to be judgment-sensitive he is vulnerable to two objections. Firstly, why think of the judgments or thoughts involved in judgment-sensitive emotions as part of a calibration file that triggers embodied appraisals rather than as constitutive causes of the emotion (Prinz 2004, 101)? Second, and relatedly, in allowing that emotion can be triggered and modified by thought, hasn't the claim of encapsulation, and with it modularity, been lost (Prinz 2004, 234–36)? In reply to the first objection, Prinz argues that we should not think of the judgment (or thought) as constitutive because there is no one judgment associated with a particular kind of higher cognitive emotion (unfaithfulness with jealousy, say), but many possible judgments (e.g. "one's lover has been staying unusually late at work"); moreover, those same emotions can be triggered by sensory states (e.g., "the smell of an unfamiliar perfume on a lover's clothes"):

> There is no internal state that always plays the role of triggering a higher cognitive emotion. Different items in our calibration files play that role on different occasions. There is, therefore, no pressure to say that any particular judgment comprises a constituent part of any higher cognitive emotion…. Instances of jealousy are united not by the fact that they share judgments but by the fact that they share similar somatic states and those somatic states represent infidelity. (Prinz 2004, 101)

This rejoinder seems to me to misdescribe how jealousy works. It is not as if the mere smell of a perfume sets it off, or the mere judgment that one's partner is late from work, or even late yet again (vary the context ever so slightly and these things will not make you jealous). They trigger jealousy just when they are seen as – I do not say "judged as" for reasons familiar from Greenspan (1988) – evidence of possible infidelity. And if that is right, then there is a thought/judgment (though perhaps not a reflective one) in play explaining why these cues are the triggers that they are.

Prinz relies on the claim that thought/judgment are not constitutive parts of even the higher cognitive emotions in arguing that his account is indeed an account of the emotions as modular. The calibration file story amounts to viewing thoughts or judgments as causal inputs into the emotion module. They are part of the "initiation pathway" and not part of the emotion itself, which consists solely in the registration of the patterned bodily change (Prinz 2004, 235). Prima facie, this rejoinder is not very satisfying. One can take *any* cognitive influence over a putative module and redescribe it as influence that happens at the input stage rather than as part of the functioning of the module itself, but this is to risk making the notion of encapsulation vacuous:

> If *any* informational influence on the internal processing of a mechanism can be reconceptualized as input to that mechanism, and if influence *via* input is consistent with encapsulation, then the notion of encapsulation is vacuous (Woodward and Cowie 2003, 329).

Perhaps, however, this objection is unfair. Grant that it is illegitimate to redescribe just any apparent cognitive influence as mere input influence in order to save a thesis of modularity; but that doesn't mean it is *never* correct to describe cognitive influence as mere input influence. Perhaps there is some reason for thinking that, in the case of the emotions, it is correct to describe the influence of cognition as input influence, while in other cases it would not be. The phenomenon of emotional recalcitrance is called on to defend the existence of encapsulation and so to underwrite describing such cognitive influence as there unquestionably is as "input" influence. Emotional recalcitrance is supposed to be analogous to visual illusions, such as seeing a straight stick that is half-immersed in water as bent, or seeing the Muller-Lyer lines as different lengths. No matter what you know about these illusions, your appearances remain unaffected. Your beliefs can't penetrate your visual processing systems to modify their operation, and they continue to output their false representations. Fodor (1983) proposes that the persistence of illusion is an acid-test for modularity. If emotional recalcitrance really does parallel visual illusion, then Prinz's move of claiming the cognitive influence emotions display is input influence only cannot be charged with being *ad hoc*. How close is the analogy between emotional recalcitrance and visual illusion? Somewhat close, but not as close as it is often supposed.

Emotional recalcitrance is the name not for a single phenomenon, but for the class of affective phenomena that range from emotional lag through to outright phobia. Emotional lag is a familiar ordinary experience: you are angry with someone for doing something then discover that they did not do it after all. Your anger nonetheless lingers longer than the belief on which it was based. Indeed, as every child knows, lingering anger is apt to go in search of some other infraction that would justify it: "You look guilty, so you must have done something!" (de Sousa 1987, 199). If emotions were not encapsulated, the argument goes, then there would be no emotional lag.

If this argument works, however, we'd be forced to say that ordinary belief-forming and revising processes are also encapsulated, something few are willing to do (but see Carruthers 2003). Emotional lag is less like visual illusion than it is like the ordinary cognitive phenomenon of beliefs outlasting acceptance of the evidential base on which they were first formed. There is strong empirical evidence that once you get a subject to form a belief – about, say, their ability to distinguish real from fake suicide notes – they will continue to hold that belief even when debriefed and told that the positive feedback they received on their performance bore no connection to their actual performance. We are not very good at revising our beliefs even when presented with information that they were wrongly formed (Gilovich 1993). Of course, we can and do revise our beliefs in the light of further beliefs about their evidential warrant, but lag here is common. We also can and do "revise" our emotions in the light of beliefs about their warrant.

Perhaps we need to go further along the continuum of recalcitrance from lag to phobia before we have a case that parallels visual illusion. While not as common as lag, everyone sometimes experiences emotion/judgment conflict, where one sincerely believes that an evoking situation doesn't merit the emotion, yet continues to feel the emotion anyway. Again there are analogous cognitive phenomenon, including the phenomenon, already mentioned, of failing to revise beliefs in the light of new evidence about their grounding: you believe you have a cognitive skill, you also believe that this belief is not warranted by your evidence, but you fail to put these two things together in the way needed to revise your belief.

Only at the far end of the spectrum of emotional recalcitrance, in phobia, do we get a phenomenon without cognitive parallel in normal individuals. (There might be analogies here with the inferential failures of people with delusional disorders such as Capgras syndrome.) But phobias are unlike visual illusions in two ways that have bearing on the issue of encapsulation: (i) phobias are treatable, though they are hard to treat and there is dispute over how best to do so; (ii) phobias are isolated emotional *disorders*, they are not part of normal emotional functioning. If emotions were encapsulated, on the model of vision, then one would expect phobias to be ineradicable, to have common themes and no individual variation, and to be more widespread than they are. Visual illusions exploit features of processing internal to the visual processing module: given the right conditions, we are all susceptible to them, and the explanation of our susceptibility is the same; no amount of training will help us avoid them, though we can train ourselves not to be mislead by them.

The two disanalogies do not establish that emotions are not encapsulated and thus that they are not modular; only that they are not modular on the model of vision. Encapsulation, like the other characteristics of modularity, admits of degrees. Certainly emotions are *relatively more* encapsulated than belief-forming processes in non-delusional subjects; clearly they are *relatively less* encapsulated than visual processing.[10] Thus it remains an open question whether there is a theoretically acceptable sense of "modularity" which is compatible with allowing the kind of cognitive influence that Prinz wishes to allow and without which the pro-emotion position is a non-starter.

Even supposing that the embodied appraisal account is an account of emotions as modular, it is another question whether it can support a pro-emotion position. That is going to depend on the possibilities for good calibration file housekeeping, a question Prinz does not address. Can we, with maturity and effort, remove an item from the calibra-

---

10 It is also possible to deny that encapsulation is a necessary characteristic of modularity: Prinz, this volume, claims that visual systems and emotions are "stimulus dependent" rather than encapsulated; that is, they are driven bottom-up so that when there is a conflict between appearance and judgment, appearance is unmodifiable by judgment. With ambiguous figures, judgment can influence perceptual appearance.

tion file and so go from immature, or just plain mistaken, emotional responses to responses that enable us to track the way our concerns are implicated in concrete choice situations? Can we get rid of some calibration files altogether? That is a difficult empirical question and the evidence is not yet in.[11]

What I have tried to argue in this paper is that there is no shortcut to a pro-emotion position, for all that making some kind of gesture towards such a position has now become philosophical (and psychological) fashion. Far from grounding an easy inference to a pro-emotion position, positing emotions as evolved modules designed to help constrained and ecologically situated agents respond quickly and reliably to their environment tends to support pessimism about their prospects for contributing positively to practical rationality here and now. If you want to defend a genuinely pro-emotion position, then you have to do the hard yards of investigating the prospects for emotional regulation, control, and transformation.[12] For what it is worth, my money remains on the pro-emotion camp.[13]

References

Antony, L. 1993. Quine as feminist: The radical import of naturalized epistemology. In *A Mind of One's Own*, ed. Louise Antony and Charlotte Witt, 185–225. Boulder: Westview Press.

Arpaly, N. 2000. On acting rationally against one's best judgment. *Ethics* 110 (3): 488–513.

Bennett, J. 1974. The conscience of Huckleberry Finn. *Philosophy* 49: 123–34.

Cosmides, L., and J. Tooby. 2000. Evolutionary psychology and the emotions. In *Handbook of Emotions* (2nd ed.), ed. M. Lewis and J. Haviland-Jones, 91–115. New York: The Guilford Press.

---

11 For a review of the literature, see Gross (1998).

12 And they are *really* hard yards. We need to know about the possibilities for ecologically situated, real-world, regulation; hence, laboratory-based studies will not get us very far.

13 Work on this project was supported by The Australian Research Council (DP 0557651). Thanks to Christine Tappolet and Luc Faucher for helpful comments and to audiences at the University of Melbourne and the University of Sydney, where an early version of this paper was presented.

Carruthers, P. 2003. The mind is a system of modules shaped by natural selection. In *Contemporary Debates in the Philosophy of Science*, ed. Christopher Hitchcock, 293–311. Oxford: Blackwell.

Clore, G. 1994. Why emotions are felt. In *The Nature of Emotion*, ed. Paul Ekman and Richard Davidson, 103–11. New York: Oxford University Press.

Damasio, A. 1994. *Descartes' Error: Emotion, Reason and the Human Brain*. New York: Gossett/Putnam.

de Sousa, R. 1987. *The Rationality of Emotion*. Cambridge (Mass.): MIT Press.

Ekman, P. 1999. Basic emotions. In *Handbook of Emotion and Cognition*, ed. T. Dalgleish and M. Power, 55–60. Chichester, NJ: Wiley.

Ekman, P. 2003. *The Face Revealed: Recognizing faces and feelings to improve communication and emotional life*. New York: Times Books.

Ekman, P., and R. J. Davidson. 1994. *The Nature of Emotion: Fundamental Questions*. New York: Oxford University Press.

Elster, J. 1999. *Alchemies of the Mind: Rationality and the Emotions*. Cambridge: Cambridge University Press.

Flanagan, O. 1991. *Varieties of Moral Personality*. Cambridge (Mass.): Harvard University Press.

Fodor, J. 1983. *The Modularity of Mind*. Cambridge (Mass.): MIT Press.

Frijda, N. 1994. Emotions are functional, most of the time. In *The Nature of Emotion*, ed. P. Ekman and R. Davidson, 112–22. New York: Oxford University Press.

Gigerenzer, G. 2000. *Adaptive Thinking: Rationality in the Real World*. New York: Oxford University Press.

Gilovich, T. 1993. *How We Know What Isn't So*. New York: Free Press.

Greenspan, P. 1988. *Emotions and Reasons: An Inquiry into Emotional Justification*. New York: Routledge.

Griffiths, P. E. 1997. *What Emotions Really Are: The Problem of Psychological Categories*. Chicago: University of Chicago Press.

Gross, J. 1998. The emerging field of emotional regulation: An integrative review. *Review of General Psychology* 2(3): 271–99.

James, W. 1884. What is an emotion? *Mind* 9: 188–205.

Jones, K. 2003a. Emotion, weakness of the will and the normative conception of agency. In *Philosophy and the Emotions (Royal Institute of Philosophy Supplement: 52)*, ed. A. Hatzimoysis, 181–200. Cambridge: Cambridge University Press.

Jones, K. 2003b. Gender and rationality. In *The Oxford Handbook of Rationality*, ed. A. Mele and P. Rawlings, 301–19. Oxford: Oxford University Press.

Jones, K. 2003c. Emotional rationality as practical rationality. In *Setting the Moral Compass: Essays by Women Philosophers*, ed. Cheshire Calhoun, 333–52. New York: Oxford University Press.

Lazarus, R. S. 1991. *Emotion and Adaptation*. New York: Oxford University Press.

Lloyd, G. [1984] 1993. *The Man of Reason* (2nd ed.). Minneapolis: University of Minnesota Press.

Long, A., and D. Sedley. 1987. *The Hellenistic Philosophers: Volume 1.* Cambridge: Cambridge University Press.

Oatley, K. 1992. *Best Laid Schemes: The Psychology of Emotions*. New York: Cambridge University Press.

Prinz, J. 2004. *Gut Reactions: A Perceptual Theory of Emotion*. Oxford: Oxford University Press.

Samuels, R., S. Stich, and P. Tremoulet. 1999. Rethinking rationality: From bleak implications to darwinian modules. In *What Is Cognitive Science*, ed. E. LePore and Z. Pylyshyn. Oxford: Blackwell.

Singer, P. 2005. Ethics and intuitions. *Journal of Ethics* 9: 331–52.

Sterelny, K. 2003. *Thought in a Hostile World*. Oxford: Blackwell.

Sterelny, K., and P. Griffiths. 1999. *Sex and Death: An Introduction to the Philosophy of Biology*. Chicago: University of Chicago Press.

Tooby, J., and L. Cosmides. 1990. The past explains the present: Emotional adaptations and the structure of ancestral environments. *Ethology and Sociobiology* 11: 375–424.

Woodward, J., and F. Cowie. 2003. The mind is not (just) a system of modules shaped (just) by natural selection. In *Contemporary Debates in the Philosophy of Science*, ed. Christopher Hitchcock, 312–34. Oxford: Blackwell.

CANADIAN JOURNAL OF PHILOSOPHY
Supplementary Volume 32

Against Emotional Modularity

RONALD DE SOUSA

I. A Political Stand

How many emotions are there? Should we accept as overwhelming the evidence in favour of regarding emotions as emanating from a relatively small number of modules evolved efficiently to serve us in common life situations? Or can emotions, like colour, be organized in a space of two, three, or more dimensions defining a vast number of discriminable emotions, arranged on a continuum, on the model of the colour cone?

There is some evidence that certain emotions are specialized to facilitate certain response sequences, relatively encapsulated in their neurophysiological organization. These are natural facts. But nature, as Katherine Hepburn remarked to Humphrey Bogart, is what we were put in the world to rise above. I shall suggest that we can consider the question not merely from a scientific point of view, but from a *political* point of view. And so I will try to explain how to reconcile the evidence of emotional modularity – which, as some of the contributions to the present volume illustrate, is not devoid of a certain ambiguity – with a reasonable plea for an attitude of disapproval towards the rigidities of our taxonomy.

It may seem bizarre to speak of a political stance, since modularity is a scientific issue. And so it is: but we may have choices in the matter in two ways. First, it is far from clear just what it *means* to speak of modular emotions. So there is at least a choice of what version of the doctrine to focus on. Secondly, one can still ask whether thinking in terms of modular emotions in the relevant sense is a "good thing" or not. The facts don't determine the attitude we take to them. There's a long tradition that recommends accepting the

Universe;[1] but one can find reasons to endorse some parts more full-heartedly than others.

In the history of philosophy, there are well-known examples of the politicization of factual and conceptual issues. Aristotle's and Aquinas's views on nature illustrate how one might make distinctions in the natural world between how things go and how they are *meant* to go. Aquinas can tell just by thinking, for example, what the sexual organs are *for*, and doesn't have to be distracted by any facts about what people and animals actually do. And if that's unreasonable in the light of the claim that what nature intends is what happens "always or for the most part,"[2] well, you can afford that in the Vatican, Mother of Theme Parks, because you have God on your side.

Without divine backing, the issue of what actually counts as a natural function needs to be somewhat more responsive to facts; but contemporary naturalistic philosophy can still distinguish in theory, among an organ's actual effects, those that are its functions. Effects merely occur, from a variety of causes. But some effects are privileged by the role played by natural selection in securing the reproduction of the mechanisms that produce them, and only those count as functions (Wright 1973; Millikan 1989).

This perspective raises a fresh problem, however, stemming from the fact that what evolution selects does not, even in the most metaphorical sense, have the goal of benefiting *me* – or you, or any other organism *as such*. Whatever view of genetics or fashionable stance on evo-devo you adopt, any particular organism remains a means for the transmission of heritable patterns. Indeed, the individual organism is strictly expendable where those larger "goals" might prove incompatible with the welfare of some particular vehicle such as you or me. So inasmuch as I can identify goals of my own, as distinct from those of natural selection, there is no guarantee at all that the pursuit of goals I identify as my own will necessarily be fostered by a policy of living according to nature (Buss 2000; de Sousa 2007).

---

1 ("I accept the universe!" – Margaret Fuller; – "By God, she'd better!" – Ralph Waldo Emerson)

2 Aristotle, *Met.* VI–6.

Where emotions are concerned, then, it may be the case that certain forms of modularity are indeed in place as a result of natural selection, but that we have reasons to think that a *bad thing* and seek to correct it. That is what I mean to convey by speaking of the "politics" of emotional modularity.

II. 'Modular' and 'Basic': Multiple Senses

There are two ways of approaching the meaning of 'modularity.' One begins with Fodor's fairly elaborate account (Fodor 1983). The other returns to basics, in the sense of taking its cue from the vernacular and in the sense of looking at what might be meant by "basic emotions." The latter sometimes speaks of "Darwinian modules" and is associated with evolutionary psychology.[3] Fodor laid down very specific criteria, on the basis of which he argued that the senses are modular but general cognition is not. Instead of quoting from that text,[4] I'll adopt Peter Carruthers' (2003) summary of the defining features of modularity. In a strict sense, applicable without modification to sensory systems, modules are stipulated to be:

1. domain-specific
2. innately specified processing systems,
3. with their own proprietary transducers, and
4. delivering 'shallow' (non-conceptual) outputs; ...
5. mandatory in their operation,
6. swift in their processing,
7. encapsulated from and inaccessible to the rest of cognition,

---

3 In the words of Edouard Machery, "by contrast with Fodorian modules, Darwinian modules need not be fast, automatic, cognitively impenetrable, or informationally encapsulated." (Machery, forthcoming, 5)

4 Fodor's own list is as follows: modular input systems or their operation are: (1) domain-specific; (2) mandatory; (3) limited in the access to the representations they compute by the central system; (4) fast; (5) informationally encapsulated; (6) shallow in their outputs; and endowed with (7) fixed neural architecture, (8) characteristic breakdown patterns, and (9) characteristic pace and sequencing in their ontogeny. All this applies to functions that are or incorporate transducers, though Fodor does not explicitly limit his modules to systems incorporating transducers.

8.   associated with particular neural structures,
9.   liable to specific and characteristic patterns of breakdown, and
10. developed in accordance with a paced and distinctively arranged sequence of growth.

On the face of it, emotions are candidates for criteria 2, 6, 7, 8, but do not meet 3 or 4. They may – at least in some cases – meet 9, though what counts as a breakdown of any particular emotional module is likely to be difficult to pin down. Criterion 10 is also probably satisfied for most common emotions, though modulated in important degrees by the role of individual experience in determining the characteristic triggers and typical manifestations of a given emotion in each individual. Criterion 1 is difficult to assess, for the modularity of emotions is supposed to relate to output, whereas most of the modules on which Fodor originally focused were sensory modules, defined by the domain of their input. But insofar as a type of triggering situation for one sort of emotion or another can be identified, according to the hypothesis of evolutionary psychology, the difference between the range of possible inputs and the range of possible outputs is narrowed. Criterion 5 is also complicated by the distinction between input and output aspects of emotions. On the face of it, it demarcates two classes fairly clearly among the conditions we think of as emotions. Although emotions in general are often described as invading a merely passive subject with a power that is *"inescapable"* (cf. Ekman 2003, 65, citing Zajonc), that does not fit all emotions equally well, particularly if we think of the output manifestations of emotions such as facial and verbal expressions. Even in the case of the cognitive analogues of basic emotions – fear of giving offence, or fear of losing one's job, for example – the outward manifestations of the emotion can generally be fully suppressed even if the feeling of the emotion can't be evaded. Furthermore, insofar as the first and fifth criteria imply some form of innateness, this needs to be interpreted not as determining a fixed pattern, but as an "open" as opposed to a "closed" program in the sense defined by Ernst Mayr (1997, 694). It is not the full functioning of the mechanism that is held to be innate, but a learning bias likely to construct variants of such a mechanism in normal environments. Once the criteria are relaxed in this manner, the sharp contrast on which Fodor insisted fades, for this opens the way for cognitive modules that meet criteria 5, 6, 7 (partly), and 9. That would bring emotion modules very close to the cognitive ones, save for just one feature, namely the applicability of criterion 8. Cognitive modules are unlikely to involve dedicated neurophysiological structures of the sort now associated with "basic emotions."

The less stringent characterization of modularity just sketched is closer to the vernacular uses of the word, as applied to devices, machines, the construction of buildings, and so forth. That yields the far more relaxed criterion, which has allowed people to construe cognition and "the mind" itself as modular.[5]

The "modularity of emotions" is an ambiguous phrase. It could mean that emotions are themselves modules. But it could also mean that emotions are put together out of modular constituents more elementary than themselves. Both notions are interesting, but for now I'm going to concentrate on the first. In a moment I'll draw attention to one way of interpreting the second.

One way of taking the concept of an emotion module coincides more or less with "basic emotions," though that usage too admits of many interpretations. Paul Ekman first identified as basic emotions a small set of emotions that proved universally recognizable in facial expressions (Ekman and Friesen 1975). In that sense, basic emotions seem to be both modular and innate. But basic also has several other senses: including what is *foundational*, or *atomic*, or (like "Basic English") *frequent and important* or important because frequent.

This last conception would fit in well with that of evolutionary psychology, for trifling differences will leave no trace: *de minimis non curat selectio*. The structures that evolution has specifically erected are liable to have been worth the trouble, hence to have been sufficiently frequent and important. But as I have already implied (this will be crucial to my "political" stand) what is important to *me now* may have little

---

5 The expression often used with reference to cognitive processes is "massively modular," implying that the mind is made up of literally thousands of modules in something like the looser (non-Fodorean) sense characterized above. (For an extended defence, see Carruthers 2006). Even where that position about cognitive functions has come under strong criticism, however, as in Buller (2005), it is generally conceded that a much smaller number of emotional modules may have a more robust psychological reality as well as being grounded in more specific neural circuitry.

in common with the concerns of my ancestors in the Environment of Evolutionary Adaptation (EEA).

I'll come to the functional approach in a moment. But for now let me mention a perspective on emotions in which they are viewed as (very loosely) modular rather than as modules. On this view, emotions are constructed out of elements or features that are not yet emotions.

I refer to one way in which Klaus Scherer's school of appraisal theory might be construed. Emotions might be seen as emergent phenomena that supervene on a number of appraisals, each of which defines a separate dimension.[6] Some of the regions of this multi-dimensional state space are recognizable emotions. This sort of view need make no reference to the neurology of emotions; and no emotions are basic in the foundational sense, though attractors or "hot spots" in the space could be claimed to be "basic" in the sense of most frequent and important. Of course, since Scherer's methods tell us nothing about the underlying mechanisms that are responsible for the shape of the space, including the existence of hot spots, it is entirely compatible with the evolutionary psychology hypothesis that those hot spots are actually wired in, or wired-to-be-learned. In other words, it is not incompatible with the hypothesis of evolutionary psychology that affect programs, "inherent central mechanism[s] that direct emotional behavior" (Ekman 2003, 65) have been shaped by evolution to fulfill specific functions.

That hypothesis, however, leaves open the question of whether and how affect programs have been selected *as such*. That hangs on the answer to two questions. First, was the affect program selected *as a unit*? Second, was it *selected for*, and not merely *selected*?

To see the point of the first question, here is an analogy. Lewontin (1978) once remarked that *the chin does not exist*. What he meant was that changes in the shape of the chin resulted from relative lags in the extent of neoteny in two independent growth fields (alveolar and mandibular), subject to independent selective pressure. That makes the chin, however expressive of manly virtue or – in the "weak-chinned" – of lack of character, a mere accident, a "spandrel" of evolution. As for the second point, it was nicely illustrated by a toy con-

---

6 (Scherer 1993; Scherer et al. 2001). I do not claim that the interpretation is the one Scherer himself intends. On the contrary (Scherer 2005) seems to favour a low-dimensional model which stresses "salient" emotions if not "basic" ones,

ceived by Elliott Sober (Sober 1984, 99). The toy consists of a cylinder with graded sieves. Small green and large red balls are placed in the device. When the cylinder is shaken up, only the green balls get to the bottom. So they have been *selected* by the device. But since their colour plays no part in the causal explanation of that fact, what they were *selected for* is size, not colour.

An emotional module in the fullest sense, then, will be one that has been selected for, as a unit. That doesn't mean that an emotional module won't have been, like any other product of selection, cobbled together from all kinds of diverse sources. But it does imply that if it is legitimate to ascribe to it a function in the full sense, such a module will have been, at some stage of evolution, distinct enough to be favoured over some genetically and developmentally possible alternative.

To get the flavour of what it might mean in practice for some emotional characteristic to have resulted from selection without having been selected for, consider Paul Ekman's intriguing recent suggestion that moods, unlike emotions, fail the test of full functionality:

> [...] emotions are necessary for our lives, and we wouldn't want to get rid of them. I am far less convinced that moods are of any use to us. Moods may be an unintended consequence of our emotion structures, not selected by evolution because they are adaptive. Moods narrow our alternatives, distort our thinking, and make it more difficult for us to control what we do, and usually for no reason that makes any sense to us [...]. I would gladly give up euphoric moods to be rid of irritable and blue moods. But none of us has that choice. (Ekman 2003, 50–51)

This passage is interesting in several respects. Notice first that Ekman's argument appeals to the apparent utility of moods from the point of view of an agent in the present world. This has little bearing on the question of whether moods were selected as such.[7] Moods may be

---

7 In a recent review, Nesse (2006) discusses various hypotheses, all speculative and uncertain, about the evolution of moods. If moods can be shown to result from integrated operations in neurotransmitters and neural circuits, the search for therapy in mood disorders would be facilitated. Thanks to the Editors for alerting me to Nesse's paper. See also Charland (this volume) about depression as a possible example of a disordered modular mood.

a good example of a biological adaptation that for most people are experienced as mere nuisance. Thus Ekman's remarks illustrate the distinction I want to stress, while at the same time underscoring the limited usefulness of making it. For let us suppose that moods are indeed more trouble than they're worth *now*, but that they had, in fact, been carefully packaged as such by natural selection, in the sense just described. That would mean they could be adaptations in the full sense, but that fact would be irrelevant to the evaluation of their present value for us. It would make no difference to the wisdom of looking for some sort of generalized lithium-like chemical agent, where the mood's triggering conditions cannot be evaded, to achieve the result that Ekman says he would prefer.

III. The Two-Track Mind

Moods are remarkably unitary, and share several features with paradigm emotions: they control salience in what is perceived or in preferred patterns of inference, and they lend a "style" to a whole lot of manifestations in body language, tone of voice, and dispositions to behaviour. But leaving moods aside, let us return to the small list of emotions for which the argument for modular affect programs has been made in the most compelling form. This turns essentially on two kinds of evidence. One is the identification by Joseph LeDoux (2000) and Jaak Panksepp (2001) of distinct neural pathways or "cell assemblies" and physiological profiles for affect programs. The other is the often-noted cognitive recalcitrance or "refractory" nature of emotions (D'Arms and Jacobson 2003). I'd like to set these arguments in a more inclusive context, viewing them as constituents of a larger argument for thinking of humans as language-using animals, as endowed with a *two-track mind*. By that I mean some version of the idea, broached half a century ago by Paul MacLean in several articles about the "Triune Brain," that we have distinct "systems" in the brain that yield responses – sometimes mutually incompatible – to standard situations (MacLean 1975). The idea is compelling, but elusive, and it has taken many forms. In his recent book, Keith Stanovich lists twenty-three other versions of such "dual-process theories." In summarizing his own version, he stresses, as central features of one system, "automaticity, modularity, and heuristic processing," while the other is characterized as "rule-based, often language based, computationally expensive" (Stanovich 2004, 34–36).

The idea of the two-track mind has proved most controversial when applied to cognitive processes, particularly inference strategies, leading to a wide range of systematic irrationalities of the sort made notorious by Amos Tversky and Daniel Kahneman (Kahneman and Tversky 2000). Against them, Gerd Gigerenzer (2000) and others have taken what Stanovich (2004) calls the "Panglossian" view that natural selection in its wisdom has actually done everything for the best, and that the irrationalities alleged by Tversky and Kahneman are only apparent. Still others, notably Buller (2005) have rejected the arguments offered by evolutionary psychologists (Barkow et al. 1995) for the proliferation of cognitive modules under the influence of natural selection. My own view of that controversy is what Stanovich endorses as the "meliorist" view: that while the "fast and frugal" cognitive strategies favoured by natural selection (whether through hardwiring or by the medium of learning biases) may well have been statistically optimal in the EEA, this doesn't make them rational in every individual case. One reason for this is obvious: the EEA is not our environment, although, as I will shortly explain, this consideration may not be as powerful as it is often taken to be. Second, and more important, is the fact mentioned in section I above: that the benefits conveyed by natural selection are not measured by the success of any individual, but only by the reproduction of key patterns through generations of expendable organisms.

What holds for cognition holds also for emotion. I can concede the wisdom of nature, and equally the social wisdom that may be responsible for some of the constraints under which I live, as a member of a social group. Long tradition has the phenomenological force of given nature. Both biology and social context have lent to my emotional responses an appearance of compelling automaticity. And yet I can become aware that those emotional strategies may not be best for me. In other words, in the light of those goals that I self-consciously embrace as mine, many of my emotions may be simply irrational. The well-worn examples of fear of flying and road rage are obviously compelling here. But it can be refined and extended, by attending to the different ways in which an emotion can be appropriate or "fitting."

Look at it first from the phylogenetic point of view. In the case of an affect program, we could think of the fittingness of an emotion as stemming from the conformity of the present situation to the situation type for which the affect program was originally selected. This sort of fittingness refers to the efficiency with which an emotion serves the function for which natural selection has designed it. As I have noted, that function is at best only incidentally beneficial to the individual in whom it is manifested. On that criterion, jealousy is fitting when it serves to eliminate actual sexual rivals or sequester a mate from possible rivals. Quite obviously, the behaviours typical of jealousy have been statistically successful in propagating the genes that favour their own manifestation. (I stress, once again, that this is not to say that these behaviours are innate, only that there is an innate learning bias that favours them.) Jealousy might be said to malfunction, however, when, in a different social environment, it results in driving the potential mate into the arms of a rival.

Even in the rawest cases of basic emotions such as fear or anger, however, there is a large range of possible triggering situations as well as a large range of possible responses. As noted above, the programs remain "open" rather than closed and the specific ways in which they are originally triggered may expand because of generalization, analogy, and association. This last, in particular, may result in idiosyncratic and pathological cases such as phobias. As for the responses, they will certainly include certain obligatory features such as those facial expressions that are seen in blind people no less than in sighted ones, and thus come with reasonable evidence of their innateness; they may also have in common certain characteristic patterns of physiological response. So much, at least, has been claimed for "anger, fear, sadness and disgust ... all marked by different changes in heart rate, sweating, skin temperature, and blood flow" (Ekman 2003, 26). This suggests that the criterion of universality picks out a class of emotions that comprise a number of physiological characteristics, measurable independently of cognitive content, and which can plausibly be attributed to mechanisms facilitated, if not entirely controlled, by genetic factors honed by natural selection. We might say of those emotions that they are *physiologically modular*.[8] Since some basic emotions can

---

8 Despite giving a barrage of arguments against cognitive modularity, Buller concedes that "Evolutionary Psychologists may be right about some of our more

be combined, however, there may be some pairs of emotions that are phenomenologically "contrary" and yet physiologically compatible.

Even those physiologically modular emotions, however, will take forms that will reflect the specific scenarios in which the program was originally activated. Think, for example, of the range of functions that William Miller has claimed stem from that most visceral of our emotions, disgust (Miller 1997). These were aptly summarized in an *Observer* review of *The Anatomy of Disgust* by Anthony Storr, who remarked that "Miller rightly perceives that disgust helps to define our identities, create hierarchies, and order our world." (Storr 1997, 16).

Such variations will shift the affect program from phylogenetic control to ontogenetic control. This will generate a different sense of "fittingness." Where an emotion, linked to a social script, has its roots in some paradigm scenario of childhood, measures of fittingness will derive from several other criteria relating the present incident to the paradigm scenario. There will be, first, some sort of resemblance between the situation that elicits the present emotion to that original paradigm scenario. This is admittedly rather question-begging, for it is difficult to figure out what independent criteria of resemblance could be devised, besides the perceived resemblance signaled by the very fact that the emotion is elicited. But here's the sort of thing intended: Jealousy is appropriate when a rival causes my lover's attention to turn away from me, because that's what was involved in my original experience of jealousy. It might be inappropriate if it is triggered by the mere fact of being on a boat, even if the defining episode took place on a boat.

But while the script fits, that implies nothing about it's being useful, nice, or good. Whether the emotion is *morally justified*, then, is an entirely different question, pertaining to yet a third sense of "appropriateness" or "fittingness" (D'Arms and Jacobson 2000). I've argued

---

basic emotional adaptations, but nonetheless wrong in its claims that we possess a lot of *cognitive* adaptations …" (Buller 2005, 143). The difference, he claims, is due partly to the fact that the development of the midbrain and limbic system, proceeding from the ventricular zone, differs from that of the neo-cortex, which proceeds from the sub-ventricular zone. The former, but not the latter, "appears to be under rather rigid genetic control" (Buller 2005, 131).

before (de Sousa 2003) that the answer to that question is unlikely to be available without making tacit assumptions about emotions themselves and how they bear on the acceptability of conflicting moral judgments. But I will leave that question entirely aside here. Here is what I wish to stress instead: it follows from this sketch of different types of "fittingness" that there are various ways in which *my own emotions can impede my own goals*. On the other hand, my emotions also *set my goals*. What I care about, what I aim at, and what I desire are defined largely by my emotions, or sometimes at least by my beliefs – not necessarily true ones – about what my emotions would be in counterfactual situations.

The considerations adduced so far can be summed up as follows. While a limited number of "basic emotions" are plausibly regarded as governed by "Darwinian modules," we can't infer that the emotional dispositions concerned are currently adaptive from the biological point of view. Neither can we assume that they serve social cohesion, let alone the individual interests of any given person. The main reason for that is that all such modules belong to the "first track" mind, which is relatively impervious to language-mediated reasoning and to the individual and social goals elaborated on the basis of explicit deliberation. Considered from the philosophical point of view, moreover, our emotional capacities can be expected to yield a vast number of different experiences. What I have called the "political" approach encourages us to seek different criteria of fittingness, ranging from biological fitness proper to the promotion of subjective individual well-being. In matters of emotion, as in matters of belief, the only option is to seek in reflection a gradual harmonizing of ends and means, of long-term goals and short-term impulses, all of which are driven by different emotions. In the next section, I will ask what are the criteria that should guide our reflection in the search for reflective equilibrium about the most desirable emotional life.

IV. PEGGing Emotions

We will need, at some point in the process of reflection, a taxonomy of emotions, and that will require us to decide how important the existence of modular affects or other emotions should be to our taxonomy. A few years ago, Paul Griffiths (1997) insisted that a viable taxonomy could be grounded only in genuine homologies; but this rather dogmatic view has been fairly demolished by Louis Charland (2002), and it also faces a plausible alternative in Dick Boyd's reconstruction of a functional concept of homeostatically stable kinds (Boyd 1999). Rather than embark on that debate, let me take a different tack and suggest a bifurcation of emotions based on the roles that they play in our lives. The two classes are non-exclusive, overlapping, and somewhat vaguely defined; nevertheless, the distinction is of paramount importance.

Among my goals and interests, some involve the cultivation of desirable emotions of the sort that contribute intrinsically to happiness. The pursuit of such emotions isn't necessarily purely selfish. It may include the cultivation of desirable emotions for my children, my friends, and others. But the pursuit I have in mind under this heading aims essentially at the cultivation of emotional *quality*. My emotions, under this heading, matter for their own sake.

Contrasting with those, I have goals and interests that necessitate accurate *Predictions, Explanations, and Generalizations in Gossip*, or *PEGGing* of how others will act and respond.[9] Here the *communicative* function of the emotional expressions comes into its own. It is in general to the subject's advantage, at least for the class of emotions linked to affect programs, to allow others to see what they are feeling. Hence the hard-wired universal expressions that Paul Ekman has anatomized. Unlike language, the second-track device given to humans, as Talleyrand reportedly quipped, for the purpose of concealing one's thoughts, facial expressions require a special effort to control. And perfect control is seldom achieved, at least for the first microseconds of any episode of emotional arousal. Furthermore, from the point of view of folk psychology, it is handy to have the simplest possible toolbox of explanatory concepts under which the behaviour of others and their states of mind can be PEGGed.

So here is the hypothesis I propose:

> *Hypothesis H*: Insofar as I am interested in PEGGing the behaviour of others, a neat scheme involving relatively few elementary states (which

---

9 The importance of gossip in the development of a larger and more powerful brain has been argued convincingly by Robin Dunbar (1996).

could then be combined to make more complex states) will serve me best. It will be a scheme which as much as possible will involve a digital system of representation.

A digital system of representation is one in which every state of what is represented is forced into one or another of a finite number of pre-assigned possibilities. The alphabet is a good if imperfect example. Providing we assume that it was intended as a piece of English, any handwritten squiggle will be assigned to one or another among our 26 letters, 10 numerical symbols, and a few other marks standing for punctuation or mathematical operations. An 'a' may be confused with a 'd,' but there is nothing between an 'a' and a 'd' that an ambiguous mark can be assigned to. What such a system does, in effect, is to construe resemblance between any two letters not as a two-term relation, but as a three-term relation involving the two squiggles and the paradigm, the actual letter or symbol A, of which they are both meant to be instances.[10]

As these examples suggest, though, there are – unfortunately for the apparent neatness of the distinction – degrees of digitality when a system of representation is envisaged as a whole through a period of time. Language, for example, changes much faster than genes: linguistic mutations large or numerous enough to affect the entire population occur in timespans of the order of decades, not millions of years. And our conceptions of emotions, once we go beyond affect program modules, may be subject to gradual change, more like a traditional dance than a phoneme.

Our conceptions of emotions may be even more difficult to analyze than the evolution of linguistic forms. The elements we start with are more complex, and the combinatorial possibilities more numerous.

---

10 This scheme is just a new version of Plato's Theory of Forms. Plato failed to grasp its true significance, however, which is that it is invaluable in any case of *serial reproduction*. It pre-empts the Xerox effect, which is the degradation of copies of copies at the end of a long line of copying operations. For since reference is made to the paradigm at each stage, even the ten millionth copy is still just two steps away from the original. It is not surprising, then, that the two most spectacular examples of digital representation in the natural world are language and DNA, both of which are in the business of limitless reproduction requiring a staggering level of fidelity.

Yet if Hypothesis H is right, there will be additional pressure to pare down our vocabulary of emotion in order to simplify our mastery of that complex domain. A corollary of the dominance of the context of PEGGing over the context of contemplation and experience is that we will, out of sheer sloth, likely come to use the same vocabulary in thinking of our own emotions, as if it comprised an adequate taxonomy of emotions for situations in which multiple reproduction is not at issue, but only *experience*.

Here is one more reason for the dominance of the needs of explanation and prediction over the value of quality of experience. Emotions are typically thought of as motivating, or as involving characteristic "action tendencies" (Frijda 1986). Insofar as emotions motivate behaviour, we can think of them as just pushing and pulling: swayed by the totality of your emotions at any particular time, either you act or you don't. The way we *experience the world* can be as complicated or as subtle as you like, but in the end, where agency is in the offing, they have to be funneled into a single sequence of exclusive decisions. Each decision is a matter of acting or not acting; it is the black-and-white of yes or no. If we focus on the experience of emotions, on the other hand, they are so diverse as to constitute no single *kind* of thing at all. (Think again of the multidimensional space of appraisals which, on Scherer's scheme, is the matrix of emotions.) Each carries a wealth of specific meanings enriched by an immensely large class of contrasts: call it the polychrome vision of the emotional field.

V. The Aesthetic Model

On such a full-colour view of emotions, geared not to the requirements of agency but to the realities of emotion as experience, it could be argued that there are no practical limits to the number of distinct emotions that can be experienced, any more than there are limits to the number of thoughts one can have (Campbell 1998). This view seems particularly compelling when we consider aesthetic experience, a domain in which, as we have all learned from Kant, we are able to contemplate aspects of the world for their own sake, in abstraction from practical considerations. To that extent, the emotions aroused by works of art are not directly tied to any goals. (Or, if you prefer, they are tied only trivially to the goal of continued contemplation.) Reading poetry, looking at paintings, watching dance, or listening to music would be largely pointless activities unless they aroused emotion.

But what sort of emotions? The observation that art evokes emotion is threatened with two unequal and opposite forms of triviality. On the one hand, one may be tempted to think that the emotions expressed in art are "the grand emotions" that we can all list on demand: anger, fear, love, awe, jealousy, sadness, desire. But if that is the point of them, then why go to all the trouble of making (or consuming) new and original art? If works of art exist merely to evoke standard emotions, and if there are no significant differences between any two instances of "fear," or "anger," and so forth, it hardly seems likely that works of art in all their diversity should be sustaining our interest for their representation of *emotion*, rather than for some other reasons. On this view, it's difficult to see why most art isn't superfluous. (Most mediocre art is indeed superfluous in just this sense: once you've seen one scary alien-invasion movie, you've seen them all.) The alternative view is that each different moment in music, dance, or literature that evokes emotion is actually expressing an emotion *sui generis*, or better *sui ipsius*: not merely of a certain sort but in its own unrepeatable individuality.

But then the role of art is trivialized again: for if every piece of art necessarily expresses its correlative emotion, no more and no less, then that seems to remove the possibility that some forms of art might be better or worse at expressing emotion, or that the emotions evoked by some work of art might be more worthwhile, more interesting, more deeply felt, more authentic than others. For all those evaluative judgments seem to presuppose that there is something beyond the expression of emotion, in terms of which a given expression can be judged.

This objection can be overcome if we give up the assumption that each work of art or literature is seen as conveying a ready-made emotional "message." If instead art is thought of as creating and embodying a particular emotion of its own, valued for its own sake, then there can be numberless emotions, and every work of art is more or less interesting in accordance with the quality of the unique emotion it conveys. There are then indeed literally *innumerable* emotions.

But now we face a problem of a different sort.

In the exploration of an aesthetic domain, we learn to discriminate, to compare, and to retain what most seems of significance. Present experience guides the superior refinement of future experience. Now if we concentrate on the unique features of each situation, on the specific qualities of each individual, and on the singularity of each emotion, it is difficult to see how they could provide any guidance at all. Comparisons require similarities and differences, classified and conceptualized in terms that necessarily return us from the particular to the general. Learning, in short, requires repeatable patterns. Taken literally, then, the suggestion that each particular situation in life (as well as each episode in a work of art) gives rise to an unrepeatably unique emotion is self-defeating. (Particular) percepts without (general) concepts cannot be refined.

If that problem seems rather unreal, it is because it takes the particularity of emotions too far. Experience, like all forms of cognition, is intrinsically *general*. It can be indefinitely *specific*, and it can have particulars as its objects, but it can't contain the infinite properties of any particular as such. Even in the experience-centred utopia I am envisaging, then, non-conceptual contents of experience can be assessed along a variety of continua: valence, intensity, similarity to some paradigm scenario, and the set of associations that give them meaning. That field of emotional existence would not necessarily be devoid of privileged "hot spots," but it has no need of being digitized, that is, of being conceptualized in terms of a finite number of pre-defined emotions.

The last few paragraphs have described a utopia of liberated emotional experience. Yet the reality is that we are all too ready to settle for a simplistic taxonomy, modeled on modules, with its set stack of standard labels. Such a schema will not serve my own quest for a rich and nuanced emotional life. Yet as I have suggested, we are liable to assume that if the scheme works for us when PEGGing the emotions of others, it has to be right for ourselves. Unless I explicitly question it, I'll ascribe to myself the same limited set of possible emotions that I use to make sense of the lives of others. I may tend to take it for granted, furthermore, that the basic scenarios emotions are geared to are well understood and pretty much permanent. And in this, as in most things we are inclined to take as "natural," there may be a strong component of social pressure – possibly a mere special case of some general rule of conformism (Dugatkin 2001) – that forces anomalous cases into a marginal status.

For that reason, the effect of the difference between our own environment and the EEA is less important than it would seem. The way we interpret our objective situation depends on the reactions we observe in others. (The classic psychological experiment that shows this, though it doesn't show most of what it's usually dragged in to show, is that of Schachter and Singer 1962.) So as we watch others *interpret* the current situation in terms of atavistic scripts, we may assume that such scripts fit all. And that, in a sense, will *make* it fit, or at least will make it true that it fits in the minds of those agents PEGGing the interactions concerned.

Here is an analogy. We commonly take it for granted that there are just two sexes. On strictly biological grounds, Anne Fausto-Sterling (1993) has urged us to recognize at least five sexes, while noting that this is still a crude simplification of what in practice is really a *continuum*. "I would argue further," she writes, "that sex is a vast, infinitely malleable continuum that defies the constraints of even five categories" (Fausto-Sterling 1993, 21). But in the medical world as well as in the public consciousness, this is simply denied. Infants born androgenous are "assigned" or "reassigned" to one or the other of the two obligatory sexes. And, needless to say, in the public discourse surrounding the current debate about "same-sex marriage," there is little consideration of bisexuality, and virtually none at all of intersexuality or of the potential multiplicity of sexes and genders. To be sure, the biological and functional reasons for sexual dimorphism in both nature and discourse are fairly plain – though the details remain obscure enough to give rise to conflicts of medieval irrationality.[11] But the result, for those who don't easily fit either of the two obligatory options, is a brutal denial of the emotional truth of their experience, indeed of their very identity.

---

11 As sadly exemplified by the outrage over some speculative remarks by the President of Harvard, even among sophisticated scientists presumably familiar with Bell curves, but who behaved as if an allusion to differences in *variances*, implying overlapping continua, connoted rigidly separate classes. See Murray (2005) for a discussion of the ramifications of that case.

VI. Conclusion

I have suggested that there are two sources of potential conflict between the modularity of emotions, whether stemming from phylogeny or from social conformism, and our aspiration to a life of greater emotional richness. The first source is the existence of pre-programmed affect syndromes. These encourage our tendency to respond in ways that may frustrate our own goals and self-image. The second stems from the undeniable usefulness of a clear schema for PEGGing other people's behaviour. This falsely instills the conviction that the representational scheme simply represents reality, and that (to put it excessively simply) the number of our emotion words is a sure guide to the number of emotions it is possible to experience.

There's not much we can do about either of these constraints on our capacity to enlarge our emotional repertoire, though some techniques have been plausibly recommended. Paul Ekman (2003, 76) reports, for example, that attentiveness, reappraisal, and "mindfulness meditation" have had some success in increasing the "impulse awareness" that may enable an agent to control the automatic responses of the intuitive track. But for my purposes, I am more interested in the way that literature and art can place us at one remove from our impulses, enable us to play down the importance of action tendencies, or simply perhaps view them as merely another aspect of intrinsically interesting experience. Reading Proust, D.H. Lawrence, or Henry James, or for that matter, if you can bring yourself to do it, the Marquis de Sade, we can be made aware of ranges of emotions lying outside the standard repertoire. This is a point made repeatedly by Martha Nussbaum, who has stressed the capacity of literature to present us with fully imagined emotions and particular characters, as contrasted with the bloodless abstractions customarily paraded in philosophical examples (Nussbaum 1992). The emotions evoked by art, music, and literature are typically enjoyed in abstraction from the practical considerations in terms of which standard emotions are deemed more or less appropriate. They need not carry with them any specific action tendencies. Instead, they constitute a "full-colour," multidimensional field of possible emotional experience that provides a model for the emotional richness that might be afforded by ordinary day-to-day existence.

Such a field would not necessarily be devoid of privileged hot spots but has no need of being digitized or conceptualized in terms of a finite number of pre-defined emotions. Armed with such examples, we might be better equipped to *resist* our own tendency to think of our own and others' emotions in terms of the limited vocabulary we use to PEGG people's motivations and behaviour.

And that – here in capsule is my political message – would be a Good Thing.[12]

References

Barkow, J. H., L. Cosmides, and J. Tooby. [1992] 1995. *The Adapted Mind*. Oxford: Oxford University Press.

Boyd, R. 1999. Kinds, complexity and multiple realization: Comments on Millikan's "Historical Kinds and the Special Sciences." *Philosophical Studies* 95: 67–98.

Buller, D. 2005. *Adapting Minds*. Cambridge (Mass.): MIT Press.

Buss, D. M. 2000. The evolution of happiness. *American Psychologist* 55(1): 15–23.

Campbell, S. 1998. Interpreting the personal: Expression and the formation of feeling. Ithaca: Cornell University.

Carruthers, P. 2003. The mind is a system of modules shaped by natural selection. In *Contemporary debates in the philosophy of science*, ed. C. Hitchcock, 293–311. Oxford: Blackwell.

Carruthers, P. 2006. *The Architecture of the mind*. New York: Oxford University Press.

Charland, L. C. 2002. The natural kind status of emotion. *British Journal for the Philosophy of Science* 53(3): 511–37.

D'Arms, J., and D. Jacobson. 2000. The moralistic fallacy: On the 'appropriateness' of emotion. *Philosophy and Phenomenological Research* 61: 65–90.

D'Arms J., and D. Jacobson. 2003. The significance of recalcitrant emotion (or quasi-judgmentalism). In *Philosophy and the Emotions*, ed. A. Hatzimoysis, 127–45. Cambridge: Cambridge University Press.

de Sousa, R. 2003. Paradoxical emotions. In *Weakness of Will and Practical Irrationality*, ed. S. Stroud and C. Tappolet. Oxford: Oxford University Press.

---

12 My thanks to the editors and to anonymous referees for many suggestions on an earlier draft.

de Sousa, R. 2007. *Why Think? Evolution and the Rational Mind.* New York: Oxford University Press.

Dugatkin, L. A. 2001. *The Imitation Factor: Evolution Beyond the Gene.* New York: Simon & Schuster.

Dunbar, R.I.M. 1996. *Grooming, Gossip, and the Evolution of Language.* London: Faber and Faber.

Ekman, P. 2003. *Emotions Revealed: Recognizing Faces and Feelings to Improve Communication and Emotional Life.* New York: Henry Holt.

Ekman, P., and W. Friesen. 1975. *Unmasking the Face: A Guide to Recognizing Emotions From Facial Expressions.* Englewood Cliffs (NJ): Prentice-Hall.

Fausto-Sterling, A. 1993. The five sexes: Why male and female are not enough. *The Sciences* 33(2): 20–25.

Fodor, J. 1983. *The Modularity of Mind.* Cambridge (Mass.): MIT Press.

Frijda, N. 1986. *The emotions. Studies in Emotion and Social Interaction.* Cambridge, Paris: Cambridge University Press, éditions de la maison des sciences de l'homme.

Gigerenzer, G. 2000. *Adaptive Thinking: Rationality in the Real World.* New York: Oxford University Press.

Griffiths, P. E. 1997. *What Emotions Really Are: The Problem of Psychological Categories.* Chicago: University of Chicago Press.

Kahneman, D., and A. Tversky, ed. 2000. *Choices, Values, and Frames.* Cambridge, New York: Cambridge University Press.

LeDoux, J. E. 2000. Emotion circuits in the brain. *Annual Review of Neuroscience* 23: 155–84.

Lewontin, R. C. 1978. Adaptation. *Scientific American* 293: 156–69.

Machery, E. Forthcoming. Massive modularity and brain evolution. *Philosophy of Science.* http://www.pitt.edu/AFShome/m/a/machery/public/html/papers/Evolutionary%20Psychology%20and%20Brain%20Evoluti on_PSA_2006_machery.pdf.

MacLean, P. D. 1975. Sensory and perceptive factors in emotional functions of the triune brain. In *Emotions: Their Parameters and Measurement,* eds. L. Levi. New York: Raven Press.

Mayr, E. 1997. Behavior programs and evolutionary strategies. In *Evolution and the Diversity of Life : Selected Essays,* 694–711. New York: Belknap Press.

Miller, W. 1997. *The Anatomy of Disgust.* Cambridge (Mass.): Harvard University Press.

Millikan, R. G. 1989. In defense of proper functions. *Philosophy of Science* 56: 288–302.

Murray, C. 2005. The inequality taboo. *Commentary* September: 13–22. Fully annotated version at http://www.commentarymagazine.com/production/files/murray0905.html.

Nesse, R. M. 2006. Evolutionary explanations for moods and mood disorders. In *American Psychiatric Publishing Textbook of Mood Disorders*, ed. D. J. Stein, J. Kupfur and A. F. Schatzberg. Washington (D.C.): American Psychiatric Publishing.

Nussbaum, M. 1992. *Love's Knowledge*. Oxford: Oxford University Press.

Panksepp, J. 2001. The neuro-evolutionary cusp between emotions and cognitions implications for understanding consciousness and the emergence of a unified mind science. *Evolution and Cognition* 7(2): 141–63.

Schachter, S., and J. Singer. 1962. Cognitive, social, and physiological determinants of emotional states. *Psychological Review* 69: 379–99.

Scherer, K. R. 1993. Studying emotion-antecedent appraisal process: An expert system approach. *Cognition and Emotion* 7(3–4): 325–55.

Scherer, K. R. 2005. What are emotions? And how can they be measured? *Social Science Information* 44(4): 695–729.

Scherer, K. R., A. Schorr, and T. Johnstone, eds. 2001. *Appraisal Processes in Emotion: Theory, Methods, Research*. Oxford: Oxford University Press.

Sober, E. 1984. *The Nature of Selection*. Cambridge (Mass.): MIT Press.

Stanovich, K. 2004. *The robot's rebellion: Finding meaning in the age of Darwin*. Chicago: Chicago University Press.

Storr, A. 1997. Why we don't like dog turds. Not even chocolate ones. Review of W. Miller 1997. *The Observer*, London, April 13.

Wright, L. 1973. Functions. *Philosophical Review* 82: 139–68.

2. Modularity and Basic Emotions

CANADIAN JOURNAL OF PHILOSOPHY
Supplementary Volume 32

Emotions Are Not Modules[1]

JAMES A. RUSSELL

Jane is calmly strolling through the forest one lovely day. Suddenly, a large spider drops in front of her face. She immediately freezes; her heart races; her hands tremble; her face broadcasts "fear." She screams and runs away. Both before and after, she concedes that spiders in this forest are harmless.

Jane's reaction to the spider contrasts greatly with the way she normally reacts to events. Normally, or so the story goes, Jane weighs her options thoughtfully, choosing a course of action consistent with her beliefs and with the greatest benefit. Indeed, her reaction to the spider contrasts so greatly with calm, rational, deliberate, belief-consistent action that traditional folk psychology supposed two different kinds of mechanism are at work: animal-like emotion (located in the heart and gut) versus human reason (located in the mind). Her emotion explains her reaction to the spider. Her emotion made her do it.

This common-sense folk theory has grown into a plausible and productive scientific research program in which emotions (now relocated to a primitive part of the brain) are assumed to be fast-acting instinctual reflex-like responses honed through evolution to provide ready-made solutions to problems recurrent in our ancestors' day. I refer here to this research program as Basic Emotion Theory (BET).

BET implies that emotions are modular, meaning that they show many or all of the following features: unique output; fast; innate; subject to an evolutionary explanation; produced by a dedicated neural

1 This article is based on a talk given at the conference on modularity of emotion, Montreal, May, 5–7, 2005. I thank Christine Tappolet, Luc Faucher, Giovanna Colombetti, Jose Miguel Fernandez Dols, Peter Zachar, and Louise Sundararajan for their comments on a draft of this article. This work was supported by NSF grant # 5000590.

processor; mandatory (automatic and involuntary); and information-ally encapsulated and hence beyond cognitive control (free from influence by certain seemingly relevant information).

This article briefly sketches my reasons for doubting BET. In doing so, I draw on an alternative account, one that poses the question of modularity in a different way. The key concept in my alternative account is Core Affect. I first characterize Core Affect and then turn to a brief critique of BET.

I. Core Affect

Core Affect is a neurophysiological state accessible to consciousness as the simplest feelings: feeling good or bad, lethargic or energized (Russell 2003). When prolonged, these feelings are the basis of mood. Core Affect differs from specific emotions in a number of ways. A person is always in some state of Core Affect. Although Core Affect is involved in specific emotions, more typically Core Affect is a simple feeling. Core Affect is not necessarily directed at anything (it is non-intentional). Core Affect responds to too many simultaneous influences to mentally track its causes with certainty. As a consequence, although we sometimes have a good idea of why we feel the Core Affect we do, we often don't, as in free-floating moods. One influence on core affect is virtual reality (art, fantasy, music) as when a song makes us feel good or not so good.

Core Affect is an ingredient of (but not the whole of) specific emotions. Would we understand someone's grief without understanding (in addition to which facial expressions, changes in the Autonomic Nervous System, appraisals, actions, and so on occur) whether the griever feels good or bad? Would we understand joy without understanding whether the joyful person feels good or bad? (My claim is not that all cases picked out by English words such as *grief* or *joy* entail a *specific* value of Core Affect, but that Core Affect is an ingredient in our emotional lives. For example, a very atypical case of grief might include feeling numb rather than bad.)

II. Evidence on Basic Emotion Theory

Reviewing evidence on BET is difficult because BET is a broad class of theories (or perhaps a framework or research program) that remains a mix of folk and scientific psychology. There are different versions, even by the same theorist. These theorists differ in how (or whether) they define *emotion, anger, fear,* and other key terms. Theorists disagree on what makes an emotion basic, how to account for non-basic emotions, how many emotions are basic, the role of cognitive processes, and so on. They differ in whether emotion is explicitly a causal entity or not. I cannot here consider every version, but rather those basic assumptions that implicitly or explicitly underlie many of the versions. I therefore examine a stark generic prototypical version, depicted in Figure 1.

On the version of BET in Figure 1, an event triggers an "affect program" (Ekman 1972; Tomkins 1962, 1963), which is a specific neural pattern to be found in the lower regions of the brain. The affect program then triggers a coordinated set of manifestations (often also called components), consisting of a unique subjective experience, a pattern of activity in the Autonomic Nervous System, facial and vocal expression, and characteristic overt behaviour. Because on BET they stem from a common cause, these manifestations are assumed to be correlated in time and intensity. Figure 1 is a schema into which any one of the basic emotions can be substituted. If *anger program* is substituted for *affect program* in Figure 1, then it becomes a BET for anger. There is a specific small number of basic emotions. All the rest are subcategories, mixtures, or blends of the basic emotions.

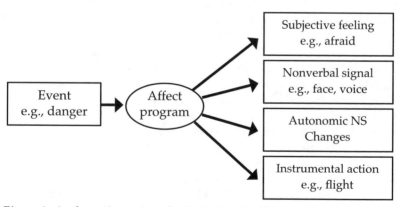

Figure 1: A schematic version of a Basic Emotion Theory.

BET implies various hypotheses about emotions, its components, and patterns among them. BET has generated a fair amount of evidence. I now discuss eight specific problems in a necessarily cursory way. Although BET is intuitively plausible, scientific evidence for it is surprisingly weak.

II.i. Facial Expression

Figure 1 implies that emotions are expressed in the face. Indeed, the most celebrated evidence for BET allegedly shows universal facial expressions for the basic emotions (Ekman 1972). Much of this evidence concerns *recognition*. That is, the evidence bears on the claim that, whatever their cultural heritage, observers agree among themselves in attributing the same emotion to certain facial expressions. Scrutiny of the primary (rather than secondary) sources reveals many problems with this evidence (Russell 1994). These studies typically relied on methods with a series of features that likely artificially inflated the amount of agreement: posed exaggerated expressions, highly pre-selected expressions, and all observers seeing all the expressions within the context of deciding which one from a short list of emotions to associate with each face. For example, substituting spontaneous for posed expressions substantially reduces the amount of agreement among observers. Similar reductions occur when other features of method are altered. With aboriginal societies, the studies likely also included experimental demand. Even if each such method factor alone exerted only a modest effect; together, these problems may cumulatively account for much of the agreement. It is not clear, especially for non-Western groups, whether agreement among observers would be much greater than chance if all method factors that exaggerate the amount of agreement were replaced with more neutral ones. People universally make reasonable interpretations of facial expressions, but it is far from clear that they universally attribute the same emotion to the predicted expressions. It is not even clear that people universally think of emotions in the same terms.

Evidence on the "universal recognition" hypothesis is unconvincing. Even if it were convincing, evidence on recognition would not show that having an emotion *produces* facial expressions. Surprisingly little evidence is available on this issue. Of course, human beings (young and old, sighted and blind, etc.) move their facial muscles. The question is the relationship of these movements to emotion. What little evidence exists on this question is not encouraging. For example, Camras (1992) examined one child for over a year and failed to find the predicted facial expressions in specific emotional circumstances. Fernandez-Dols and Ruiz-Belda (1995) found that persons in a clearly ecstatic state (having just won a gold medal at the Olympic Games) failed to smile except in specific social circumstances. When people in a certain emotional state do produce a facial expression, it may not be the full pattern presented in BET but a part of that pattern or a different pattern (Carroll and Russell 1997).

Proponents of BET can counter by pointing to non-emotional influences on facial movements. Consider one such influence: "display rules" – a notion that Ekman (1972) borrowed from Klineberg (1940). A display rule is a culture-specific norm dictating when the natural expression is allowed or is to be altered (inhibited, masked, or exaggerated). Display rules are problematic as a lifeline for BET for two reasons. First, it is not clear just how display rules account for the current evidence on production. Display rules are implausible with the young child studied by Camras or in the culturally heterogeneous group studied by Fernandez-Dols and Ruiz-Belda. Second, invoking display rules *ad hoc* whenever the BET-predicted facial expression fails to occur renders the BET account of faces non-falsifiable in the absence of a more detailed and predictive theory of display rules than we now have.

In addition, even when a part or whole of a BET-predicted facial expression does occur in the expected emotional circumstances, there are alternative explanations for that occurrence. Faces move as part of pretty much everything we do. Faces move as we speak, listen, attend, look away, shout, etc. We wrinkle our noses while smelling; we raise our brows while looking up. Faces change with the general arousal and positive versus negative quality of Core Affect (Lang et al. 1993). Specific facial signals may exist that evolved to guide social interactions, such as threat, greeting, and submission (Fridlund 1994). Fridlund pointed out that evolution is unlikely to have produced automatic veridical signals of emotional state (which would be indiscriminant altruism) but could have produced (and in many species did produce) signals that influence another's behaviour to the signaler's advantage. Thus, signaling one's fear would be non-adaptive in a hostile encounter (just as veridical signaling would be non-adaptive in poker), but a threat face could be useful. From all this information from the face, an observer can make a good guess about the express-er's situation, intention, and so on – including emotion. (This process may explain what agreement there is among observers on the emotion "expressed" by a given face.)

II.ii. Patterns in the Autonomic Nervous System

Studies by Ekman et al. (1983) found that three clusters of emotion could be differentiated by activity in the autonomic nervous system (ANS, which controls such peripheral activities as blood pressure and sweating). This finding suggested that each basic emotion would leave an identifiable fingerprint in the ANS, but no study has found them. But even if a study had done so, a methodological issue would then arise: In any one study, each specific emotion is confounded with vari-ous co-occurring events. Between, say, an anger and a fear condition in such a study, much is different: different eliciting circumstances, different memories, different thoughts, and so on. The ANS finger-print should be common to various instances of the emotion, however elicited. The key question is therefore whether the same ANS finger-print for each emotion emerges *across* different studies (i.e., across dif-ferent ways of creating the emotion, different memories, and so on). What is required is a meta-analysis, which is a statistical method for finding consistencies across studies. Meta-analyses examining this question (Cacioppo et al. 2000; Zajonc and McIntosh 1992) showed little evidence of such fingerprints for individual emotions or for the clusters of Ekman et al. (1983).

Of course, the ANS changes as one's circumstances change. But the explanation for those changes need not involve emotion concepts. ANS activity is ongoing, with both general features and specific chores to do. The ANS is influenced by Core Affect (Lang 1995; Lang et al. 1990). It is influenced by whether the eliciting situation is perceived as a threat or a challenging opportunity (Tomaka et al. 1997) or whether one is preparing to approach or avoid (Cacioppo et al. 2000; Lang et al. 1993). Tellingly, different ANS activity occurs for the same emotion elicited differently (Hamm et al. 1992) or with different behavioral implications (Hamm et al. 2003).

II.iii. Overt Behaviour

In folk psychology, flight is explained by fear, fight by anger. And human raters can reliably associate specific emotions with specific actions (Frijda and Tcherkasoff 1997). However, BET theorists have abandoned the claim that fear entails flight, anger entails fight, or other specific emotions entail other specific instrumental behaviours. Counter-examples are clear: fear without flight, anger without fight, and so on. Actual instrumental behaviour is not triggered automatically. Instead, behaviour is guided by the specific situation. Encountering the spider, Jane might simply flee; but afraid of a car accident, she might put on the brakes; afraid of a disease, she might telephone her doctor; afraid that her child is in danger, she might run toward the child. Animals can be constrained in cages such that freezing or flight is the only available response to a sign of danger, but given fewer constraints, monkeys explore the danger (MacDonald and Pinel 1991) and mother rats pick up their pups and move them to safety (Pinel and Mana 1989). Given such observations, BET's claim now is that emotions produce action *tendencies* (Frijda 1986). Still, Frijda's list of action tendencies does not match one-to-one his list of basic emotions. The move from action to action tendencies leaves actual action unexplained.

People do sometimes fight or flee or otherwise behave emotionally. It is unclear how BET contributes to an explanation of that behaviour, which can instead be explained in other ways. There are reflexes: startle, orienting, blinking, gag, etc, but these reflexes are more specific than emotions. Some behaviour is stimulus- and hormone-bound (Numan 2006), but again more specific than emotions. A person is usually engaged in pursuit of a hierarchy of goals through execution of plans. Goals and plans may be activated automatically (Bargh 1997). Emergencies arise, which call for hasty planning and quick execution of the plan. Even hasty instrumental behaviour is complexly determined and sensitive to situational demands (Bouton 2005). Fleeing a danger is a hastily constructed and executed plan.

II.iv. Subjective Feeling

People sometimes consciously *feel* angry, or afraid, and so on. BET accounts for such experiences through the assumption that each basic emotion entails a specific primitive subjective conscious experience:

the "feeling of" that emotion – much as the detection of light of a certain wavelength entails a unique primitive subjective conscious experience of red. The subjective feeling of an emotion has sometimes been called a "readout" or even "essence" of that emotion. Such terms suggest that the feeling is a veridical detection of the emotion. On BET, the number of such universal primitive emotional feelings equals the number of basic emotions.

Available evidence, however, does not support this account. Consider how emotions are categorized in different languages (Russell 1991; Wierzbicka 1999). One might think that if emotional feelings come in a small number of universal basic primitives, then all languages might lexicalize them; this is not the case. Or, even if not all are lexicalized, what words for emotions do exist in the world's languages would correspond to BET's basic emotions; this is not the case. Linguistic categories into which emotions are divided do not correspond one-to-one across languages.

Consider as well factor analytic studies of self-reported emotional experience. Factor analysis is a statistical technique designed to uncover the separate causal "factors" of the reported feelings. Such studies have not found factors of anger, fear, sadness, and so on, but instead found broader dimensions such as positive vs. negative and degree of arousal (Feldman Barrett and Russell 1999; Watson and Tellegen 1985). (This research led to the hypothesis of Core Affect.)

Of course, people do sometimes feel angry, sad, and so on. For many, acceptance of BET stems mainly from this simple fact. Such conscious feelings surely occur, but we need not accept BET's assumption of a small number of simple universal primitives. On my alternative account, such experiences are perceptions, no different in kind from other perceptions. Percepts are often compelling but they are not simple or primitive. They are rich complex end-products of processes involving concepts, learning, and context. They can be mistaken. They are not necessary for the occurrence of other components. There is an uncountable number of such percepts, family resemblance categories of which can be found. One prediction therefore is that these experiences vary to some degree with culture. Let me cite just one piece of evidence obtained in a study by Levenson et al. (1992). In their effort to find a universal ANS fingerprint for each basic emotion, they studied the Minankabau of West Sumatra. Participants were instructed to contract facial muscles into the prototypical configurations hypothesized for basic emotions. Doing so, in turn, alters ANS activity. For North Americans, this combination of facial muscle contractions and ANS activity resulted in some reports of the experience of the targeted emotion. For the Minankabau, however, the same procedure failed to produce the emotional experience.

II.v. Neuroscience of Affect Programs

Every psychological state or event is produced by the brain; different psychological states therefore imply different patterns of brain activity. This truism must be presupposed in any account of emotional episodes. BET provides the additional hypothesis of a unique pattern for all cases of each basic emotion.

Consistent with BET, research with non-human animals led Panksepp (1998) to postulate a discrete circuit for each basic emotion. However, Panksepp's list of basic circuits (seeking, fear, rage, lust, care, panic, and play) does not correspond to Ekman's (1972) list of basic emotions (happiness, surprise, fear, anger, disgust, and sadness). Panksepp circuits might best be thought of as mechanisms of basic mammalian behaviour, which may or may not be recruited in any given emotional episode. Despite its name, the "rage circuit" would not be unique to anger. The rage circuit might be recruited for aggressive behaviour in some cases of anger, but not others (anger over the injustice of war). The same circuit might also be recruited in some cases of fear (Jane might swat the spider in defensive aggression), joy (triumphant dominance over others), fun (rough-and-tumble play), or excitement (competitive sport).

With humans, neuroimaging has been used to search for neural correlates of discrete emotions. Such studies are subject to a methodological issue similar to the one described earlier in regard to an ANS fingerprint for each emotion. Two events that are different psychologically must be different neurally. *Within* any given study, different emotions (each with a different eliciting event, different memories, and so on) will therefore be associated with different patterns of brain activation, but the key question is whether the brain activation pattern for a given emotion remains constant *across* different studies (i.e., across different ways of eliciting the emotion, different types of accompanying memories, etc.). Two recent meta-analyses found only modest consistency across studies (Murphy et al. 2003; Phan et al. 2002). The two analyses did not agree with each other on the most likely brain pattern for some emotions. Further, no brain pattern has been found unique to a given emotion.

II.vi. Encapsulation

Basic emotions are said to be encapsulated from general cognition (Griffiths 1997). That Jane was afraid of a spider she knows to be harmless illustrates the idea. Many people have experienced fear watching a film, even though they know that no real danger exists. Prinz (2004) gave as another example sadness resulting from the experience of art (reading a novel, listening to music, or even hearing a D minor chord); in each case, the sad person knows that no real loss has occurred but feels sad nonetheless.

BET does not generally include encapsulation and, indeed, theorists typically endorse a contrary view: that emotions are determined by (or include) cognitive appraisal processes (Frijda 1986; Lazarus 1991; Ortony et al. 1987; Roseman 1991). More generally, in the examples cited, some perception and cognition are involved (Jane *saw* the spider; people must *see* and *understand* the film or *hear* the music.). So, the first question is what precisely is encapsulated from what. The idea that basic emotions are encapsulated from general cognitive information has not been translated into a scientifically testable hypothesis.

Equally important, support for encapsulation is largely limited to anecdotes such as those I cited. The next question is therefore whether the anecdotes are real and reliable. If real and reliable, then the question is this: to which classes of event can the cases of encapsulation be generalized? After all, people's beliefs, desires, and actions are sometimes inconsistent with one another. Therefore the real cases would need to be examined carefully to show that it is emotion, rather than something else, that is encapsulated.

To illustrate, return to Jane and the spider. The story I told is fiction, but readers find it believable because it is consistent with our folk theory, and, of course, people do get frightened by spiders. So, such events would have to be examined to find out what precisely occurs. We need to know whether the entire BET fear reaction occurs, or if what is encapsulated is, for instance, simply the startle reflex. Or return to the anecdotes of emotion in response to art. Core Affect responds to the contents of consciousness irrespective of one's knowledge of whether the contents are real or fiction. Core Affect responds to virtual reality. A horror film may create a Core Affect of upset, rather than the full-blown BET emotion of fear: people do not flee the theatre; indeed, they pay to attend. Similarly, the sadness from reading a novel, listening to music, or hearing a D minor chord may be limited to Core Affect. So, cases of encapsulation do not necessarily entail BET. It might be that what is encapsulated and beyond certain kinds of cognitive control is a reflex, Core Affect, or something else.

II.vii. Scope of Basic Emotion Theory

BET is a theory of emotion. This broad but vague scope is problematic. Many important emotions – love (of a romantic partner, of offspring, of humanity), hate, envy, jealousy, depression, anxiety, sympathy, empathy, regret, hope – have not been satisfactorily accounted for by BET. The term *emotion* is limited to a small number of languages (Russell 1991) and is ill-defined (Fehr and Russell 1984). I see no reason to believe that *emotion* is a homogeneous class and there is reason to suspect the opposite (Griffiths 1997). Such features make emotion a problematic concept as a scientific tool (although as a concept, *emotion* remains an object of scientific study). For example, it is unclear in investigating BET which events provide a test for BET and which are outside its scope.

The same problem arises with the subcategories of emotion clearly within the scope of BET: anger, disgust, fear, happiness, surprise, and sadness. These categories appear not to be homogeneous classes (Russell and Fehr 1994). Humans tend to think in terms of anecdotes and prototypical exemplars, but we must not assume that what is true of one member of a category is true of other members of that category, especially for everyday folk categories. Even if some examples of anger (flash of anger at being punched), disgust (at rotten food), or fear (of a looming spider) show a property such as speed or encapsulation, it does not follow that the same is true of other examples of anger (long-held indignation at an injustice), disgust (at taboo violations), or fear (of developing cancer).

II.viii. Coherence and the Existence of Patterns

Suppose for the sake of argument that the alternative explanations I've mentioned so far for each separate component are plausible such that no one component entails BET. One might still argue that basic emotions are implied by the patterns among those components. The single most important prediction of BET therefore is this: the manifestations/components (the right column in Figure 1) of an emotion are highly correlated with each other in time and intensity. This prediction follows from the model of Figure 1 because all manifestations stem from a single cause. But this prediction also follows from the definition of a basic emotion as a pattern of components.

Research has repeatedly uncovered surprisingly weak correlations among these manifestations (Lang 1968, 1995; Mandler et al. 1961; Rachman and Hodgson 1974). In the most sophisticated set of laboratory studies on this topic, Reisenzein (2000) examined the intercorrelations among four components of surprise: cognitive appraisal, self-reported experience of surprise, reaction time, and facial expression. Correlations were modest, with the exception of one relation that is close to a tautology: a correlation between self-reported feeling of surprise and self-reported appraisal of the stimulus as unexpected.

A single central mechanism (the affect program) is not the only possible explanation of what correlations do exist. There are three alternatives. First, environmental features can be correlated. If two correlated environmental features each elicit a separate response, then those two responses will be correlated – even if there is no internal link between the two responses. To illustrate, suppose that friends tend to be more predictable in their behaviour than are strangers. Suppose further that friends elicit smiles of greeting and that predictability elicits an ANS pattern of cardiac deceleration. If so, smiling and cardiac deceleration will be correlated. There need be no internal common cause or internal link between smiles and cardiac response.

Second, one component process can influence another. For example, suppose that forming the face into an intense expression (such as the "anger face" or "threat face") alters breathing and muscle tension, which in turn alters ANS activity, perhaps cardiac acceleration. The consequence would be that the threat face is correlated with cardiac acceleration.

And, third, two components will be correlated when they are both influenced by a central mechanism other than emotion. For example, suppose that a person makes the calculated decision to be friendly to a stranger. This decision leads to both smiling and behavioural approach.

In short, the existence of patterns of weakly correlated components does not imply that these patterns stem from an affect program or any other single source. Proponents of BET might reply that patterns among the components do occur nonetheless, and I agree. The question is the nature of these patterns, how to define them, how they come about, how frequently they occur, and whether they naturally divide into a small number of universal categories.

Here is an alternative way to think about patterns. Each of the many component processes that make up the emotion pattern is ongoing. The ANS is always in some state; facial muscles often move; people are always behaving; and so on. The component processes therefore always form some pattern. As the processes change, new patterns form. Most such patterns are uninteresting and have no name. Even if the processes were completely independent of one another, interesting and nameable patterns would occasionally form by the laws of chance. Most poker hands are uninteresting and have no name, but even when cards are dealt randomly in a fair game, interesting and nameable hands (such as a royal flush) arise from time to time. To the extent that the component emotion processes are somewhat correlated with each other, certain patterns are that much more likely to form. The occasional formation of an interesting and nameable pattern of emotion components, or of cards in poker, does not imply that these patterns are anything more than happenstance.

My alternative proposal is not actually happenstance, but this: an uncountable number of patterns occur because the components change in response to circumstances. Each such token event (each specific combination of components occurring in a specific person, time, and place) is psychologically constructed to suit the immediate circumstances. The events are constructed on the fly rather than pre-formed. If so, one might ask, how is it that we perceive a small rather than uncountable number of emotions?

II.ix. Perception of Emotion

The lack of evidence for BET is surprising because BET seems obviously true. Emotion is not ordinarily thought of as a hypothesis, but as something we see. We witness events such as Jane's fear of the spider and we experience fear ourselves. BET is implicit in the words – *emotion, fear, anger,* and so on – that we use to ask questions and formulate answers. These observations and experiences of emotions do not, however, entail BET. Instead, they are further events that require explanation.

In observing other persons or ourselves, we bring to the task a set of concepts inherited from our linguistic ancestors – for English speakers, these are concepts such as *emotion, fear, anger,* and so on. These everyday concepts lack necessary and sufficient features but entail heterogeneous clusters with fuzzy borders. Members of the category resemble one another along different dimensions. A concept such as *fear* is a prototypical script that specifies a temporal and causal pattern among its various components, but exemplars of the concept need not fit the script exactly.

A person witnesses a pattern of components in another or in him- or herself. Many such patterns will seem random and go nameless, but sometimes the pattern will resemble the script/concept for a specific emotion. Resemblance is a matter of degree, and so while some cases will be excellent examples of the script/concept, many will be mediocre examples, and some will be borderline such that one is not sure if it belongs inside or outside the category. The same event can resemble more than one script, albeit typically to different degrees. When resemblance is sufficient, we see the emotion in another or experience it in ourselves. Such sightings and experiences are not veridical detections but after-the-fact labelings.

II.x. Interim Conclusion and Retrenchment

As a research program, BET is faring poorly. Perhaps the version portrayed in Figure 1 can be accused of being a straw man. Perhaps the same complaint would be made of any explicit version of it. Because there are many possible versions of BET, no one problem found with it is lethal. Thus, the evidence does not rule out BET. New revised versions can always be created.

For example, faced with failure to find an ANS fingerprint for each basic emotion, one could propose that emotion-specific ANS finger-prints exist but are hidden by measurement difficulties or by the demands of simultaneously occurring behaviour. Or the ANS finger-prints could be moved to their origin in the brain with only shadows seen in the periphery. Or the ANS component could be abandoned altogether, leaving the rest of BET intact. Similarly, one could abandon the idea of a central organizing mechanism (the affect program in the centre of Figure 1) and simply think of emotion as a pattern directly produced by the stimulus.

A major conceptual retrenchment is also possible. BET's scope could be limited to a few basic emotions, anger, fear, and a few more (Griffiths 1997). And, for scientific purposes, anger, fear, etc, could themselves be re-defined. No such re-definitions for BET's central concepts have been developed, but suppose that with re-definition all cases of *anger, disgust,* and *fear* and other hypothesized basic emotions necessarily have certain of the properties listed in Figure 1. It is not clear what proportion of cases of what is now called *fear* or *anger* and so on would have to be excluded. Depending on the definition, many, most, or even nearly all cases might have been excluded. Given the surprising heterogeneity within the current categories of anger, etc., re-defined limited homogeneous categories would be very different from what we have today. Further, even with re-definition, it remains a scientific question whether BET provides the best account of these limited cases. A more general question is whether the reconceptual-ized BET has much to say about human emotional life.

III. Modularity Revisited

The concept of Core Affect opens up an alternative perspective on our emotional lives, of which blue ribbon emotions of BET are but a tiny part. This perspective has many implications, but I limit myself here to its implications for modularity. The heterogeneity and highly variable nature of the basic emotion categories of BET do not support modularity of those categories. On my alternative, the question of modularity is asked not of the pattern/emotion category but of each component process separately. Questions about instrumental behav-iour, facial behaviour, the autonomic nervous system, and so on can be referred to the appropriate branch of psychology. Each component may or may not be modular. After farming out these questions, we are left with but one process: Core Affect.

Core Affect too may or may not be modular. It does have certain modular-like features: unique output, fast, an evolutionary explanation, and so on, although encapsulation merits some discussion. Some examples of Core Affect strongly suggest information encapsulation. Core Affect is changed directly by chemicals, both uppers and downers and euphoric and dysphoric drugs. Indeed, it is precisely the Core-Affect-altering properties of drugs that make them objects of abuse or avoidance. We often experience feelings for which we have no name or explanation. Encapsulation is also suggested by Core Affect's responses to virtual reality in art, memory, fantasy, imagination, and so on. Knowledge that the circumstances are not "real" does not diminish the Core Affect.

On the other hand, cognitively processed information can be a powerful influence on Core Affect: news of winning a lottery, learning of the death of a loved one, reading about injustice, and pondering a distant danger such as global warming all require cognition. These examples also have another feature in common: conscious attention to the information. Let me speculate that general cognitive appraisals per se do not alter Core Affect (or not much) unless we are conscious of them. Consider the excitement of winning the lottery. If the news continues to invade consciousness (obsessive thoughts, reminders), then it continues to shape Core Affect. But if one is distracted and thoughts about the win are pushed out of consciousness, then the excitement fades. On this speculation, Core Affect is encapsulated from general information, with the major exception of information – real or fictive – seen through the window of consciousness.

References

Bargh, J. A. 1997. The automaticity of everyday life. In *The Automaticity of Everyday Life: Advances in Social Cognition*, ed. R. S. Wyer Jr., 10: 1–61. Mahwah: Erlbaum.

Bouton, M. E. 2005. Behavior systems and the contextual control of anxiety, fear, and panic. In *Emotion and Consciousness*, ed. L. F. Barrett, P. M. Niedenthal and P. Winkielman, 205–27. New York: Guilford.

Cacioppo, J. T., G. G. Berntson, J. T. Larsen, K. M. Poehlmann, and T. A. Ito. 2000. The psychophysiology of emotion. In *Handbook of Emotions*, 2nd ed., ed. M. Lewis and J. M. Haviland-Jones, 173–91. New York: Guilford.

Camras, L. A. 1992. Expressive development and basic emotions. *Cognition and Emotion*, 6: 269–83.

Carroll, J. M., and J. A. Russell. 1997. Facial expressions in Hollywood's portrayal of emotion. *Journal of Personality and Social Psychology*, 72: 164–76.

Ekman, P. 1972. Universals and cultural differences in facial expressions of emotions. In *Nebraska Symposium on Motivation 1971*, ed. J. K. Cole, 207–83. Lincoln: University of Nebraska Press.

Ekman, P., R. W. Levenson, and W. V. Friesen. 1983. Autonomic nervous system activity distinguishes among emotions. *Science* 221: 1208–1210.

Fehr, B., and J. A. Russell. 1984. Concept of emotion viewed from a prototype perspective. *Journal of Experimental Psychology: General* 113: 464–86.

Feldman Barrett, L., and J. A. Russell. 1999. The structure of current affect: Controversies and emerging consensus. *Current Directions in Psychological Science* 8: 10–14.

Fernandez-Dols, J. M., and M. A. Ruiz-Belda. 1995. Are smiles a sign of happiness? Gold medal winners at the Olympic Games. *Journal of Personality and Social Psychology* 69: 1113–1119.

Fridlund, A. J. 1994. *Human Facial Expression: An Evolutionary View*. San Diego: Academic.

Frijda, N. H. 1986. *The Emotions*. Cambridge: Cambridge University Press.

Fridja, N. H., and A. Tcherkassof. 1997. Facial expressions as modes of action readiness. In *The Psychology of Facial Expression*, ed. J. A. Russell and J. M. Fernandez-Dols, 78–102. New York: Cambridge University Press.

Griffiths, P. E. 1997. *What Emotions Really Are: The Problem of Psychological Categories*. Chicago: University of Chicago Press.

Hamm, A. O., M. Gerlach J. Globisch, and D. Vaitl. 1992. Phobia specific startle reflex modulation during affective imagery and slide viewing. *Psychophysiology* 29: S36.

Hamm, A. O., H. T. Schupp, and A. I. Weike. 2003. Motivational organization of emotions: Autonomic changes, cortical responses, and reflex modulation. In *Handbook of Affective Sciences*, ed. R. J. Davidson, K. R. Scherer and H. H. Goldsmith, 187–211. Oxford: Oxford University Press.

Klineberg, O. 1940. *Social Psychology*. New York: Holt.

Lang, P. J. 1968. Fear reduction and fear behavior: Problems in treating a construct. In *Research in Psychotherapy*, ed. J. Schlien, 3: 90–103. Washington (DC): American Psychological Association.

Lang, P. J. 1995. The emotion probe. *American Psychologist* 50: 372–95.

Lang, P. J., M. M. Bradley, and B. N. Cuthbert. 1990. Emotion, attention and the startle reflex. *Psychological Review* 97: 377–95.

Lang, P. J., M. K. Greenwald, M. M. Bradley, and A. O. Hamm. 1993. Looking at pictures: Affective, facial, visceral and behavioral reactions. *Psychophysiology* 30: 261–73.

Lazarus, R. S. 1991. *Emotion and Adaptation*. New York: Oxford University Press.

Levenson, R. W., P. Ekman, K. Heider, and W. V. Friesen. 1992. Emotion and autonomic nervous system activity in the Minangkabau of West Sumatra. *Journal of Personality and Social Psychology* 62: 972–88.

MacDonald, S. E., and J.P.J. Pinel. 1991. Information gathering: A component of the defensive behavior of rats and Old-World monkeys. *Psychological Record* 41: 207–15.

Mandler, G., J. M. Mandler, I. Kremen, and R. Sholiton. 1961. The response to threat: Relations among verbal and physiological indices. *Psychological Monographs* 75(513).

Murphy, F. C., I. Nimmo-Smith, and A. D. Lawrence. 2003. Functional neuroanatomy of emotion: A meta-analysis. *Cognitive, Affective and Behavioral Neuroscience* 3: 207–33.

Numan, M. 2006. Hypothalamic neural circuits regulating maternal responsiveness towards infants. *Behavioral and Cognitive Neuroscience Review* 5: 163–90.

Ortony, A., G. L. Clore, and A. Collins. 1987. *The Cognitive Structure Of Emotions*. New York: Cambridge University.

Panksepp, J. 1998. *Affective Neuroscience*. New York: Oxford University.

Phan, K. L., T. D. Wager, S. F. Taylor, and I. Liberzon. 2002. Functional neuroanatomy of emotion. A meta-analysis of emotion activation studies in PET and f MRI. *NeuroImage* 16: 331–48.

Pinel, J.P.J. and M. J. Mana. 1989. Adaptive interaction of rats with dangerous inanimate objects: Support for a cognitive theory of defensive behavior. In *Ethoexperimental Approaches to the Study of Behavior*, ed. R. J. Blanchard, P. F. Brain, D. C. Blanchard and S. Parmigiani, 137–50. Norwell (Mass.): Kluwer Academic.

Prinz, J. 2004. *Gut Reactions: A Perceptual Theory of Emotion*. New York: Oxford University Press.

Rachman, S., and R. J. Hodgson. 1974. Synchrony and desynchrony in fear and avoidance. *Behavior Research and Therapy* 12: 311–18.

Reisenzein, R. 2000. Exploring the strength of association between the components of emotion syndromes: The case of surprise. *Cognition and Emotion* 14: 1–38.

Roseman, I. 1991. Appraisal determinants of discrete emotions. *Cognition and Emotion* 5: 161–200.

Russell, J. A. 1991. Culture and the categorization of emotion. *Psychological Bulletin* 100: 426–50.

Russell, J. A. 1994. Is there universal recognition of emotion from facial expression? A review of the cross-cultural studies. *Psychological Bulletin* 155: 102–41.

Russell, J. A. 2003. Core affect and the psychological construction of emotion. *Psychological Review* 110: 145–72.

Russell, J. A., and B. Fehr. 1994. Fuzzy concepts in a fuzzy hierarchy: Varieties of anger. *Journal of Personality and Social Psychology* 67: 186–205.

Tomaka, J., J. Blascovich, J. Kibler, and J. M. Ernst. 1997. Cognitive and physiological antecedents of threat and challenge appraisal. *Journal of Personality and Social Psychology* 73: 63–72.

Tomkins, S. S. 1962. *Affect, Imagery, Consciousness: Vol. 1. The Positive Affects.* New York: Springer.

Tomkins, S. S. 1963. *Affect, Imagery, Consciousness: Vol. 2. The Negative Affects.* New York: Springer.

Watson, D., and A. Tellegen. 1985. Toward a consensual structure of mood. *Psychological Bulletin* 98: 219–35.

Wierzbicka, A. 1999. *Emotions Across Languages and Cultures.* New York: Cambridge University Press.

Zajonc, R. B., and D. N. McIntosh, D. N. 1992. Emotions research: Some promising questions and some questionable promises. *Psychological Science* 3: 70–74.

CANADIAN JOURNAL OF PHILOSOPHY
Supplementary Volume 32

Beyond the Basics: The Evolution and Development of Human Emotions

ROBYN BLUHM

The suggestion that at least some emotions are modular captures a number of our intuitions about emotions: they are generally fast responses to a stimulus, they are involuntary, and they are easily distinguished (at least in most cases) from one another; we simply know that, for example, anger feels different than fear. Candidates for modular emotions are usually the so-called "basic" emotions – anger and fear are good examples of these. Defenders of emotion theories that focus on basic emotions, such as Paul Ekman in psychology and Paul Griffiths in philosophy, emphasize the advantages of theories that stress the evolutionary continuity of emotional expression and link emotions to the activity of neural circuits that are similar in human beings and other animals.

In this paper, however, I will examine arguments for the *discontinuity of emotions in human beings, as compared with other animals. Owing to a combination of cultural practices and neuroanatomy, both our emotional "wiring" and our emotions are unique. Moreover, contrary to the claims of evolutionary continuity noted above, the evolutionary processes that culminated in this uniqueness also have important consequences for the extent to which emotions can be said to be modular. In making this case, I will begin by outlining Griffiths' "psychoevolutionary theory" of emotion and his application of Fodor's (1983) work on modularity to emotion. I will then suggest that, at least in human beings, the "basic" emotions that are the topic of Griffiths' work are not so basic, after all. Drawing on work on psychological development during infancy by Allan Schore and by Stanley Greenspan and Stuart Shanker, as well as work on the cognitive consequences of human brain evolution by Terrence Deacon, I will show that the neural circuits underpinning Griffiths' modular "affect-programs" may not be as independent as a module is usually held to be. In the last two sections of the paper, I will return to the issue of modularity and suggest that what remains of the modular nature of emotions can also be explained with reference to the evolution of the central nervous system and that, in fact, even the modularity of emotions in nonhuman animals is limited. If my account is correct, then the psychological differences between human and nonhuman emotion reflect biological differences that are simply the most recent step in a long evolutionary process.

I. The Psychoevolutionary Theory of Emotion and the Modularity of Affect-Programs

Griffiths proposes his psychoevolutionary theory as an alternative to the cognitive conception of emotion, which he saw as dominating philosophy. On this cognitive account, Griffiths notes, emotions are held to be judgments that are made on the basis of the propositional attitudes held towards the object of emotion. According to Griffiths, "[t]he philosophical cognitivist claims that it is a necessary condition of fearing something that you believe it to be dangerous, and desire to avoid the danger" (Griffiths 2003, 257). He points out that not only is this account not sufficient to explain emotion (and that additional criteria that have been suggested to supplement the beliefs and desires seem rather *ad hoc*), it is actually not even necessary. The existence of irrational emotional responses, in which, for example, we fear something without believing it is really dangerous, shows that there is something seriously wrong with the cognitivist theory of emotions.

The psychoevolutionary theory that Griffiths proposes as a replacement is radically different from the cognitivist theory, and Griffiths is quite honest about the price that will have to be paid in adopting it. Whereas cognitivism takes as its starting point our everyday talk of emotion and the range of emotions that we describe ourselves as experiencing, on the psychoevolutionary theory the types of emotions that are allowed is restricted to those that can be cashed out in biological terms, specifically, in terms of neural circuits and of the expression of emotional behaviour. As a result, the range of emotions that will be admitted is much more restricted than that found in cognitivist accounts and, moreover, may not even consist of emotions we are used to recognizing. (Panksepp's [1998] proposed "expectancy" response is an example of such an emotion.)

These differences are due to the fact that the psychoevolutionary account of emotion is designed to answer a different range of questions than is the cognitivist view. Griffiths is primarily interested in identifying the "basic" emotions common to all human beings, and found in at least some other species, rather than the complex and culturally influenced experiences that make up a significant part of our emotional experience. He argues that this "folk" categorization will not be likely to survive scientific scrutiny and that a philosophical theory of emotions should therefore pay careful attention to those emotions that *are* able to figure in a scientific theory. Scientific work to date suggests that these emotions are those that are: fast (lasting on the order of seconds, as opposed to moods, which are longer lasting), universal across cultures, and associated with particular motor responses (of facial musculature, vocal musculature, skeletal musculature, and of the autonomic nervous system). While Griffiths does not give a definitive taxonomy of emotions, he points to the work of Ekman and his colleagues as providing one possible breakdown, which consists of anger, fear, surprise, joy, disgust, and sadness (see Griffiths 2003, 269); Griffiths adopts these categories as "affect-program responses." Affect-programs are what trigger the motor responses that characterize an emotion, and it is these affect-programs that Griffiths suggests are likely to be modular.

In describing the modular nature of affect-programs, Griffiths draws on the work of Jerry Fodor. In *The Modularity of Mind* (1983), Fodor describes nine characteristics that he suggests are typically possessed by modular systems. Griffiths' discussion of affect-programs centres on the claim that these responses possess at least several of these characteristics. In particular, affect-programs are fast, they are associated with specific neural circuits, they operate in a mandatory fashion (at least in some cases), and, most importantly, they are informationally encapsulated. This last characteristic, according to Fodor, is the essence of modularity (at least for the input systems on which Fodor's own discussion centres) and is also the source of the analogy between modules and reflexes (Fodor 1983, 71). Griffiths borrows the analogy with reflexes in describing affect-programs, and he argues that they, too, are informationally encapsulated. What this means in

Fodor's account is that the operation of input systems draws only on a limited domain of inputs and thus occurs independently of what the system, as a whole, knows. Fodor's examples, though, are generally given in terms of vision or of language perception, so what informational encapsulation means in these areas is that what we see does not depend on what we expect to see; the words we hear do not depend on what we might expect an individual to say under the circumstances. The informational encapsulation of affect-programs is also important in Griffiths' theory of emotions, as this characteristic is supposed to explain cases in which we experience irrational emotional responses. Someone with a phobia about earthworms, for example, has a fear response despite the fact that, rationally, he knows that worms are harmless. Because the fear affect-program does not receive information from the individual's stock of rational beliefs about worms, the phobic response occurs anyway.

There is very likely some truth in Griffiths' account of emotions; however, I believe that it is too narrow in its scope and, as a result, can never hope to capture the complexity of even our basic emotional experiences. To begin with, note that my concern is with Griffiths' failure to account for emotional *experience*; his discussion is couched instead in terms of emotional *responses*. By concentrating solely on the motor responses associated with basic emotions, Griffiths leaves out entirely something that most people would likely see as the quintessential characteristic of emotions, namely, their phenomenology. We know what it is like to *feel* anger, or joy, or disgust, and it does not seem unreasonable to expect that a theory of emotions should take these feelings into account. Moreover, even Griffiths' account of emotional responses is inadequate, since it involves only "shallow" emotional responses. While the psychoevolutionary theory emphasizes that emotions inherently involve a motor response, the extent of this response is very limited; the triggering of an affect-program causes changes to posture, facial expression, and vocal musculature, as well as to autonomic functioning. These affect-programs, however, do not account for the complex behaviours that are triggered by emotions (and that are sometimes, though not always, tempered by further judgment).[1]

---

1 I will distinguish between the motor changes resulting from the operation of Griffiths' affect-programs and more complex, often voluntary, responses, by

Both of these shortcomings, the focus on shallow responses and the lack of interest in phenomenology, could perhaps be justified on the grounds that Griffiths wishes to emphasize the evolutionary aspects of emotion; because of this he focuses on (as mentioned earlier) cross-cultural universals and similarities with emotion in other animals. Certainly the behavioural responses to emotional stimuli may differ widely between individuals in the same culture, let alone across cultures, and of course at least some human responses are unique to our species. It could also be argued that many or all non-human animals do not have emotional experiences, that phenomenological aspect of emotions is unique to human beings. (Joseph LeDoux, in *The Emotional Brain* (1996) appears to take this line.) I believe, however, that both of these shortcomings must be addressed. Because of this, I propose to revise Griffiths' discussion of the neural circuitry of emotions in order to provide framework for a richer and more complex account of emotions. I am interested primarily in human emotion, and what makes it different from emotions in other animals; however, I also think that Griffiths' affect-programs fail to do justice to emotions experienced by other animals. In the next section of the paper, I will look at qualities of human emotions that are most likely unique to human beings. In particular, I stress the importance of postnatal development of the human brain, specifically the prefrontal cortex, for human emotions. In the following section, I point out that the evolutionary changes that underlie the unique aspects of human emotion are simply the most recent step in the evolution of the nervous system; Griffith's emphasis on reflexive "affect-programs" means that his theory leaves out important aspects of emotion in non-human animals, as well as in human beings. The result will be an account that builds on Griffiths' insights about the evolutionarily derived affect patterns that underlie basic emotions, but that permits a richer and more complex understanding of our emotional life, one that has the potential to do justice to the intuitions about our own emotions that Griffiths had to discard.

---

referring to the former as "emotional responses" and to the latter as "emotional behaviour"

II. Human Emotion

Part of the discontinuity between human emotions and those of other animals is that human emotions are, at least to some extent, culturally mediated. Griffiths does acknowledge this point, stressing that the details of human emotional experience are influenced by culture. Cultural forces modify the expression of emotions, lead us to describe our emotions in particular ways, and in some cases even affect the emotions that we feel and the extent to which we feel them. (For example, Griffiths cites "piety" as an emotion the experience of which is more common in some cultures than others – and at different times in the same culture.) Griffiths, however, wants a theory of emotion to distinguish these "folk" emotional categories from those emotions that can be studied by physiologists and evolutionary theorists; his theory thus advocates a split between the natural expression of emotion (which he claims is similar in humans and in many other animals) and the modification of this natural expression in human beings by cultural forces. Yet there may well be reason to question the validity of this distinction. And even if we do want to, for at least some purposes, preserve this distinction, perhaps in order to divide the explanatory burden between biologists and social scientists, it is surely part of the biologist's job to explain the factors in virtue of which "natural" emotions can be so altered. What is it about human emotion, in other words, that is *different* from emotion in other animals?

The answer, I suspect, is that human emotion is profoundly influenced by our social interactions with other human beings. Not merely the sophisticated, culturally mediated aspects of appropriate social behaviour, but the very expression of Griffiths' affect patterns depends on social factors. In making this case, I draw on Griffiths' discussion of the role of the limbic system in emotion and on work on the importance of early childhood relationships in the development of emotion and of the brain itself.

I noted earlier that one of the characteristics of modules is that they are associated with specific neural circuits. This feature plays only a limited role in Fodor's discussion of modularity but is central to Griffiths' views on emotional modules. Griffiths describes the neural basis of his modular affect patterns in terms of MacLean's theory of the triune brain (MacLean 1950). MacLean noted that, from an evolutionary perspective, the brain can be divided into three main regions. The brain stem is concerned with maintaining basic survival functions and is the oldest region of the brain. Most recent in evolutionary development is the cerebral cortex, which occurs in mammals and is by far the best developed in human beings. In between these regions in both evolutionary and anatomical terms is the limbic system, which shows up first in reptiles. It is this region that appears to be most closely connected with emotional responses and that Griffiths suggests is "the natural place to look" (Griffiths 2003, 268) for emotional circuits in human beings as well. He cautions against too readily assuming that inheritance of structure means inheritance of function but suggests that it does provide a rational basis for a research strategy and one that has been supported by evidence by MacLean and others.

It appears, though, that MacLean's influence on Griffiths goes beyond this acceptance of the limbic system as the locus of emotional response. MacLean further believed that the functional relationships between the three brain regions were, at best, incomplete and, at worst, dangerously incomplete. "It cannot be overemphasized that these three basic brains show great differences in structure and chemistry.... The wonder is that nature was able to hook them up and establish any kind of communication between them" (MacLean 1973, 7). In fact, MacLean's early work (1949), even predating the triune brain theory, focused on the psychological problems that arise because of imperfect communication between the limbic and neomammalian brain regions. In particular, he suggested that associations made at the level of the limbic system might not be open to modification by higher cortical centres, resulting in, for example, phobias. This point is reminiscent of Griffiths' discussion of irrational emotions, such as fear of a harmless earthworm. It appears that Griffiths' conception of modular affect patterns that link a stimulus directly with an emotional response relies on a functional separation between these limbic circuits and the cortical centres involved in rational belief. Griffiths further suggests that it is only a matter of coincidence – literally, temporal coincidence – that results in the majority of our emotions being compatible with our rational beliefs. "The judgment that [a] current stimulus is dangerous can occur in two ways. First, it can arise through the normal process of belief fixation. Secondly, the modular triggering system may class a stimulus as falling into one of the emotion-evoking categories and trigger the affect-program response. If these processes run in tandem, as they often do, the subject will both exhibit the symptoms of fear, and assert that the cause of his fear is dangerous" (Griffiths 2003, 272).

But it does not seem likely that the relationship between emotional and cognitive responses is so tenuous, nor that the neural circuits subserving them are as distinct as MacLean believed (and as Griffiths seems to accept). An alternative, and I believe more reasonable, account of the connections between these regions is provided by work by Allen Schore and by Terrence Deacon. These authors emphasize the intimate relationship between the anatomy of the neomammalian brain (specifically the prefrontal cortex) and the limbic system. Schore is concerned with the experience-dependent maturation of the prefrontal cortex in early infancy. Drawing on work in psychological attachment theory, neuroanatomy, and clinical psychology, Schore suggests that the early relationship between a mother and her infant sculpts the development of the prefrontal cortex, particularly the orbitofrontal regions. Critical to my argument in this paper is the specific nature of the interaction; during this period, the mother is teaching the infant how to regulate her emotions. This process is described by Greenspan and Shanker (2004):

> Babies, older nonhuman animals and barroom brawlers usually experience affects or emotions in a 'catastrophic' way. Catastrophic emotions are intense global emotional states, such as massive rage, fear or emotional hunger or neediness, that press for direct discharge in fixed actions. These intense global feeling states are often tied to the flight or fight reactions, massive avoidance, approach, seeking behaviors, or other basic responses.... In human development, however, infants can learn to 'tame' catastrophic emotional patterns. Early to midway in the first year of life, caregivers help babies begin to learn how to transform catastrophic emotions into interactive signals. (Greenspan and Shanker 2004, 27–28).

These encounters result in "back-and-forth" signaling between the child and the caregiver and are the basis for the child's learning to signal intent, rather than launching directly into action. The caregiver's response to the infant's intent in turn fosters the infant's development of skills in emotion regulation. "The baby is learning to show a little annoyance, to negotiate, and to get his needs met. There is, therefore, less of a tendency to explode into desperate action" (Schore 1994, 32). This lessening tendency, according to Schore, is associated with the development and maintenance of neuronal connections between the limbic system and the prefrontal cortex. During this period of infancy, environmental influences shape the development of the limbic system (Joseph 1999), input from which in turn is required for the normal development of the (neomammalian) prefrontal cortex. Thus, the structure of the prefrontal cortex depends critically on environmental, specifically social, input.[2]

However, the development of neural connections is only part of the story, as it has been well established that a large part of early neural development involves *losing* neurons and the connections between them. This process functions on a "use-it-or-lose-it" basis: connections that are not used wither away and cells that do not make an adequate number of connections also die off. Terrence Deacon, in his analysis of the importance of the prefrontal cortex for uniquely human capacities such as language and other symbol use, emphasizes the fact that, compared to even our closest evolutionary relatives, human beings have a great deal of prefrontal cortex. The prefrontal cortex accounts for approximately 29 per cent of the total cortex in human beings, and 17 per cent in chimpanzees (compared with 7 per cent in the dog and 3.5 per cent in the cat; Brodmann, cited in Fuster 1989, 3). Deacon argues that the massive changes in the relative size of this structure means that it plays an important role in the developmental "sculpting" of the brain. "In general terms, relative increases in certain neuronal populations will tend to translate into the more effective recruitment of afferent and efferent connections in the competition for axons and synapses" (Deacon 1997, 207). That is, the prefrontal cortex, due to its size, ends up being involved in a proportionately large number of the synaptic connections between different brain regions. Moreover, because the development of the brain during infancy involves the selective development and maintenance of neural connections, the degree of functional separation between the limbic and cortical regions that MacLean and Griffiths endorse does not seem very plausible. In

---

2 Later in life, these prefrontal structures will also be important in the cognitive control of emotion; see Ochsner and Gross (2005).

fact, the prefrontal cortex is strongly connected, via the orbitofrontal regions, with areas of the limbic system, including the basal amygdala, hippocampus, and hypothalamus (Groenwegen and Uylings 2000).

Thus it appears that the *structural* separation of the neomammalian and limbic brains is over-emphasized in MacLean's work, and given that functional connectivity is necessary for the preservation of structural connectivity, it also appears that the operation of these two regions is much closer than might be suggested by Griffiths' theory. The question, then, is *how* close their operations actually are. One possible interpretation of these developmental and neuroanatomical findings is that it is the relationship between the limbic system and the prefrontal cortex that allows human beings to experience – *in addition* to the basic emotions we share with other animals – complex emotions. A number of authors have suggested that there is a fundamental distinction between these two types of emotion. Griffiths, in his 2003 paper, "Basic emotions, complex emotions and Machiavellian emotions" describes these theories as the revival of the early twentieth-century James/Lange theory and notes that the recent work of Antonio Damasio has contributed to its renewed popularity. Supporters of this view claim that

> ... the phenomenology that accompanies basic emotions is the perception of bodily changes caused by the subcortical circuits that drive those responses. They argue further that these "somatic appraisals" play important functional roles in cognition and action. More complex emotions involve subtly different somatic appraisals and cognitive activity realized in the neocortex that accompanies some combination of basic emotions (Griffiths 2003, 48).

Despite attempts to account for the complexities of human emotion, this approach to building on the basic emotions still takes the distinction between primary and secondary emotions as fundamental. As Griffiths describes it: "Primary emotions are part of our evolutionary inheritance, shared by all normal humans and tied to specific types of stimuli. Secondary emotions are acquired during development, show cultural and individual variation and are sensitive to more complex and abstract features of the stimulus situation" (Griffiths 2003, 49). While I am not, in this paper, concerned with the fairness of Griffiths' appraisal of philosophical advocates of this theory,[3] it is true that the primary/secondary distinction plays an important role in Damasio's work. His "somatic marker hypothesis" suggests that primary emotions, which are "innate, preorganized and Jamesian" and are dependent on limbic circuitry (Damasio 1994, 133) must be contrasted with secondary emotions, which "occur once we begin experiencing feelings and forming *systematic connections between categories of objects and situations, on the one hand, and primary emotions on the other*" (Damasio 1994, 134; italics in original). In other words, only secondary emotions are influenced by experience and cognition. And again we see the suggestion that the limbic system simply acts as input to these higher cognitive processes.

The developmental work I described earlier, however, suggests that the distinction between primary and secondary emotions may well be overemphasized in these theories. As Greenspan and Shanker note, part of what we learn in early development is how to modulate our own "catastrophic" emotions, so that our emotional experiences as normal adults is much different than that of infants, non-human animals, and the emotionally immature barroom brawler. The revised James/Lange theory suggests that this difference is due entirely to differences in the cognitive appraisal of bodily changes (caused by limbic systems subserving affect-programs). However, given that there is good evidence that there is *reciprocal* connectivity between the prefrontal (or neomammalian) brain regions subserving cognitive appraisal (Groenwegen and Uylings 2000) and the limbic regions governing immediate emotional response, it seems quite likely that the activity of the latter circuits is itself modified by the activity of the former. There is, then, a significant "top down" modulation of the functioning of the affect-programs mediated by limbic structures. Put slightly differently, basic emotions are quite possibly not so basic, after all.

If I am correct about the reciprocal nature of the influence between limbic- and cortical-level processing and about the importance of social experiences for the development of the prefrontal cortex (and thus for human emotions), then one question that needs to be

---

3 In particular, he points to Louis Charland and Jesse Prinz as advocates of this type of theory.

addressed is how to account for those aspects of emotion that appear to us to be modular. One strength of Griffiths' theory is that it allows the study of emotions to be situated in an evolutionary framework along with other biological processes. At the same time, however, by focusing on "shallow" emotional responses that appear to have been evolutionarily conserved, Griffiths' theory does not address the variability in even so-called "basic" emotions that is a result of evolutionary changes in the nervous system.

III. Modularity and Evolution

Having just finished arguing that a philosophy of emotion should take into account the discontinuity between human emotions and those of other animals, I now suggest that the influence of the pre-frontal cortex on human emotions, which is responsible for this discontinuity, represents nothing more than a particularly dramatic step in an evolutionary process that has been continuing since the nervous system first appeared. The earliest nervous systems served to co-ordinate sensory information with appropriate motor responses. The evolution of increasingly complex nervous systems has simply allowed motor responses to become more complex and more subtly attuned to alterations in environmental stimuli. In human beings, they are more open than in other animals to the effects of learning and also open to some degree of conscious control. In making this case, I will develop an insight of Rudolpho Llinas (2001), who describes the increasing complexity of the nervous system throughout evolution as the "internalization of movement" – or, in the terms I have been using, as the ability to conduct increasingly complex processing between sensation and motor response. This insight is far from new; however, its implications for the concept of modularity have not been sufficiently understood.

How is the increasing complexity of the nervous system relevant to the claim that at least some emotions are modules? Both Griffiths and Fodor suggest that one characteristic of modules is that they are subserved by dedicated neural circuitry. Both also suggest that modules are analogous to reflexes. This latter claim is a good place to start in understanding the link between the evolution of the nervous system and the modularity of emotions.

The simplest reflexes, such as the knee-jerk (or patellar reflex) require only two neurons, one sensory and one motor. More complex reflexes involve one or more interneurons mediating between the sensory and the motor neurons. These extra cells serve to increase the flexibility of the motor response to the sensory stimulus. In many cases, reflexes do not even require a brain; the synapses occur in the spinal cord. As Llinas explains:

> If one irritates a patch of skin on the back of a frog, a reflex to scratch is set into motion. The hind leg will swing out and up in a very stereotypical fashion, circling around to land the foot on the distressed area; this is readily repeatable and is the same across all frogs. Furthermore, this reflex may be activated and runs exactly the same in the absence of the brain and brainstem. (Llinas 2001, 134)

The simplest reflexes found in complex nervous systems, like the simplest nervous systems, presumably resemble the nervous systems of our distant evolutionary ancestors. In all three cases, there is a fast, simple and stereotypical link between stimulus and response. Clearly, this is not the type of reflex meant by Fodor and Griffiths. To the extent that modules are reflexes, they are reflexes that require a more complex nervous system – a brain as well as a spinal cord.

Yet Fodorian modules do resemble reflexes in that they are generally fast and involuntary. Also like reflexes, the "input systems" in which Fodor is interested, have "shallow outputs"; however, the nature of the output is different. Whereas reflexes have motor output, the output of Fodorian modules is to "central cognition." Fodor does suggest that there may be motor modules analogous to his input systems. These would presumably receive input from central cognition and "deliver" their output to motor neurons, or perhaps to the neurons innervating the autonomic nervous system.

Llinas explicitly discusses motor modules, which he describes as "sets of well-defined motor patterns, ready-made 'motor tapes' as it were, that when switched on produce well-defined and co-ordinated movements: the escape response, walking, swallowing, the prewired aspects of bird songs, and the like" (Llinas 2001, 133). It should be noted, though, that even among these examples, some motor modules are more reflexive than others. Whereas swallowing is, at least much of the time, under conscious control, the module, once initiated, runs automatically to completion. On the other hand, the module that mediates walking is flexible – it can be modified either unconsciously or consciously as the environment demands. Llinas points out that, if we are walking in the woods and must carefully pick our way through the terrain, we can modify the stereotypical motor sequences as the environment demands. The key is that the basic motor activity is modular, even though it can, when necessary, be modified by unconscious processes or by conscious control. To return to Fodor's criteria, Llinas's motor modules are automatic, stereotypical, and (again) subserved by dedicated neural machinery. Because their execution must be sensitive to the demands of the environment, they are under some degree of central control; however, they are still largely cognitively impenetrable: we have no more insight into how we walk or catch a ball than we do into how we see or hear.

In terms of the issue of the increasing complexity of the nervous system, I suggest that both of these types of module – Fodorian input systems and Llinas's motor modules – can be understood as the vestiges of reflexes. Input systems are more complex versions of the sensory end of the type of reflex that mediates the frog's scratching; motor modules are more complex versions of the motor end of the reflex. And what remains of the reflexive nature of sensorimotor systems also has an analogue in emotional systems. In fact, Griffiths specifically likens his affect-programs to motor modules. He suggests that the mismatch between emotional and cognitive responses exemplified by phobias occurs because "there are processes that trigger affect-programs which are 'informationally encapsulated.' In that case, there would not be free flow of information between them and the rest of the mind" (Griffiths 1990, 266).[4] This explanation means that Griffiths' affect-programs are closer in character to reflexes than are Fodorian input systems, as they explicitly link a particular sensory stimulus with the operation of a set of motor systems: though not quite as fixed a reflex as the frog's scratching (since affect-programs responses can be modified slightly by culturallymediated learning),

---

4 He further suggests that, like Fodorian input systems, affect-programs are mandatory in their operation, cognitively impenetrable, and associated with the operation of distinct neural (limbic) circuits.

they do not link up significantly with higher cortical processes in between their sensory input and their motor output. Affect-programs, remember, result in facial and bodily and vocal expressions character- istic of an emotion, and in changes to autonomic functions. Together, these responses serve to signal the animal's state and ready it for an appropriate response to the stimulus that elicited the emotion.

These affect-program responses, though, are far from being the complete story about even nonhuman emotional responses. In fact, there is an analogue in many animals of the kind of subtle, back-and- forth signaling pattern described by Greenspan and Shanker as occur- ring between a human infant and her caregiver. (What is unique to humans is not the existence of subtle emotional signals, but the extent to which these signals are learned.) For example, many animals regu- late aggressive behaviour,[5] particularly toward conspecifics, through an elaborate process of mutual signaling, in which behaviour by one of the pair acts as a "releaser" for a response by the other. While the individual behaviours are themselves stereotypical, the sequence as a whole does not result in an inevitable conclusion. In some cases, the level of aggression rises to a point where physical conflict occurs; in others, the pair's signals serve to defuse their initial aggressive response and ultimately avert physical conflict.

This type of behaviour has implications for both of the problems that I identified with Griffiths' psychoevolutionary theory. First, the interaction between the animals is an example of what I have termed "emotional behaviour," rather than of "emotional responses." While the exchange that occurs between the animals consists entirely of ste- reotypical behaviours that resemble Griffiths' affect-programs, they exhibit a level of behavioural complexity that Griffiths' theory ignores in favour of simple, physiological responses. In fact, it is likely that these complex behaviours are in part the result of conflict between different drives:

> [E]thologists have been fairly successful in analysing the diversity of behaviour shown in threat and courtship in terms of ambivalence among a relatively small number of behavioural tendencies. The usual

---

5 Courtship behaviour is similarly regulated.

approach is to postulate three basic tendencies, one of which, if acting alone, would lead to sexual behaviour, one to attack, and one to fleeing (McFarland 1999, 414)

While Griffiths' affect-programs treat each basic emotion in isolation, associating one affect-program with one stereotypical set of responses, the above discussion shows that important emotional behaviours may be the result of the combined effects of different (and competing) programs. Although a number of neural circuits may be triggered, the behavioural outcomes cannot be easily reduced to the motor outputs that characterize affect-programs. If we accept the argument that the resulting emotional behaviour reflects the operation of more than one affect-program, then we must give up on the claim that the generation of affect-program responses is informationally encapsulated. It also calls into question the extent to which the operation of an affect-program is mandatory. Reflexes are generally held to be mandatory to the extent that, once initiated, they must run to their conclusion. In the case of Griffiths' affect-programs, the conclusion – the stereotypical motor responses that characterize an affect-program – often does not occur in any straightforward way.

In addition to calling into question the modularity of Griffiths' affect-programs, the ritualistic emotional behaviours described above may also have implications for the second shortcoming that I have identified with Griffiths' theory, that is, of the lack of a place for the phenomenology of emotion. The subtle variations in behaviour are accompanied by changes in the animals' level of arousal. Given the importance of this arousal in guiding the animals' behaviour, it seems no more likely that they simply act as if they experience emotions than that their response to visual stimuli suggests that they simply act as if they can see. Llinas argues that sensory experiences (including emotional experiences) are actually central to action. He suggests that, as the nervous system became more complex, it became necessary to co-ordinate information from numerous sensory systems (and from memory). This co-ordinative neural activity is experienced as sensation and is itself an input that guides action. Whereas Griffiths' affect-programs reflexively link a stimulus and a response, Llinas's account of sensation suggests that the experience of emotion actually does play an important role in shaping the response.

In summary, then, Griffiths' psychoevolutionary theory is an attempt to find "basic" emotions by finding common circuitry underlying emotional responses in humans and in other animals. The theory, however, requires that we leave out much about emotion that is worth explaining. I have argued in this section that, rather than focusing on reflexive affect-programs that act largely in isolation, we should expand our theory of emotion to include an explanation of complex emotional behaviours and of the phenomenological aspect of emotions. My alternative account also takes seriously the evolution of emotion but opposes Griffiths' view in suggesting that the relevant neural circuits are both more complex and less isolated than the ones that Griffiths hopes to find. Even non-human emotions are more complex – and more interesting – than Griffiths' affect-program responses.

IV. Human Emotions and Modularity

The discussion above of modularity and the evolution of emotions described the gradually increasing complexity of the nervous system and its effects on the amount of processing that can occur between a stimulus and a response. Griffiths' affect-program responses are stereotypical emotional responses that are similar to reflexes but that are mediated by circuits that are complex enough to allow flexibility of motor output in response to subtle variations in the environmental stimuli that trigger them. Emotional behaviours, as described above, arise from the combined activation of various competing modules but cannot be readily reduced to them.

Human emotions are still more complex. In one sense, they are continuous with those of nonhuman animals, in that the human nervous system, including the circuits involved in emotion, is a product of the evolutionary trend towards increasingly complex nervous systems. In another sense, as the preceding discussion of human emotions shows, they are radically different from animal emotions in the extent to which they are shaped by the social environment. While it may seem that these two descriptions are incompatible, in fact it is because of the increasing size and complexity of the brain that environmental factors have become so important in determining the wiring of the human brain. Human beings are born at an earlier stage of neural development than other animals, so our brains are much more open to – and even require – fine-tuning from the environment, particularly the social environment. Moreover, if the implication of Schore's and Deacon's theories are correct, it is because of the developmental sculpting of our neuroanatomy that we become able to exert some degree of control over our emotions. The limbic system that mediates emotional functioning in nonhuman animals functions together with the prefrontal cortex, which means that we can in, at least in some instances, consciously modulate both our emotional responses and our emotional signals. We may explicitly choose our tone of voice, our body posture, or (most often) our words with a view to their intended effect.

At the same time, human emotions do betray their evolutionary roots, in that they involve behaviours that are mediated by all three of the types of response I have characterized. Some emotional stimuli trigger shallow and involuntary behaviours like the emotional reflexes Griffiths discusses: reddening of the face, change in vocal pitch, a smile or a gasp of fear may all be examples of these behaviours. Prolonged exchanges tend to involve such further unconscious (or perhaps subconscious) changes in vocal pitch, changes in bodily posture, etc. Finally, some behaviours are learned habits, either inculcated through the teachings of others or self-taught. Given, however, that I have already argued for the uniqueness of human emotions on the grounds that in our species the prefrontal cortex (and so cognition) exerts a huge influence over the limbic system, I should probably now address the problem of why our emotions are not governed entirely by our cognitions. And here again, my suggestions appeal to the developmental sculpting of the brain. The fact that the prefrontal cortex commands a significant number of synaptic connections during early development by no means means that it commands them all. The limbic circuits that Griffiths suggests underlie affect-programs are still connected with structures that subserve autonomic and motor functions (as Griffiths' description of affect-programs requires) and also with those cortical and subcortical structures that are required (in both humans and other animals) for the more flexible behaviour patterns. Thus while Griffiths' affect-programs play a role in human emotion, their function is not merely as simple reflexes linking a stimulus (whether innately triggered or learned) with an emotional response. Rather, the activity of the "motor end" of these reflexes is modified by a number of inputs, including those subserving competing emotional responses and, in humans, those derived from higher cognitive processes.

If my account is correct, though, then it seems to have implications for the extent to which emotions can be said to be modular. As noted above, the shaping of emotional behaviour by a number of drives and emotions appears to suggest that the information encapsulation and mandatory operation of affect-programs is probably overemphasized in Griffiths' theory. Griffiths appears to recognize this point; he explicitly focuses on the cases in which affect-programs are triggered in a reflexive, modular manner and notes: "It may be the case that affect-programs can be triggered by other routes, in addition to their modular one. The existence of a relatively unintelligent, dedicated mechanism does not imply that higher-level cognitive processes cannot initiate the same events" (268). Here Griffiths suggests that there are alternate routes to triggering the same motor responses; my suggestion, instead is that it seems more likely that the evolution of the nervous system has altered the very circuitry that Griffiths describes as modular, making it responsive to a broader range of inputs. This suggestion strikes me as inherently more plausible than Griffiths' alternative explanation that a separate triggering system evolved with the evolutionary expansion of the cerebral cortex. It also appears to be supported by the work of Deacon and of Schore on neural development.

This same work also points to two characteristics of modules that may not be possessed by affect-programs. Whereas affect-programs, like Fodorian input systems, are associated with the operation of distinct neural circuits, in human beings the neural circuits subserving emotion are not limited to the limbic regions involved in affect-programs. As the nervous system evolved to permit increased processing between a stimulus and a response, the opportunity increased for input from other systems to influence the eventual response, making the neural circuits that subserve a given module less "distinct." Moreover, affect-programs are unlike "classic" Fodorian modules in that they do not exhibit a characteristic pace and sequencing in their ontogeny (Fodor 1983, 100). Vision and other sensory capacities, as well as language, all develop relatively independently of environmental stimuli. While extreme cases of deprivation (such as experimental deprivation of certain kinds of visual stimuli in animals, or the cases of "wild children" raised without social and linguistic interaction) show that development of these systems have some sensitivity to the environment, their development can be understood on an analogy with the development of limbs and organ systems in the presence of adequate nutrition. Only a minimal input is required. However, developmental neurobiology suggests that this is not the case with the systems that subserve emotional experience in the normal adult human.

Further, it is because of this characteristic of brain development that emotional systems are even less informationally encapsulated than those of other animals: cognition *can* change the emotions that we feel, and it does so not merely by affecting future "cognitive appraisals" of our basic or primary emotions. Because prefrontal circuits subserving cognition have input to the limbic system, cognition also changes the limbic-level response to emotional stimuli that was held to characterize primary or basic emotions. This can occur not only within a single emotion episode, in which the activity of limbic circuits is modulated upon cognitive appraisal of a situation; it can also occur over time. Repeated exposure to the same (or similar) emotional stimuli may well evoke different immediate responses in limbic structures at different times; recall the infant described by Greenspan and Shanker, who learns over time to tame the catastrophic signals (that reflect the motor patterns of emotional response described by Griffiths) of emotion into signals that more subtly signal emotional response.

In summary, the account of the evolution and development of human emotion that I have sketched has implications for the extent to which emotions can be said to be modular. They are not as informationally encapsulated or as mandatory in their operation as Griffiths' account seems to suggest. Nor are they subserved by a distinct set of neural circuits, as a module would generally be expected to be. Finally, their development, at least in humans, is dependent on interactions with the environment to a much greater degree than that of input systems. These considerations may not suffice to disprove that emotions are modular; Fodor, for example, notes that many modules may possess their defining characteristics in degrees, being "more or less" informationally encapsulated, or "more or less" mandatory in their operation. The point of this paper, though, is not to disprove the modularity of emotions, but rather to show that the extent to which they qualify as modular depends on the way in which we define them. By narrowing our definition of emotions to the immediate and isolated responses considered by Griffiths, we are also essentially viewing them as strongly modular. If, instead, we decide our definition of an emotion be broad enough to encompass the emotional behaviours and complex human emotional responses that I have emphasized in this paper, as well as to allow a place for the phenomenology of emotions, these decisions have implications for the extent of the modularity of emotions. This paper has argued for a broader definition of emotions and so also has implications for the extent to which emotions are modular. It also raises a question about the nature of modularity in general: at what point do modules which have modular characteristics to a lesser, rather than a greater, extent, cease to be modular at all?

While Griffiths' psychoevolutionary theory provides an important approach to the understanding of emotions, it is, as Griffiths himself acknowledges, incomplete. I have argued that, even in nonhuman animals, emotional behaviour is more complex than Griffiths' theory would allow. In the case of human emotions, it is even more complex, as the circuits that mediate complex emotional exchanges are shaped by social experiences early in life. My arguments in this paper are compatible with two central aspects of Griffiths' theory: the need to give an evolutionary explanation of emotion and to discuss emotions in terms of neurophysiology. At the same time, they reject Griffiths' narrow focus on affect-program responses and basic emotions in favour of an account that better reflects the complexity and richness of emotional behaviours and experiences.

References

Damasio, A. 1994. *Descartes' Error: Emotion, Reason and the Human Brain*. New York: Avon Books.

Deacon, T. 1997. *The Symbolic Species: The Co-evolution of Language and the Human Brain*. New York: W.W. Norton.

Fodor, J. 1983. *The Modularity of Mind*. Cambridge (Mass.): MIT Press.

Fuster, J. M. 1989. *The Prefrontal Cortex: Anatomy, Physiology and Neuropsychology of the Frontal Lobes*. New York: Raven Press.

Greenspan, S. I., and S. G. Shanker. 2004. *The First Idea: How Symbols, Language and Intelligence Evolved from Our Primate Ancestors to Modern Humans*. Cambridge (Mass.): Da Capo Press.

Griffiths, P. E. 1990. Modularity and the psychoevolutionary theory of emotions. Reprinted in *Philosophy and the Emotions: A Reader*, ed. S. Leighton. Peterborough: Broadview Press, 2003.

Griffiths, P. E. 2003. Basic emotions, complex emotions, and Machiavellian emotions. In *Philosophy and the Emotions*, ed. A. Hatzimoysis. Cambridge: Cambridge University Press.

Groenewegen, H. J., and H.B.M. Uylings. 2000. The prefrontal cortex and the integration of sensory, limbic and autonomic information. *Progress in Brain Research* 126: 3–28.

Joseph, R. 1999. Environmental influences on neural plasticity, the limbic system, emotional development and attachment: A review. *Child Psychiatry and Human Development* 29(3): 189–208.

LeDoux, J. E. 1996. *The Emotional Brain: The Mysterious Underpinnings of Emotional Life*. New York: Simon and Schuster.

Llinas, R. 2001. *I of the Vortex: From Neurons to Self*. Cambridge (Mass.): MIT Press.

MacLean, P. D. 1949. Psychosomatic disease and the visceral brain: Recent developments bearing on the Papez theory of emotion. *Psychosomatic Medicine* 11: 338–53.

MacLean, P. D. 1973. *A Triune Concept of the Brain and Behavior*. T.J. Boag and D. Campbell, Eds. Toronto: University of Toronto Press.

MacLean, P. D. 1990. *The Triune Brain in Evolution: Role in Paleocerebral Functions*. New York: Plenum Press.

McFarland, D. 1999. *Animal Behaviour: Psychobiology, Ethology and Evolution*. 2nd ed. Oxford: Oxford University Press.

Ochsner, K. D., and J. J. Gross. 2005. The cognitive control of emotion. *Trends in Cognitive Sciences*. 9(5): 242–49.

Panksepp, J. 1998. *Affective Neuroscience: The Foundations of Human and Animal Emotions*. New York: Oxford University Press.

Schore, A. N. 1994. Affect Regulation and the Development of the Self: The Neurobiology of Emotional Development. Mahwah (NJ): Lawrence Erlbaum Associates.

Empathy, Primitive Reactions and the Modularity of Emotion

ANNE J. JACOBSON

Are emotion-producing processes modular? Jerry Fodor, in his classic introduction of the notion of modularity (Fodor 1983), holds that its most important feature is cognitive impenetrability or information encapsulation.[1] If a process possesses this feature, then, as standardly understood (Currie and Sterelny 2000), "what we want or believe makes no difference to how [it] works" (147).

In this paper, we will start with the issue of the cognitive impenetrability of emotion-producing processes. It turns out that, while there is abundant evidence of emotion-producing processes that are not cognitively impenetrable, some nonetheless are. We will look at two sorts of case. The first concerns emotional reactions to observed faces, and the second involves what we can call "primitive emotions," emotions that can be activated by non-doxastic input into regions of the brain we share with more primitive animals.

In seeing how some emotion-producing processes can be cognitively impenetrable while others are not, we need to use two commonsensical theses. First, a discussion of modularity must in general operate with a taxonomy that allows for sub-processes or stages of processes. Second, we cannot infer from the fact that some emotion-producing processes have or lack a general characteristic, such as that of impenetrability, that they all do.

The examples we will consider are less easy to understand than they may seem at first. With each sort of case, we need to raise questions about the content of the emotional reactions. The philosophi-

---

1 There are qualifications in later work (Fodor 1998).

cal notion of representational content may obscure the psychological import of what is being uncovered in some very important areas of cognitive neuroscience. Accordingly, our investigation into modularity includes an examination of emotional representations.

I. Cognitive Impenetrability

Visual illusions are often appealed to in order to illustrate the phenomenon of cognitive impenetrability or informational encapsulation. Two lines may persist in looking curved even though we know they are not. In such a case, the visual input is processed independently of our beliefs or desires.

So understood, cognitive impenetrability is very closely related to the familiar contrast between top-down and bottom-up processing. We can think of the process as taking inputs and yielding outputs. A bottom-up process is wholly stimulus- or input-driven; its operations and output are not affected by information other than that carried by the input. As Fodor notes, there is an analogy between modular systems and reflexes, which "are informationally encapsulated with bells on" (Fodor 1983).

The question of cognitive penetrability in the case of emotions is involved in important issues. One concerns the extent to which human emotions are rationally and morally assessable. It sometimes seems right to appraise emotional reactions as rational or irrational, and even to censure those who have some emotional reactions. Thus, for example, one might be told that it is irrational to be afraid of flying or that it is shameful to be delighted when an opponent in some competition falls seriously ill. In short, there's a wide-spread presumption that emotions are responsive to rational and moral standards, and, if so, the processes producing them are certainly not completely encapsulated.

A second but related issue concerns the extent to which emotions are something like socially shaped, or even constructed. To what extent is one's emotional reaction to a kind of event the product of social standards and expectations? Some emotional reactions that appear as automatic reactions to events can turn out to be more like behavioural tools employed to serve some goal. For example, as little children quickly learn, raging hysterics may give one considerable power.

Similarly, feeling disgust can allow one to present a form of social disapproval. Such reactions may be highly sensitive to contextual influence and accompanying beliefs; they may go away if it becomes clear they are counter-productive. Despite appearances, they can turn out to be far from the mandatory reactions of modular systems. Rather, to adapt Hacking's felicitous reading of some mental syndromes, they are socially available ways of dealing with problems (Hacking 1995). In still other cases, we can find emotions infected by all sorts of beliefs about what is, for example, appropriate behaviour for a member of one's class or gender and about how versions of that behaviour need to be modulated to fit class or gender norms.

The Fodorean notion of cognitive impenetrability is introduced as a feature of sensory systems, and it comes as part of the modularity package, which gives us a number of other features, including the process's having domain specificity, being rapid, mandatory, innately specified, and having characteristic breakdowns and shallow outputs. With emotions, it may not be clear that the cases are analogous enough to the original sensory processing to provide genuine instances of some robust conception of modularity. For example, given the extremely wide range of things to which we can react with anger, domain specificity of input comes under question. Perhaps a solution here would be to ascend to a higher level of generality in describing the input.[2] On the other hand, one could argue for domain specificity in the sense of there being a computational mechanism that operates with emotions and in no other cases.

More troubling for the issues of cognitive impenetrability, the process resulting in an emotional reaction may start not as some reaction to basic sensory stimulation, but rather as a reaction to features of one's environment that can be discerned only because of a great deal of background learning. One may not need much learning to be delighted at the scent of baking chocolate, but a similar emotional lift at the sight of a package from Tiffany's in one's mailbox is clearly unlikely without a great deal of cultural experience.

---

2 I believe that in fact the problems I raise below for the relation between fear and danger will dog any attempt to specify the proper objects of specific emotions; however, I will not be pursuing this problem here.

The situation is in fact quite complex. It is true that a reaction that has a highly culturally specific input may still be informationally encapsulated, a conditioned reflex for which there are specific triggers. Certainly, one's reaction can look like an reflex, as, say, one's heart lifts at the sight of that Tiffany's blue in one's mailbox; just as animals can have what appear to be automatic reactions to highly culturally specific objects, such as, in the notorious case of cats, the sound of a tin of cat food being opened. Nonetheless, such reactions can still become sensitive to accompanying beliefs, if one learns, say, that someone is putting anthrax into boxes from Tiffany's, or the cat realizes that opening a tin has become a way of luring it toward the carrier used on trips to the vet.

We will revisit the issue of the complexity of emotional triggers in a later section when we consider the well-researched case of fear as a "primitive emotion." For now it is important to emphasize a point made at the beginning of this paper, that we should not think that there is some one kind of process, "producing an emotion," all instances of which have the same general features.

II. Emotional Contagion and Cognitive Impenetrability

We can pick up emotions from others; we mirror their emotions by getting a feeling of the same type, though not with all the same features. The extent to which we do this varies among human beings, but it is a familiar experience to find that a cheerful person cheers us up, while a depressed person can cause us to feel down. This feature of human social situations has recently been called "emotional contagion" (Hatfield et al. 1994); it is a phenomenon many people have been aware of independently of any recent scientific research. Centuries ago, Hume observed that we appear to pick up emotions from others. As he says,

> As in strings equally wound up, the motion of one communicates itself to the rest, so all the affections readily pass from one person to another, and beget correspondent movements in every human creature. When I see the effects of passion in the voice and gesture of any person, my mind immediately passes from these effects to their causes, and forms

such a lively idea of the passion as is presently converted into the passion itself. (Treatise.3.3.1.7)

The potential significance of emotional contagion for accounts of emotion is considerable. While it may appear that emotional reactions that are typically reported as reactions to our environment are highly cognitive, it turns out that at least a considerable part of an emotion can be obtained in cases where we do not have the corresponding cognitive attitudes. When we pick up on the fear in the faces of others who are expressing fear, our neural and behavioural dispositions can come at least close to ones found in states of fear, and they can do so without our thinking we are in danger. This can happen when we are watching a play or a film.

One might think that there is some sort of inference going on when we see a fearful face; namely, that we infer there is something frightening in the environment and so feel warned and frightened ourselves. There is no evidence that this needs to happen, and some evidence that it does not. First, a great deal of psychological data comes from cases in which the subjects are looking at pictures and film clips. But in such cases, a picture of a frightened face is no evidence about one's present environment. Secondly, there have been backward-masking experiments and these again suggest that the emotional arousal starts before anything like conceptual engagement (Williams 2005).[3] That is, the experiments are such that one's perceptual experience of a frightened face is blocked or masked before conceptualization gets engaged. Hence, there is no cognitive classification of the face as a frightened one, and still less any inference about anyone's circumstances. Such experiments strongly suggest that some simple information about the emotional expression in a face is carried along a sub-cortical route to the emotional centres in the brain, in much the same way as we know the experience of a snake can be (LeDoux 2000). To say this is not to say one's own sense of one's environment is irrelevant to what one reacts to; there is good evidence that heightened anxiety increases one's reaction to pictures of fearful faces (Cools et al. 2005).

The importance of such studies from the point of view of modularity is that the fledgling emotion aroused appears to have belief inde-

---

3   Early work on affect and masking can be found in Zajonc (1980).

pendence. Once emotions are so aroused, they may go in search of appropriate beliefs. For example, a crowd aroused to anger can turn on a selected target, and the fear stirred up by a frightening film can lead one to the conviction late at night that someone is trying to get into one's house. Emotions can be belief-hungry, in addition to belief-saturated.

Though we have concentrated on fear, we should be clear that recent imaging studies, including particularly fMRI studies, have looked at people's reactions to a range of emotions as expressed by viewed faces and other reactions, such as pain (Avenanti et al. 2005; Jackson et al. 2005). For example, anger, fear, happiness, sadness, disgust, and surprise have been studied. The common finding in these studies is that the perception of faces expressing an emotion commonly activates at least some of the neural substrate also involved in feeling the emotion in reaction to one's own environment. Thus:

> We performed an fMRI study in which participants inhaled odorants producing a strong feeling of disgust. The same participants observed video clips showing the emotional facial expression of disgust. Observing such faces and feeling disgust activated the same sites in the anterior insula and to a lesser extent in the anterior cingulate cortex. (Wicker 2003)

What is being uncovered is the neural basis of emotional contagion. And emotional contagion can lead to genuine emotion, as Hume noted. The sight of a cheerful face is cheering; a speaker's anger can spread through a crowd. Hence, what is being discussed is at least one pathway for the arousal of genuine emotion. More generally:

> In recent years, abundant evidence from behavioral and cognitive studies and functional-imaging experiments has indicated that individuals come to understand the emotional and affective states expressed by others with the help of the neural architecture that *produces such states in themselves.* (Decety and Jackson 2006)

Taking cognitive impenetrability as the central characteristic of modularity, we have seen that some instances of emotions can be replete with beliefs while others are not.

III. Emotion Representations

Studies regarding reactions to facial expressions can be seen as part of a large project in cognitive neuroscience to uncover a neural basis for our capacity to understand one another. Given the evidence that is emerging, we have the capacity to get in neural synchronization with one another with regard to both action and feeling. As one research group puts it, "Thus, as observing hand actions activates the observer's *motor representation* of that action, observing an emotion activates *the neural representation of that emotion*. This finding provides a unifying mechanism for understanding the behaviors of others" (Wicker 2003, 655).

Hume's discussion anticipates some of this recent account. That is, for Hume, the process of picking up someone else's emotion involves acquiring an idea which in turn becomes so enlivened that it changes into an impression or real feeling. Suppose, then, one sees a face of someone who is expressing considerable fear. When our idea of fear gets enlivened enough, we end up with an impression of fear, which is fear itself. The difference between an idea and an impression is merely one of liveliness, and to have an idea enlivened into an impression of fear is to feel fear. There is an important point underlying this. Our idea 'of their fear' is not about them in any philosophical sense. Rather, the idea when enlivened is just fear, not fear-about-them. It does not have the intentional content of representations as they are theorized in recent philosophy.

Hume's view can provide an insight into what is meant by "motor representations" and "neural representations" of emotions. Let us first note that the research on action that describes "motor representations" is largely concerned with "mirror neurons," that fire similarly with the execution, observation, or imagination of an action. A "motor representation" refers to this neural substrate of an action. What makes the activation of a motor program be a representation?

Little follows of philosophical interest merely from the fact that the word "representation" is used by the cognitive neuroscientists. A use of "representation" or "encoded" in cognitive neuroscience may have effectively nothing to do with philosophy's representations, which are about something and have intentional content (Jacobson 2003). For example, the belief that today is Monday or the desire to eat that last piece of cheese are commonly counted as having intentional content. In contrast, when cognitive neuroscientists speak of how pain is represented or encoded in the brain, what they are at least often talking about is how pain is processed or realized in the brain, or that part of the brain forming the neural substratum. Thus in the following quote from the abstract of Hofbauer et al. (2001), "represents" can be replaced without any loss of sense by "processes," as the third sentence makes clear: "It is well accepted that pain is a multidimensional experience, but little is known of how the brain represents these dimensions. We used positron emission tomography (PET) to indirectly measure pain-evoked cerebral activity…. This double dissociation of cortical modulation indicates a relative specialization of the sensory and the classical limbic cortical areas in the processing of the sensory and affective dimensions of pain."

Over the last thirty-plus years, philosophy of mind has concentrated on a modern conception of representation that derives from the Chisholm's work, which involves his misreading of Brentano on intentionality (Jacobson 2003; Crane 2003). These more recently theorized representations have content and satisfaction conditions. A paradigm case of such a representation is a syntactically structured belief. They are part of a general picture of the mind as *directed toward* external objects.

In contrast, in the history of philosophy, there is another view of representation that we can call "Aristotelian representations," which is based on a model of the mind's duplicating features existing in the world external to it. This view is in Aristotle and the Aristotelian philosophy of Thomas Aquinas. Aquinas held that the features of the world reduplicated in the mind had an intentional existence, and this is the origin of Brentano's conception of intentionality, which Chisholm misunderstood.

Aristotelian representations can arguably be found in early modern philosophers such as Descartes, Locke, and Hume (Jacobson 2006), and they are clearly in recent neuroscience (Jacobson 2003). Aristotelian representations are sometimes thought merely to be the products of a mistaken similarity theory of modern representations. It is well recognized that similarity theories cannot account for modern representations, and Aristotelian representations share at least some of their difficulties. One problem concerns accounting for thought about specific individuals. The problem arises because the features that Aristotelian representations reduplicate may occur in many individuals in the exterior world. The fear that one picks up in one person may be felt by many others in the room; there is nothing about one's feeling to make it that one person's emotion other than its cause, which is now generally taken to be insufficient to make one's state refer to that person or be about some one person.

While Aristotelian representations thus fail to have the aboutness that modern representations are supposed to have, they nonetheless succeed at a different task. In the cases we are looking at, having the Aristotelian representation is feeling the same; it constitutes an emotional rapport that having information about someone's emotions does not. Accordingly, others' feelings become shared, at least to some small extent, and, as a consequence, their goals become more salient.

How this works out in individual cases can vary greatly. If someone is visibly very sad and that makes us very sad, we may be motivated to help alleviate that person's sadness, but we might also be motivated to get rid of the sad person. Thus some self-help books counsel us to avoid unhappy people. If someone is obviously very angry and we pick up the anger, the anger we then feel may acquire the same target and we may all coordinate an assault on the target. Or, feeling someone's fear, we may become very alert to features of our environment in a way that aides us both. In many such cases, one need not recognize that the emotion is picked up from the other; rather, one may just be reacting to the feeling.

Though on this account the feeling that matches that of another person is not about that other person, Aristotelian representations fit well with environmental, enactive approaches, which can seek to locate having aboutness and satisfaction conditions not in an internal vehicle but rather in statements available to observers. Statements of the form "X feels Y's fear" is made true in cases we are looking at by X's fear's being caused by Y's expression, and not by X's having some internal state that is about Y.

Thus a "neural representation" of an emotion that is caused by observing an expressive face need be understood only as the activation of some of the neural substrate of that sort of emotion. It is not a representation that is about the emotion, still less about the other person. This representation does not come, as it were, requiring a theory of mind about others, as a representation full of intentional content about the other's emotions might.

IV. Primitive Emotions

Primitive emotions are responses to the environment that may involve merely sub-cortical parts of the brain that we share with creatures who split from our evolutionary line very early on. A central example of a primitive emotion is the fear that a glimpse of a snake can cause. They appear to answer quite well to a Jamesian conception of emotion (James 1884), at least as far as the cases are generally described in the literature. For James, an emotion is a belief-independent reaction to the environment which itself causes feelings and beliefs. While an adequate description of such emotions may not mandate treating the feeling as simply an effect of the emotion, rather than a part of it or even its defining feature, it is important that these emotions, or their evolutionary predecessors, occurred in creatures who had something like important aspects of the emotion without much of a conceptual repertoire or much consciousness.

Primitive emotions also coincide with those described by theories of "affect programs." Such theories identify basic or core emotions, such as anger, fear, disgust, sadness, joy, and surprise; though there are variations in the members of the list, the one just given, from Griffiths (1997) is typical. Equally common is Griffiths' description of them (16): "The affect program states are phylogenetically ancient, informationally encapsulated, reflexlike responses which seem to be insensitive to culture."

We need to be cautious in how we understand these descriptions of basic emotions that we will discuss. However, before we look at the problems, we should consider a particularly well-developed account in some more detail. Joseph LeDoux has an account of the neural processes that lead to one primitive emotion, fear. What stands out in LeDoux's account is the role of subcortical, and so clearly subdoxastic, processing. When one sees a snake, for example, a basic fear response is initiated in the amygdala as a result of signals sent through the thalamus. The thalamus also signals the cortex, which will signal back to the amygdala. There are, then, two pathways, a thalamo-amygdala pathway and a thalamo-cortico-amygdala pathway, with the second providing more processed information about the stimulus. However, the first pathway is quicker and it is sufficient for a fear response.

There are two particularly important features of this account. First of all, the thalamo-amygdala pathway transmits only a simple and select range of sensory signals. The cause of one's fear reaction may still be a snake all right, but the reaction is independent of any complex integration of sensory signals that would enable one to categorize the object. Still further, the reaction is independent of any conceptualization one could bring to bear. Nonetheless, through conditioning, the range of simple sensory cues that one can respond to can be considerably increased. A culturally very complex object may set off a very primitive action that uses this pathway if there is a regular, simple sensory cue. Thus, perhaps, a certain smell or curve of the cheek may induce a very primitive reaction to a schoolyard bully, for example. And Tiffany's blue might come to signal a pleasure ahead.

However, many things we fear do not have these simple sensory cues. As Heilman observes, "Although conditioned stimuli, similar to those used by LeDoux, may induce emotion without cortical interpretation, there is overwhelming evidence that in humans the neocortex is critical for interpreting the meaning of many stimuli, especially those stimuli that are complex and rely on past learning" (Heilman 2000). There may be simple sensory cues that alert us to some difference outside one's apartment at night, but the more complex sensory synthesis and conceptualization that informs one of a vandal, and so makes one frightened that one's car is going to be stolen or one's windows used to gain access, is not wholly sub-cortical. Similarly, the reactions to these more complex cues do not appear to have cognitive impenetrability; hence, the realization that the lurching figure is actually a friend with an injured back brings a halt to the mounting fear.

A case can be made, then, that instances of fear – and presumably other emotions in the affect program list – do not all share the same neural substrate, and this fact is reflected in the differences in whether or not they possess cognitive penetrability. Fear can be instinctive or it can be more considered. In Griffiths' later terminology, an instance of fear may be a basic emotion or it may be a complex one (Griffiths 2004).

We have, then, found a second class of emotion some instances of which appear to be cognitively impenetrable, but it seems also to bring along with it a problem for the theory of emotions. Our classificatory words that divide emotions into kinds do not pick out a kind of neural substrate, and the differences in neural substrate are significant ones since they create a difference in properties such as cognitive penetrability.

Is there another kind of unity we might find to all instances of fear? Do they all represent the world in a particular way, for example? This is not an idle question, since there is in fact an extended account of fear as representation (Prinz, this volume; 2004). We can see it as grounded in LeDoux's (2000) observation that "The ability to detect and respond to danger ... is the function that the fear system evolved to perform," I shall argue that the view that such emotions detect general features of our environment is seriously problematic.

To count as detecting danger, a feature or a system must be more than sometimes caused by the relevant danger. More precisely, at least according to the central account of representation that tends to be invoked in these discussions, the causation must be reliable (Prinz 2004). If the fear response is reliably caused by danger and is, as LeDoux says, the function that it evolved to perform, then we can make a strong case, given this account of representation, for saying that fear represents danger.

But is the fear system reliably activated by danger? Was it even reliable in the prehistoric times during which it evolved? The fear system appears to start off reacting to very selective cues that can be processed extremely rapidly along a sub-cortical route. While it may be that most things that could activate the fear system were dangerous, many things would not activate it for reasons such as those advanced by Heilman (2000), quoted above. To say this is not to say that there are no affect programs as Griffiths described them. But the mechanism that is cognitively impenetrable is not capable of registering the wide and complex array of environmental factors we need to react to.

We can find another kind of evidence in the effects of evolution that fear did not reliably indicate many of the dangers our ancient ancestors faced; this evidence comes from the fact that other indicators of danger also evolved. Among them are disgust, anger, and, arguably, depression. These reactions may be reactions to different kinds of danger, but the point is that fear at best was a reaction to some subset of dangers. That we have other primitive reactions to dangers is some evidence that this is so.

The fact that some processes producing fear are cognitively impenetrable and some are not might well suggest we should give up on a science of emotions. As Griffiths (1997) argues, terms that feature in a science need to be capable of supporting the generalizations that are at the heart of a science; there cannot be a science of emotions unless emotions are natural kinds. There may, however, be a way to find a place for emotion-kinds in psychology and neuroscience. For scientific purposes, the taxonomizing of emotions might be done through the taxonomy that neuroscience makes available to us, with the usefulness to science of a psychological term depending on how unified its class of neural realizers is. For example, "mental illness" has so many different kinds of realizers that it really is unsuitable for any generalizations. "Fear" looks different; there is a limbic system core to it. But this is a project that can only be adumbrated here, though some of the underpinnings for such a view may be found in Bickle (2003) and my comments on it (Jacobson 2005).

V. Emotions, Representations and Social Understanding

This paper has been shaped by two main theses. The first is that emotional kinds do not track modularity; some cases of an emotional kind may be cognitively impenetrable while others are not. The cases of modularity that we found involve what are called "neural representations of emotions," which led to the topic of the second thesis. This is the thesis that the "neural representation" of an emotion can be understood as an Aristotelian representation. In this section, we will conclude by considering how understanding emotional contagion in terms of Aristotelian representations can help explain how emotional mirroring contributes to our social understanding.

We have already seen one kind of contribution, that by which we get into emotional synchronization with others. Shared emotions may lead to shared goals, for example. However, there is another kind of important social understanding; namely, being able to identify the other's emotions. What sort of explanatory role can we assign to Aristotelian representations in this second task?

The neural activations we are looking at may impinge just at the edge of consciousness, and they may not come into conscious awareness at all. They seem paradigmatically lacking in conceptual content, and theorizing them as Aristotelian representations emphasizes this feature. It has been argued that only conceptualized items can function as reasons for belief (McDowell 1994; Brewer 2005).[4] However, even if non-conceptualized experiences cannot provide one reasons for belief, they may enter into causal relations with beliefs in other ways such as, for example, in a priming relation.

An experience can prime a reaction and thereby make it more likely without playing any sort of reason-giving or evidential role. For example, hearing a dog behind one bark may prime one to see a vague figure on the horizon as a dog without in any way being evidence. Such primes are, as I termed them elsewhere, pure facilitators of belief, actions, and emotions (Jacobson 1992, 1993).

Primes may be unconscious and, at least in the case of priming for colour identification, priming may draw on purely physical (as opposed to psychological) similarities (Breitmeyer et al. 2004). What this means is that an experience can prime one without being in psychological space at all. We do not need the notion of priming to describe every way emotional mirroring contributes to our social understanding, but it is still important to note that when we do employ that conception, it does not necessarily bring in a reference to intentionality. There is abundant evidence that emotions prime one's use of emotional ascriptions. Priming, then, can take us from the emotional representation to our finding a particular description of emotion salient.

We can also relate emotional representations understood as Aristotelian representations to a more general picture of social understanding. There are very good reasons for thinking that human beings employ sub-conscious and automatic internal forward models of other people rather than updating beliefs by continuously checking on the others (Gallese 2004; Iacoboni et al. 2005). Without such models, it has recently been argued, we would have to waste a great deal of energy and time in consulting the external environment to find out what the actual people are doing (Montague 2006). Human social life is much

---

4 This view, which may have Kantian origins, in turn has been disputed by others (Peacocke 1992).

too quick for that to be a plausible construal of it, and human cognition is too efficient.

That our modelling of others appears to involve our feeling their feelings – and, with mirror neurons, experiencing their motor programs – strongly suggests that one's model for another person is oneself. Indeed, as parents of small children can testify, one has to teach children to modulate what seems to be a strong sense that the emotions being expressed by someone in their environment are theirs too. It is also likely that the need to distinguish clearly one's emotions from those of others around one varies quite considerably from occasion to occasion. However, when one does make the distinction, priming seems to play a considerable role; indeed, those incapable of picking up others' emotions (perhaps because of an inability to mirror facial expressions) do have deficits in recognizing them (Oberman et al. 2005; Bohannon 2005; Sebanz et al. 2005; Archibald 2006). In addition, once one is primed to an identification, other sensory cues and even background knowledge are available as further resources to draw on. Given one is primed to call his reaction anger, one may see one has good reasons for that ascription, based on how he looks and what kind of person he is.

Though it does not addressed the use of "representation" in neuroscience,[5] Alvin Goldman's recent book (Goldman 2006) on simulation theory has a reading of the literature on the neural basis of emotional contagion very similar to that I have presented here. However, there are two important differences that should be noted. Goldman holds that the attribution of emotional states to others involves two steps: classification of the state and then projection. My emphasis on the pre-conceptual feelings and the phenomena of shared feelings and goals leads to a picture in which mind-reading may occur without the classification. Accordingly, awareness of emotional sharing may tell one a great deal about another person without going through beliefs about the emotions shared. One can, for example, be aware that one has "clicked" with another, and so be able to make quite accurate assessments of how that person will react to further interactions. Even if the assessments are not accurate, one may still

---

5 However, Chapter Eight, especially Section 8.10, addresses a very closely related question.

find emotional contagion accompanied by a considerable array of beliefs about others' attitudes without one's understanding what the core shared feelings actually are.

Secondly, the hypothesis that priming is at work means that the beginning of the conceptualization does not necessarily involve a self-ascription of the emotion. This raises questions about Goldman's view that the ascription of the emotion to others is based on classifying one's emotion and then projecting it. The situation may often be the more complicated one described above, where other sensory cues and background knowledge are also in play.

We should conclude by noting that Aristotelian representations and modern representations place us in very different epistemological situations in developing an account of social understanding. The most promising account of how modern representations acquire their content involves appeal to their evolutionary benefit (Prinz 2004). However, it is not clear what evolutionary benefits led to the selection of emotional mirroring, if indeed it persisted through evolutionary development for such a reason. But the system clearly has benefits, and perhaps it was selected for the way it helps in cementing the social lives of social creatures. Alternatively, insofar as emotional reactions signal that the environment has some quite salient features, emotional contagion may have been selected for as a very powerful way of conveying environmental information. Finally, whatever the benefit that determines the hypothesized content, given how low level and subdoxastic the emotional mirroring may be, it is difficult to see how the conjectured intentional content of pre-conscious experience would add to our social understanding.

To say this is not to say that one could not work up a plausible story about the details of the evolutionary development of emotional mirroring and, from that, derive an account of the content such mirroring emotions have. Nothing said here shows one cannot attribute intentional semantical-like features to neural states. Rather, much of this essay has been concerned with building a robust picture of social understanding on a theoretically much more austere base. Though the topic of modularity leads to the subject of "emotion representations," we are able to understand them without attributing to neural states the factors that recent philosophy has taken to be definitive of representing.

References

Archibald, S. 2006. Mirror image. *Nature Reviews Neuroscience* 7(1): 4–4.

Avenanti, A., D. Bueti, G. Galati, and S. M. Aglioti. 2005. Transcranial magnetic stimulation highlights the sensorimotor side of empathy for pain. *Nature Neuroscience* 8(7): 955–60.

Bickle, J. 2003. *Philosophy and Neuroscience: A Ruthlessly Reductive Account, Studies in Brain and Mind*, vol. 2. Dordrecht: Kluwer.

Bohannon, J. 2005. Faulty "emotional mirror" may help explain autism. *Science Now*: 1–2.

Breitmeyer, B. G., T. Ro, and N. Singhal. 2004. Unconscious priming with chromatic stimuli occurs at stimulus- not percept-dependent levels of visual processing. *Psychological Science* 15: 198–202.

Brewer, B. 2005. Does perceptual experience have conceptual content? *European Journal of Philosophy* 14(2): 165–81.

Cools, R., A. J. Calder, A. D. Lawrence, L. Clark, E. Bullmore, and T. W. Robbins. 2005. Individual differences in threat sensitivity predict serotonergic modulation of amygdala response to fearful faces. *Psychopharmacology* 180(4): 670.

Crane, T. 2003. *The Mechanical Mind: A Philosophical Introduction to Minds, Machines, and Mental Representation*. 2nd ed. London: Routledge.

Currie, G., and K. Sterelny. 2000. How to think about the modularity of mind-reading. *Philosophical Quarterly* 50(199): 145–60.

Decety, J., and P. L. Jackson. 2006. A social-neuroscience perspective on empathy. *Current Directions in Psychological Science* 15(2): 54.

Fodor, J. A. 1983. *The Modularity of Mind: An Essay on Faculty Psychology*. Cambridge (Mass.): MIT Press.

Fodor, J. A. 1998. *In Critical Condition: Polemical Essays on Cognitive Science and the Philosophy of Mind, Representation and Mind*. Cambridge (Mass.): MIT Press.

Gallese, V. 2004. Intentional Attunement: The Mirror Neuron system and its role in interpersonal relations. Review of reviewed Item. *Interdisciplines*. http://www.interdisciplines.org/mirror/papers.

Goldman, A. I. 2006. *Simulating Minds: The Philosophy, Psychology, and Neuroscience of Mindreading*. Oxford: Oxford University Press.

Griffiths, P. E. 1997. *What Emotions Really Are: The Problem of Psychological Categories*. Chicago: University of Chicago Press.

Griffiths, P. E. 2004. Is emotion a natural kind? In *Thinking About Feeling: Contemporary Philosophers on Emotions*, ed. R. Soloman. Oxford: Oxford University Press.

Hacking, I. 1995. *Rewriting the Soul: Multiple Personality and the Sciences of Memory*. Princeton (N.J.): Princeton University Press.

Hatfield, E., J. T. Cacioppo, and R. L. Rapson. 1994. *Emotional Contagion, Studies in Emotion and Social Interaction*. New York: Cambridge University Press.

Heilman, K. M. 2000. Emotional Experience: A neurological model. In *Cognitive Neuroscience of Emotion*, ed. R. D. Lane and L. Nadel, 328–44. Oxford: Oxford University Press.

Hofbauer, R. K., P. Rainville, G. H. Duncan, and M. C. Bushnell. 2001. Cortical representation of the sensory dimension of pain. *Journal of Neurophysiology* 86(1): 402–11.

Hume, D., D. F. Norton, and M. J. Norton. 2000. *A Treatise of Human Nature, Oxford Philosophical Texts*. Oxford: Oxford University Press.

Iacoboni, M., I. Molnar-Szakacs, V. Gallese, G. Buccino, J. C. Mazziotta, and G. Rizzolatti. 2005. Grasping the intentions of others with one's own mirror neuron system. *PLoS Biology* 3(3): 529–37.

Jackson, P. L., A. N. Meltzoff, and J. Decety. 2005. How do we perceive the pain of others? A window into the neural processes involved in empathy. *NeuroImage* 24(3): 771.

Jacobson, A J. 1992. A problem for naturalizing epistemologies. *Southern Journal of Philosophy* 30(4): 31–49.

Jacobson, A J. 1993. A problem for causal theories of reasons and rationalizations. *Southern Journal of Philosophy* 31(3): 307–21.

Jacobson, A J. 2003. Mental representations: What philosophy leaves out and neuroscience puts in. *Philosophical Psychology* 16(2): 189–203.

Jacobson, A J. 2005. Is the brain a memory box? *Phenomenology and the Cognitive Sciences* 3: 271–78.

Jacobson, A J. 2006. Hume's theory of ideas. In *The Pre-History of Cognitive Science*, ed. A. Brook, 97–114. New York: MacMillan/Palmgrave.

James, W. 1884. What is an emotion? *Mind* 9: 188–205.

LeDoux, J. 2000. Cognitive-emotional interactions: Listen to the brain. In *Cognitive Neuroscience of Emotion*, ed. R. D. Lane and L. Nadel. Oxford: Oxford University Press.

McDowell, J. H. 1994. *Mind and World*. Cambridge (Mass.): Harvard University Press.

Montague, R. 2006. *Why Choose this Book? How We Make Decisions*. New York: Penguin.

Oberman, L., E. M. Hubbard, J. P. McCleery, E. L. Altschuler, V. S. Ramachandran, and J. A. Pineda. 2005. EEG evidence for mirror neuron dysfunction in autism spectrum disorders. *Cognitive Brain Research* 24(2): 190–98.

Peacocke, C. 1992. Anchoring conceptual content: Scenarios and perception. In *Cognition, Semantics and Philosophy*, ed. J. Ezquerro, 293–322. Norwell, MA: Kluwer.

Prinz, J. J. 2004. *Gut Reactions: A Perceptual Theory of Emotion*, Philosophy of Mind Series. Oxford: Oxford University Press.

Sebanz, N., G. Knoblich, L. Stumpf, and W. Prinz. 2005. Far from action-blind: Representation of others' actions in individuals with autism. *Cognitive Neuropsychology* 22(3–4): 433.

Wicker, B. 2003. Both of us disgusted in my insula: The common neural basis of seeing and feeling disgust. *Neuron* 40(3): 655–755.

Williams, L. M., B. J. Liddell, A. H. Kemp, R. A. Bryant, R. A. Meares, A. S. Peduto, and E. Gordon. 2005. Amygdala-prefrontal dissociation of subliminal and supraliminal fear. *Human Brain Mapping* 27: 652–61.

Zajonc, R. B. 1980. Feeling and thinking: Preferences need no inferences. *American Psychologist* 35: 151–75.

Biological Modules and Emotions

PAUL DUMOUCHEL

> But as for most genes, they are not the units of interest once we get to the network level: it is the whole conspiracy we care about. (von Dassow and Meir 2003, 27)

I. Biologists and Modules

Biologists, more precisely evolutionary biologists, and not only psychologists and philosophers also speak of modularity. However the way in which this theoretical construct functions in their discipline is relatively different from the role it obtains in evolutionary psychology and cognitive science. Rather than postulating modules to explain particular traits of organisms, such as the specificity of input systems or limitations of human reasoning abilities, biologists originally simply assume that some form of modularity constitutes a precondition of evolution.[1] They argue that, in order for natural selection to fine tune organisms to their environment, different traits must be able to evolve independently from one another. This implies modularity in one form or another. Organisms will only be able to adapt if they do not come all in one piece, so to speak. It must therefore be possible for changes to occur in one characteristic of an animal without those changes having repercussions throughout the whole organism. It seems that evolution requires that organisms be modular; it requires that they be made of relatively independent building blocks that are nonetheless in some way integrated. How is this delicate bal-

---

1 Sloman (2002) applies a somewhat similar understanding of modules to emotions and the cognitive domain in general.

ance achieved? Is it possible to identify, describe, and analyze these modules?[2]

As it turns out, biologists have been quite successful in their search for modules, perhaps too much so. They have come back with many different kinds of modules and more questions than they started out with. Among other things, some types of modules appear to be obstacles to continuing evolution and adaptation rather than necessary conditions for it to take place. Furthermore, it should be added that at this point in biology many questions concerning modules still remain unanswered. Biologists disagree as to how many different types of modules there are; they disagree concerning which conditions and how many conditions something must satisfy in order to qualify as a module; they disagree about the role and importance of modules in evolution; finally, they even sometimes disagree as to whether this or that object is a module or not. What they do agree on is that there are such things as modules in organisms, and they can exhibit a fairly long list of objects that have a good claim to being called modules. By saying "objects that have a good claim to being called modules," I mean to insist upon the fact that, even if biologists resort to definitions and conceptual analysis, they essentially work with biological objects, organisms, processes, and structures. Rather than elaborating an abstract model of what a module is and then seeing which objects qualify to be a module in view of this model, as in a sense Fodor (1983) does, they exhibit exemplars, objects to which they point as examples of biological modules.[3] Their claims are about these objects. They describe, for example, a genetic pathway, and then argue that there are good evolutionary or developmental reasons to call the object a module. They argue that considering it to be a module makes sense and that it is useful and explanatory.

In what follows, I first want to rapidly review a few examples of biological modules. These modules, or at least a sub-category of them, constitute an interesting class of objects. They are described and ana-

---

2 Granted, this is a rational or conceptual reconstruction of the search for modules rather than a historically adequate description of the way in which modules became an important topic in evolutionary biology.

3 For a similar understanding of the way biologists work with objects, exemplars, and model organisms rather than abstract models, see Kelley (2002), 51–52.

lyzed at the sub-cellular level; however, their consequence, what they are taken to explain or to do within a biological organism (or between organisms), is located at the level of a cell population, of a group. In other words, biological modules of the type described below are implemented at the sub-cellular level in the sense that they are contained within the individual cell but their effect, their role, is located at the level of a whole cell population. Emotions, or rather affective coordination, I then wish to argue, with the help of a short fiction, may be viewed as resting on a similar type of sub-personal modules that lead to consequences that are visible at the level of a group or population.

II. Biological Modules

Biologists mainly distinguish between evolutionary and developmental modules. In both cases, a module can correspond either to a structure (for example, specific types of cells or an organelle) or to a process. In what follows, I will be mainly interested in modules that are process. Classical examples of this type of module are regulatory genetic networks. Such networks are processes rather than structures inasmuch as they do not exist other than as a collection of chronologically arranged events where the activation of one gene leads, for example, to the activation of another, and the two activated together result in the inhibition of a third, and so on. There is no material structure that corresponds to the network. The network is just the sequence of interrelated events. Genetic regulatory networks qualify as biological modules when they exhibit all or most of the following characteristics.

First, they are relatively autonomous in the sense that, once initiated, the sequence of events follows its course independently of the environment, and in the sense that the network is to some extent self-sustaining. Of course independence from the environment is never absolute and there are changes in the environment that will prevent the network from functioning. Nonetheless, as long as the specific products are present, or certain parameters maintained within a definite range, the chain of events takes place unperturbed. Theoretically the advantages of autonomy are readily evident. It allows the network to be deployed in many different contexts where it can nonetheless perform correctly. Interestingly enough, this is precisely what we find.

One of these genetic regulatory networks, named the *Pax/Six/Eya/Dach* network, plays a fundamental role in differentiation of the cells that become photoreceptors in the eye of Drosophilia. Among vertebrates this same network is indispensable for the development of muscles, eyes, and ears (Kardon et al. 2003, 63). Diversity of usage is the second characteristic of biological modules. Modules are used over and over again in many different contexts, as if they were good tricks that, once hit upon, should not be abandoned lightly. This is true of the *Wg* signalling pathway which has short- and long-range functions during cell epidermal specification and the core elements of which have been preserved in many species including Drosophila, C. elegans, Xenopus, chicken, mouse, and human (Borycki 2003, 105). It is also true of the *Notch* signalling module that influences cell fate choices during the development of multicellular organisms. It has essentially been conserved in vertebrates and invertebrates, and it affects similar developmental operations in all organisms where its function has been analyzed (de Celis 2003, 81). As Strähle and Blader say:

> [W]e define a module as an assembly of biological structures that fulfill a function in an integrated and context insensitive manner. Function as defined here is not merely the interaction of molecules but an interaction that yields a biological output which is characteristic of the module. Furthermore, the application of the module is flexible. To be recognized as a module, it has to be used either in different processes in the same organism or in different organisms, exploiting its invariant functional properties in the same or different processes. A module is therefore characterized by its reiterated use. (Strähle and Blader 2003, 35)

The third characteristic, as suggested by the previous examples, is that modules are stable over very long periods of time. The same modules are not only employed in different cellular contexts within one organism or species of organism; they are found in many different species that often are phylogenetically quite distant. It should be added that a module as it exists in different contexts or species is not always strictly identical. For example, what we often find in different species is not exactly the same genetic network but a highly similar one. Such is the case of the *Pax/Six/Eya/Dach* network mentioned earlier. In vertebrates it does not mobilize exactly the same genes as in Drosophilia, but calls upon genes that belong to the same family of genes or on homologous genes. This last point is one of the reasons why biologists often disagree about the role of modules in evolution. On one hand the fact that modules evolve, that they are not always the same in different species, suggests that natural selection can fine tune them to different environmental requirements. On the other hand, the phylogenetic stability of modules, the fact that what we are dealing with nonetheless are different versions of the same modules that play similar functional roles in many different cellular contexts and species, suggests that modules constitute strong constraints that limit the paths that are open to evolution.

The fourth characteristic of biological modules is that they often are hierarchically organized in the sense that lower-level modules, i.e., signalling modules, can be part of higher-level modules. For example, the *Notch* signalling module is a necessary part of the *Basic Helix-Loop-Helix* protein domain module that plays a pivotal role in neurogenesis in both vertebrates and invertebrates (Strähle and Blader 2003, 39). As a consequence of their relative autonomy, which among other things allows them to be imbedded in higher-level modules, modules can also "frequently be triggered in a switch like fashion by a variety of inputs ... to which they are only weakly linked ... and may affect different downstream processes depending on the circumstances" (Schlosser 2003, 525). Thus, as José de Celis argues: "Although the Notch signaling pathway is a context independent module, in the sense that the molecular interactions between its members are conserved and invariant, the outcome of Notch signaling is highly context dependant" (de Celis 2003, 93). Anne-Gaelle Borycki reaches a similar conclusion concerning the *Sonic Hedgehog* and *Wnt* signalling pathways: "despite their apparent autonomy, genetic modules are subject to and part of larger signaling network, which remodels them into context-dependent modules." (Borycki 2003, 121). It follows from this, as Schlosser clearly noted, that modules can be described as being the same only if they are described in a sufficiently abstract way. For example, two processes in which the *Notch* signalling network plays a significant role are lateral inhibition and the formation of boundaries in cell populations, but both processes can lead to quite different end results depending on the context (de Celis 2003, 91). "Despite qualitative differences in inputs and outputs in these cases," says Schlosser, "the quantitative and spatio-temporal input-output transformation of the module – what could be called its *logical role* (or its intrinsic behavior ...) – stays the same." (Schlosser 2003, 525). In other words, there must be a description of the module's operation under which it remains the same, but this description will usually be in terms of intra-modular interactions and of input-output relations defined spatio-temporally, e.g., we go from this molecule to that molecule, rather than qualitatively. On the contrary, as far as its qualitative consequences are concerned, the module's result will vary from domain to domain. It is only under a sufficiently abstract description that the module can be described as "doing the same thing."

Finally, and this last point is fundamental, the operation of modules like *Sonic Hedgehog* and *Pax/Six/Eya/Dach* yields consequences that exist at a level that is different from the one at which the module is described. What I mean is that to describe a signalling pathway like *Sonic Hedgehog*, you analyze molecular events that are taking place at a sub-cellular level, but the end result of its functioning, which is often what you are actually trying to explain, or what is defined as (one of) the role(s) of the module, is something that takes place at the level of a cell population, for example, the creation of a border between two cell groups or a pattern of cellular differentiation, neurogenesis, etc. This is particularly clear for signalling modules, but it is also true of positional modules, as well as of the module that is responsible for cellular suicide (*Apoptosis*) and that has remained to some extent similar from C. elegans to us (Ameisen 1999). Overall, it is true of all the genetic regulatory networks that work together during development and that have been conserved in a wide range of metazoan taxa. There is a sense in which these modules supervene on more than one individual. It is true that they are implemented individualistically in the sense that the elements of the network exist inside one cell and the interactions between these elements are a purely internal process. Nonetheless, biologically, their result does not make sense at the level of a single individual. It does not make sense not only because, biologically, an isolated individual of one particular cell type plays absolutely no role or function within an organism, such an isolated cell is only a meaningless accident, but also because the inappropriate differentiation of a single cell normally rapidly leads to cellular suicide.[4] Furthermore, modules that are found and implemented in unicellular organisms also play the role of coordinating populations of organisms. Such modules typically constitute the basis of self-organizing processes in cell populations (Camazine et al. 2003, 91–115). These biological modules that have been maintained for a long time through a wide range of species are infra individual modules indispensable for the coordination or collective behaviour of populations of individuals. To paraphrase what Hobbes said concerning justice, the characteristic of cells supported by such modules belong to cells in society, not in solitude (Hobbes 1651).

In the remainder of this paper I wish to consider modules in the affective domain in a somewhat similar way to what biologists do. We usually understand the modularity of emotion as meaning that there are modules (in a relaxed Fodorian sense of module)[5] that underlie or constitute certain emotions. One of the problems to which this hypothesis has led is a fractioning of the category of emotions. Some instances of fear, anger, or disgust, for example, seem to correspond pretty well to the functioning of a module, but other instances apparently do not. In order to accommodate these anomalous examples, one popular strategy has been to distinguish between *basic* emotions which correspond to hardwired modules and higher-level emotions that are more cognitive and depend to some extent, in an unspecified and obscure way, on those modules. In other words, we associate modules with individual emotions, and when that association proves for some reason inadequate, we redraw the borders of the emotion leaving out for future research those instances that do not fit the modular explanation. This may or may not be good science. However the main difficulty as I understand it lies with the association of modules and particular emotions. This association is equivalent to defining the function of affective modules at the individual or personal level, given that emotions, whatever else they may be taken to be, are viewed as individual subjective events. Emotion modules are seen as playing a

---

4 I say "normally" because one thing that seems necessary for the growth of cancers is that isolated cells fail to commit suicide. Cf. Ameisen (1999), 133–50.

5 See Ronald de Sousa's contribution to this issue concerning the applicability of Fodor's conception of modules to emotions.

role for individual agents; they produce or realize certain emotions that are beneficial to the individual, or at least that are supposed to have been beneficial during the EEA (Cosmides and Tooby 2000). The idea I want to pursue is that of affective modules that are internal to an individual entity and best described at the infra-individual level, but whose consequence, role, or function is located at the level of the population or at least of coordination between individuals.What I want to focus on are affective coordination and expression. Affective modules in the above sense, if they exist, are relatively autonomous processes whose functioning remains the same in a wide range of environments. It is likely that among these there will be processes that have been around for a long time; processes that we share with some of our distant ancestors. Furthermore, we should also expect such modules to be recruited for more than one purpose or function, to be "characterized by [their] reiterated use" as Strähle and Blader write and sometimes to be hierarchically imbedded in one another. Therefore, if such modules exist, there is no reason to expect that they will map neatly onto our categories of emotions. This is because emotions are defined at the level of the individual and like biological modules that give different results in different context we should expect affective modules to do the same. In other words, affective modules, like biological modules locally at the sub-individual level, can be doing exactly the same thing, while distally, at the population level, they may be doing something entirely different. Yet emotions are defined at neither of these two levels but at the level of the individual. The thesis of the modularity of emotion as it is usually understood can be seen as an attempt to reduce what happens at the level of the individual, the emotion, to what happens at the sub-personal level, the module. If there are affective modules similar to the biological modules described earlier, they will relate the sub-personal level with the collective level, bypassing in a sense the individual.

Are there any affective modules? I am not a biologist and unfortunately I do not have any object or exemplar that I could show and say "Here! Look. This is an affective module." Furthermore the level at which the function of affective modules should be defined often remains hidden from us. Affective coordination is such a usual thing that takes place all the time that we generally do not notice it. The existence of a particular mechanism whose task would be to fulfill this function seems superfluous. One of the reasons for this invisibility of affective coordination is that we cannot step out of it in order to observe it from the outside. Unlike cell differentiation or the formation of a border that separates cell populations in the case of affective coordination, we cannot directly observe the global effect, but only its repercussion at the individual level. In an attempt to turn this difficulty, I will introduce the topic of affective coordination by way of a fiction, more precisely of a "science-fiction," specifically, by way of an extract from a conference that will be given by Vulcan scientist Yram Rekab at the Federation's Star Academy on star date 29,036 and which I have been lucky enough to discover in an ancient chest abandoned in my cellar. Rekab, you will remember, is an anthropologist specializing in non-federation species and the topic of her conference that day was (will be) the origin of the Borg.[6]

III. "Resistance Is Futile"

There has been much speculation about the origin of the Borg. Where is it from? How did it begin? Clearly this is not a biological species, at least not today. On the contrary, as we all know from painful experience, the Borg assimilates by force as many biological species as it can and transforms their members into Borg, parts of itself, things that are half living and half machine. Those that cannot be assimilated are simply killed. The goal of the assimilation of diverse species seems to be to augment the pool of technological knowledge and genetic material that is at the disposal of the Borg, thereby adding endlessly to its store of competence, knowledge, and power. When assimilation takes place, the individual's self disappears and he or she becomes one with the collective. Simultaneously, all the knowledge possessed by that individual becomes available to the Borg. The Borg only has one mind

---

6   For those who are not familiar with it, the television series *Star Trek* takes place in the future when humankind has discovered the technology of efficient space travel and is now part of a multi-galactic political organization, the Federation (the good guys) in which many different species of intelligent beings participate, for example, Humans and Vulcans. Opposing the Federation are various other species and civilizations, for example, the Klingon and Romulan empires, but also the Borg, who, as the name suggests, are Cyborgs, half mechanical and half living creatures.

that is shared by all and that is why it makes sense to say as we do 'the Borg' rather than 'Borgs' for there are not many of them but only one in spite of the fact that the Borg is not spatio-temporally continuous.

The thesis I want to defend is that the Borg is a religion, a religion that, like Christianity or Buddhism, has a universal vocation. The Borg does not reproduce; members of the collective have lost the necessary autonomy. The Borg 'converts' other people. On many planets of the Federation, religions exist that are religions of the denial of the self. The self is nothing, these religions argue. It is an illusion and the goal of spiritual exercises is to abolish the self and become one with the universal mind. The Borg can be seen as a material and technological realization of this spiritual endeavour. This is what the Borg does; it materially, technologically creates a universal mind, a mind that is shared by all and obliterates the self. Given this, it would therefore make absolutely no sense to ask this illusion, the self, whether or not it wants be assimilated. Individuals are simply errors that should be eradicated.

The greatest objection to this hypothesis, which it must be said is not entirely new, comes from those who claim that the self of members of the collective is not destroyed entirely. It is argued that, even though each one is connected to all others and shares their mind and knowledge, individual members of the collective remain to some extent as poles of initiative. That is to say, they respond to local situations and their success in dealing with them is due to the fact that, thanks to their interconnection, they have access to all the knowledge of the collective. Furthermore, it is argued that there is no technology known to us that could react in real time to so many local situations as those that confront the billions of members of the collective. This last argument, however, is moot, given that we have no idea how it is technically possible for all members of the collective to access at all times the complete stock of knowledge of the Borg. We are nonetheless certain that this happens.

What prompts me to believe that the self of organisms assimilated into the Borg is properly extinguished is that when an individual is transformed into a member of the collective it immediately loses the ability to express its emotions. It may be objected that this incapacity to express emotions is purely strategic and does not indicate that members of the collective do not feel anything. Their apparent indifference to fear and complete absence of pity, and the methodical and emotion-less way in which they proceed to their end, without rage, anger, or doubt, makes them formidable adversaries, who, it seems, can never be deterred from their goals, but only destroyed. In other words, this apparent insensitivity, it is argued, is there mainly to instill terror in the hearts of the Borg's victims. Perhaps is it true that the Borg still feels, but this objection itself illustrates precisely the point I am trying to make. The objection rests on the fact that Humans, and yes, even Vulcans, immediately interpret the Borg's absence of affective expres-sion as a sign of attitudes and dispositions that, if they are not emo-tions as such, are clearly related to them, for example, resoluteness, determination, cruelty, and indifference. The adjective "strategic" in the above objection assumes that we anticipate that the Borg's behav-iour will be consistent with what is suggested by the signs that we recognize or that we assume to be there. This in turn implies, first, that we do not understand the Borg's lack of emotional expression as affec-tive silence. We give it meaning in terms of emotions. However, this spontaneous projection informs us about the type of creatures that we are but tells us nothing about the Borg. For us, there is no behaviour that is without a certain affective quality, none to which we do not attribute an emotional dimension of some sort. The term "strategic" also implies that affective expression is directly related to behaviour. The idea of strategy as it is used in the objection supposes that the lack of affect expressed by the Borg is unmistakenly associated by us with definite behaviours. Finally it suggests that the impassivity of the Borg will spontaneously orient us towards certain affective disposi-tions, such as fear, doubt, irresolution, and perhaps terror and confu-sion, as if the insensitivity of Borg itself were an action that had direct consequences on our own behaviour.

It therefore does not really matter whether or not members of the collective feel anything, for we spontaneously interpret their expres-sive passivity as revealing definite affective dispositions. What does matter for the argument concerning the disappearance of the self, how-ever, is that (it) they do(es) not express anything. When we respond affectively as we do to the Borg's indifference, through anger, fear, repulsion, or disgust, we attempt to coordinate our actions to theirs. Unfortunately, this spontaneous effort of ours is doomed to failure because they cannot answer our affect. Unlike the action of their imagined insensitivity upon us, our emotional expression has no hold upon them. How is this failure visible? What demonstrates it is that we cannot individualize members of the collective. I do not mean by this that we cannot recognize that this "thing," half human and half machine, that is now coming towards us was not Borg half an hour ago but a data analyst working in engineering. It is, on the contrary, easy to recognize that members of the collective once were distinct individuals belonging to different species. However, what we cannot do is individualize them in action so to speak. There is nothing we can do that can evoke from a member of the collective a response that is not dictated by the collective.

Members of the collective do not react to affective expression because they do not need to. The Borg's mind is conscious of itself and the access of all to the complete store of information it contains is immediate and total. No individual needs therefore to coordinate his or her actions to those of another precisely because they are not individuals but part of a whole. The smooth functioning of the various parts of the Borg is centrally directed. There is no need for local and individual coordination in this situation because no one is uncertain about the intentions of another towards him. That is why members of the collective neither express nor recognize emotions. They have no use for that device.

IV. A Coordination Module

The manuscript is unfortunately incomplete. The Borg, unlike us, does not need to express or recognize emotions because what are called in the fiction "members of the collective" are actually its parts. They have no autonomy. Between them, there may be some room for play as in a mechanism, but none of them is a pole of initiative. We, on the contrary, are a highly social species. This means that for each one of us most of the advantages and disadvantages that we can receive in life come from other members of our own species. Each individual is a pole of initiative. Everyone can initiate a chain of action that is unpredictable to others and yet can have fundamental consequences upon them. Because of this, knowledge of the intentions and dispositions of each individual toward others is of paramount importance. Conflict, cooperation, reproduction, alliances, and sustained relations all depend to some extent on the intentions others harbour towards us and on how they understand our dispositions towards them. Given this, it would seem like a good idea if members of a species similar to ours had a way of informing one another of their mutual intentions and dispositions. This would allow them to coordinate their action and interact more frequently in ways that are mutually beneficial.

Since Adam Smith (1759)[7] and Francis Hutcheson (1726), emotions, or at least some emotions, have been viewed as playing precisely this role. Most authors, however, including modern ones like Robert Frank (1988), Alan Gibbard (1990), or Peter Strawson (1963), have usually focused on the inner sentiment rather than on the expression of affect itself. This approach leads to two important difficulties. The first, which has been extensively studied, can be called the problem of sincerity detection.[8] A device that allows one organism to inform another of his or her disposition and intentions towards that second organism will play its role only if it transmits reliable information, that is to say, if cheaters can be detected and truthful messages regularly recognized. The signal must be consistent with the inner sentiment, and the problem of sincerity detection is that of recognizing when that condition is satisfied and when it is not.

The second difficulty, has received a lot less attention but is perhaps even more important and can be called the problem of indeterminacy. As de Waal and Aureli wrote: "if two individuals compete over a particular resource, they need to take into account not only the value of the resource and the risk of bodily harm, but also the value of their relationship. Sometimes the resource may not be worth straining a cooperative relationship" (de Waal and Aureli 1999, 122). However, it is clear that for social animals that are sophisticated enough to distinguish between the partners with whom they interact the value of a given relationship for one individual is not independent of the value of that same relationship for the other individual involved. The value of a relationship is related to reiterated interaction, and how an organism behaves in a specific situation is indicative of the importance it

---

7 Adam Smith *The Theory of Moral Sentiments* (1759) (Indianapolis: Liberty Classic, 1976).

8 See, for example, Skyrms (1996), esp. chap. 5, and Frank (2004).

gives to future interaction. It is a conceptual truth therefore that the value further interaction with another organism has for one organism is not independent of the value it has for the other organism. Thus, the value my relationship with you has for me is not independent of the value your relationship with me has for you, and vice versa. More generally, my intentions towards you are not independent of your intentions towards me. They will change depending on how yours turn out to be. Given that this is true of all of us, there is a sense in which our intentions towards one another are radically indeterminate. But if this is the case, how is it possible for me to inform you of my intention towards you if it is not already determined but awaits information concerning your intention towards me in order to reach a definite form? And how is it possible for you to inform me since you are in exactly the same situation?

If this description of the situation is accurate, then there is no system of communication, classically understood as an exchange of messages carrying information, which can resolve these two difficulties. However, there is another way to achieve the desired goal of coordination and mutually beneficial interactions while avoiding these two pitfalls. It is to have the intentions of every individual partially determined by other individuals. Organisms could thus coordinate by converging towards complementary intentions and actions. From this point of view, the expression of emotion should not be seen as a system of signalling but as a way in which one organism acts upon the intentions and dispositions of another. Affective expression is a mechanism through which individuals reciprocally determine one another's mutual intentions. This interaction is not an exchange of messages or information; it contains no representation but is a form of reciprocal action of one organism upon another. This may seem strange at first, but when biologists talk about animal communication this is often pretty much what they describe, even if they do not use exactly this language. This is what bird songs and mating rituals are about; the vocabulary of messages and information is purely metaphorical in this context.[9] Furthermore, there is beginning to be quite a bit of neurological evidence that, through reciprocal expression of

9 See, for example, Hauser and Konishi (2003), 701.

affect, mammals, and primates in particular, do things to one another. When one organism perceives the expressed emotion of another, that perception modifies it own inner state (Perret 2003). It triggers the production of a hormone or neurotransmitter, or initiates a neurological or physiological reaction that is immediate and automatic. Actually, we also know that certain affective displays are necessary for the normal development of various social skills and abilities and even some neurological components (Levine et al. 1999; Wallen and Tannenbaum 1999; Perret 2003; Cheney and Seyfarth 1999; Gergely at al. 2002; Decety 2002).

The first advantage of looking at the expression of affect in this way is that the problem of indeterminacy is solved. Determinate intentions do not precede the dynamic of expression but appear at the end of the process. There is no need to presuppose them. The goal of the interaction is to determine them. How is this done? A good example of this is the regulation of voice pitch during conversation. Empirical studies have shown that during conversation the voice pitch of each speaker is closely related to that of his or her partners. The pitch of each speaker varies in response to the modulation of the pitch of others, and this close coordination is strongly related to the emotional tone of a conversation (Cowley 1997; 1998). In this way, the pitch of one speaker acts upon the pitch of another but also upon the emotional state or disposition of the other. These changes in voice pitch and tone are part of what makes a conversation progress towards anger, distress, or laughter. They do not follow but precede this progression. The process is generally wholly unconscious. Most of the time we are not aware of it and notice our reciprocal vocal adaptation only when emotions erupt on the front stage and we start shouting insults at one another. However, from the point of view of the coordination of voice pitch, there is no discontinuity between the moment when speakers would describe the situation in terms of emotions and the part of the conversation that came before. The process takes place at a sub-personal level; the coordination is taken care of by neurologically closely integrated devices of perception and expression of affect (Adolphs 2003; Perret 2003), but its consequence appears at the level of social coordination of two or more individuals.

The second advantage of looking at the expression of affect in this way is that the problem of sincerity detection is radically transformed.

If we do not start out from determined intentions but only reach them through a process of dynamic interaction in which each individual partially determines the intentions of others, then the question of the sincerity of affective expression is no longer one of knowing if an agent is cheating, in the sense of discovering whether he or she is sending out a message that is inconsistent with his or her real intentions. As Don Ross and I have argued, in this new context, the question of sincerity is not one of distinguishing truthful messages from unreliable ones but of holding agents to their commitments (Ross and Dumouchel 2004a, 2004b). This is done in two ways. First, important coordination equilibria result in strong affects. Robert Frank believes that strong affects guarantee the truth of certain messages, especially if the expression of such affect is to a large extent involuntary (Frank 1988). The reason for this is that Frank rightly assumes that strong affects increase commitment. Given this, if the coordination of intention through affective expression is associated with strong affects, then the probability that agents will be committed to that solution of coordination will also augment. The second way in which agents are held to their commitments is that standard expressions of emotions, which are the end results of the dynamic of coordination and are associated with definite intentions, have evolved as convention of coordination.[10] It is by definition to the advantage of everyone to respect conventions and those who transgress them are ostracized. In other words, agents commit themselves through the fact that they express their emotions in standardized ways that everyone associates with definite intentions. They make in short public commitments. Of course, agents can cheat and they sometimes do. They do not always live up to their affective commitments, but the fact that more or less seven standard emotional displays are universally recognizable suggests that these conventions are generally respected.

In what way can this coordination be viewed as resting on modules similar to those that were described earlier in the second section of this text? At this point the answer to this question can only be highly speculative. Nonetheless, in closing, consider the following points. First,

---

10 This is a very natural way of understanding Paul Ekman's results concerning the expression of emotion. What we recognize as *basic* emotions are fixed points of affective coordination.

it seems possible to argue that (at least some of) the devices responsible for affective coordination are autonomous in the required sense. Once initiated affective coordination follows its course independently of many other events that take place in the environment. The process is to some extent self-sustaining. Affective expression from one organism triggers a similar type of response from another organism that in turn acts upon the first until an equilibrium of coordination is found. The self-organizing aspects of affective coordination suggest that the underlying mechanisms remain stable under a wide range of environmental changes. Second, it seems that they also satisfy the requirement of reiterated use in different domains, for example, perception and action in both the visual and the audible domains. In fact it is precisely that plasticity which creates problems for our concepts of emotions. Because of that, it is only under a sufficiently abstract description that the module can be defined as the same, only in the sense that the description of its function is coordination among co-specifics.[11] The module of affective expression and perception can be applied to any situation that can be described as one where there is a need for coordination between different organisms. Thirdly, the modules are also hierarchically organized, since the expression of many emotions such as anger, fear, and disgust depend on neural systems that also seem to function as modules. Fourthly, many of these systems are relatively ancient and seem to have been doing the same thing, for example, fear conditioning, in many different species that are sometimes phylogenetically quite distant (LeDoux 1998; Adolphs 2003). Finally, just as in the case of many biological modules, the consequences or function of these modules, social coordination, takes place at the level of a group of organism while the module is described at a sub-personal level.

References

Adolphs, R. 2003. Neural systems for recognizing emotions in humans. In *The Design of Animal Communication*, ed. M. D. Hauser and M. Konishi, 187–211. Cambridge (Mass.): MIT Press.

---

11 Mostly but not exclusively since it seems clear that we can to some extent reach affective coordination with some other mammals like dogs or horses.

Ameisen, J.-C. 1999. *La Sculpture du vivant. Le suicide cellulaire ou la mort créatrice.* Paris: Seuil.

Borycki, A.-G. 2003. Sonic hedgehog and wnt signaling pathways during development and evolution. In *Modularity in Development and Evolution,* ed. G. Schlosser and G. Wagner. Chicago: Chicago University Press.

Camazine, S., J.-L. Deneubourg, N. R. Franks, J. Sneyd, G. Theraulaz, and E. Bonabeau. 2003. *Self-Organization in Biological Systems.* Princeton: Princeton University Press.

Cheney, D. L., and R. M. Seyfarth. 1999 Mechanism underlying the vocalizations of nonhuman primates. In *The Design of Animal Communication,* ed. M. D. Hauser and M. Konishi, 627–43. Cambridge (Mass.): MIT Press.

Cosmides, L., and J. Tooby. 2000. Evolutionary psychology and the emotions. In *Handbook of Emotions,* ed. M. Lewis and J. Haviland-Jones, 91–115. New York: The Guilford Press.

Cowley, S. J. 1997. Of representations and language. *Language and Communication* 17(4): 279–300.

Cowley, S. J. 1998. On timing, turn-taking, and conversation. *Journal of Psycholinguistic Research* 27(5): 541–71.

de Celis, J. F. 2003. The notch signaling module. In *Modularity in Development and Evolution,* ed. G. Schlosser and G. Wagner. Chicago: Chicago University Press.

de Waal, F.B.M., and F. Aureli. 1999. Conflict resolution and distress alleviation in monkeys and apes. In *The Integrative Neurobiology of Affiliation,* ed. S. Carter, I. Lederhendler, and B. Kirkpatrick. Cambridge (Mass.): MIT Press.

Decety, J. 2002. Neurobiologie des représentations motrices partagées. In *Imiter pour découvrir l'humain,* ed. J. Nadel and J. Decety, 105–30. Paris: PUF.

Fodor, J. 1983. *The Modularity of Mind.* Cambridge (Mass.): MIT Press.

Frank, R. 1988. *Passions within Reason: The Strategic Role of the Emotions.* New York: Norton.

Frank, R. 2004. In defense of sincerity detection: Response to Ross and Dumouchel. *Rationality and Society* 16(3): 287–305.

Gergely, G., O. Koos, and J. S. Watson. 2002. Perception causale et rôle des comportements immitatifs des parents dans le développement socio-émotionnel précoce. In *Imiter pour découvrir l'humain,* ed. J. Nadel and J. Decety, 59–82. Paris: PUF.

Gibbard, A. 1990. *Wise Choices, Apt Feelings: A Theory of Normative Judgment.* Oxford: Oxford University Press.

Hauser, M. D., and M. Konishi. 2003. *The Design of Animal Communication.* Cambridge (Mass.): MIT Press.

Hobbes, T. 1651. *Leviathan.* Indianapolis: Hackett.

Hutcheson, F. [1726] 2004. *An Inquiry into the Original of Our Ideas of Beauty and Virtue.* Wolfgang Leidhold, ed. Indianapolis: Liberty Classic.

Kardon, G., T. A. Heanue, and C. T. Tabin. 2003. The Pax/Six/Eya/Dach network in development and evolution. In *Modularity in Development and Evolution,* ed. G. Schlosser and G. Wagner. Chicago: University of Chicago Press.

Kelley, E. F. 2002. *Making Sense of Life.* Cambridge (Mass.): Harvard University Press.

LeDoux, J. 1998. *The Emotional Brain.* New York: Simon & Schuster.

Levine, S., D. M. Lyons, and F. Schatzberg. 1999. Psychobiological consequences of social relationships. In *The Integrative Neurobiology of Affiliation,* ed. S. Carter, I. Lederhendler, and B. Kirkpatrick, 83–89. Cambridge (Mass.): MIT Press.

Perret, D. I. 2003. A cellular basis for reading minds from faces and actions. In *The Design of Animal Communication,* ed. M. D. Hauser and M. Konishi, 159–85. Cambridge (Mass.): MIT Press.

Ross, D., and P. Dumouchel. 2004a. Emotions as strategic signals. *Rationality and Society* 16(3): 251–86.

Ross, D., and P. Dumouchel. 2004b. Sincerity is just consistency: Reply to Frank. *Rationality and Society* 16(3): 207–318.

Schlosser, G. 2003. The role of module in development and evolution. In *Modularity in Development and Evolution,* ed. G. Schlosser and G. Wagner, 525. Chicago: Chicago University Press.

Skyrms, B. 1996. *Evolution of the Social Contract.* Cambridge: Cambridge University Press.

Sloman, A. 2002. How many separately evolved emotional beasties live within us? In *Emotions in Humans and Aritifacts,* ed. R. Trappl, P. Petta, and S. Payr, 35–114. Cambridge (Mass.): MIT Press.

Smith, A. [1759] 1976. *The Theory of Moral Sentiments.* Indianapolis: Liberty Classic.

Strähle, U., and P. Blader. 2003. The basic helix-loop-helix proteins in vertebrate and invertebrate neurogenesis. In *Modularity in Development and*

Evolution, ed. G. Schlosser and G. Wagner. Chicago: Chicago University Press.

Strawson, P. 1963. Freedom and resentment. *Proceedings of the British Academy* 48: 1–25.

von Dassow, G., and E. Meir. 2003. Exploring modularity with dynamical models of gene networks. In *Modularity in Development and Evolution*, ed. G. Schlosser and G. Wagner. Chicago: Chicago University Press.

Wallen, K., and P. L. Tannenbaum. 1999. Hormone Modulation of sexual behavior and affiliation in rhesus monkeys. In *The Integrative Neurobiology of Affiliation*, ed. S. Carter, I. Lederhendler, and B. Kirkpatrick, 101–18. Cambridge (Mass.): MIT Press.

3. The Analogy with Perception

Is Emotion a Form of Perception?

JESSE J. PRINZ

Theories of emotions traditionally divide into two categories. According to some researchers, emotions are or essentially involve evaluative thoughts or judgments. These are called *cognitive theories*. According to other researchers, an emotion can occur without any thought. These are called *non-cognitive theories*. Some defenders of non-cognitive theories argue that emotions are action tendencies, others say they are feelings, and still others say they are affect programs, which encompass a range of internal and external events. One of the most celebrated non-cognitive theories owes, independently, to William James and Carl Lange. According to them, emotions are perceptions of patterned changes in the body. I think the perceptual theory of emotions is basically correct, but it needs to be updated. In this discussion, I will offer a summary and defence.

The question I am addressing bears on the question of modularity. Within cognitive science, there is a widespread view that perceptual systems are modular. If this is right, then showing that emotion is a form of perception requires showing that emotion is a modular process, and showing that emotion is modular could contribute to showing that emotion is a form of perception (assuming that not all mental capacities are underwritten by modular systems). Therefore, modularity will figure centrally in the discussion that follows, as it did in an earlier treatment of this topic (Prinz 2004). There is, however, a change in how I will approach this topic here. I have come to believe that perception is not, in fact, modular as that term is defined by Fodor (1983) in his classic treatment of the topic. Perceptual systems bear features in common with Fodor's modules, but Fodor's approach is, in my view, mistaken (Prinz 2006). Here I will introduce the idea of quasi-modules, which bear some things in common with Fodor's modules, and I will argue that emotions are quasi-modular. This thesis will help secure the parallel between emotion and perception.

I. What Is Perception?

To determine whether emotion is a form of perception, it would be handy to have a working definition of perception. I am not going to offer such a definition, however. Offering conceptual analyses of psychological terms is methodologically unscrupulous. It presupposes, quite implausibly, that our ordinary folk psychological terms have good definitions. There are some paradigm cases of perception, but what these have in common must be determined by careful observation and theory construction, not armchair lexicography. Still, as a starting place, we can reflect on some of the features that paradigm perceptions have in common. If we consider visual, auditory, and olfactory states, for example, we find the following characteristic features:

First, perception takes place in sensory systems. Sensory systems are systems that convert physical magnitudes into mental representations. Each sensory system has dedicated transducers that are stimulated by non-mental features of the world, and output mental representations in a modality- specific code.

Second, perception involves the generation of internal representations, and these typically represent the mind-external stimuli. Sometimes the senses represent proximal stimuli (i.e., perturbations of our sensory transducers), but they can also represent more distal stimuli (e.g., external objects) or relational properties (e.g., secondary qualities, or powers that external objects have to cause mental states in us). It is important to emphasize that sensory systems may have to do a fair amount of processing before representations of complex distal objects can be generated. When you see a giraffe, for example, the eyes first convert light reflected from the surface of the giraffe into a vast assembly of edge representations and colour patches. These are then bound together and organized into a representation of the giraffe's contours. Those contours are used to extract perceptual invariants that remain constant across various viewing positions and these are matched against stored templates in visual memory. Through this process, the visual system ends up generating a giraffe representation. It generates that representation by first representing something else: patterns of light. Giraffes are not identical to their appearances, but we detect them through their appearances. Objects are not directly given to the senses. They must be reconstructed or extrapolated from the superficial magnitudes that senses transduce.

Third, perceptions can be consciously experienced. They have phenomenal qualities. This is significant because, arguably, perceptual representations are the only internal states of which we can be conscious. When we consider our phenomenal qualities, all of them seem to be modality-specific. We can recognize a smooth surface with eyes or touch, but smoothness is not presented consciously in an amodal code; it always presents itself in consciousness as visual or tactile. Even thoughts present themselves to us in modality- specific codes. We experience thoughts as images of the facts they represent or, more commonly, as strings of words in the languages we speak. When thinking about philosophy, for example, we usually hear auditory images of sentences running through our heads. There is no uncontroversial example of a phenomenal quality that is not perceptual in character. I will assume throughout that only perceptual states are phenomenally conscious, and I will also suggest below that perceptual states become phenomenally conscious in exactly the same way.

Fourth, perception is quasi-modular. I add the ugly prefix because, as I remarked at the outset, I do not think perception is modular in the way that the term is defined in Fodor's (1983) influential book. I have argued against Fodorian modularity at length elsewhere (Prinz 2006). Rather than rehearsing those arguments, I will be a bit more constructive here. For even if perceptual systems are not modular in the standard sense that has been given to the term, they share some features in common with modules. I will describe these features and label any system that has them *quasi-modular*.

A mental capacity is *quasi-modular* to the extent that it is:

1. Functionally specialized
2. Subject to characteristic breakdowns
3. Capable of automatic processing
4. Built up from a system of innate rules and representations
5. Stimulus-dependent

On the face of it, all of these criteria are consistent with Fodor's definition of modularity. He talks about domain specificity, characteristic breakdowns, automatic processing, and innateness. But the last item on my list, stimulus-dependence, is introduced to replace the aspect of his definition that he considers most fundamental to modularity: informational encapsulation. By stimulus-dependent, I mean to suggest that modules are constrained by their inputs. Top-down influences cannot fully determine what happens inside a module. In terms of perception, the idea is that we cannot simply choose what we perceive. But stimulus-dependence is consistent with the possibility that top-down influences can significantly affect what happens in perceptual systems. And this is an important departure from Fodor's idea of "encapsulation." Fodor insists that perceptual systems do not let in any information from systems further up the information-processing hierarchy, and I think he is mistaken about this (see Prinz 2006). There is overwhelming evidence that cognitive systems can communicate with perceptual systems (as in the case of mental imagery), and that perceptual systems can communicate with each other (as with the McGurk effect [McGurk and MacDonald 1976] and other forms of intermodal accommodation).

Fodor argues for informational encapsulation by appeal to perceptual illusions. Consider the Müller-Lyer illusion, in which equal lines appear different in length. This illusion persists even after we learn that the lines are the same, which leads Fodor to conclude that knowledge cannot penetrate the perception system. But this conclusion is too strong. An alternative explanation is that bottom-up inputs *trump* top-down inputs when the two come into conflict. After all, when there is no conflict, there can be top-down influences. Consider the duck-rabbit. Cognition can lead us to reconstrue the image as a duck after seeing it as a rabbit, because both interpretations are consistent with the stimulus. I think we should drop talk of encapsulation and appeal to the notion of trumping when describing perceptual systems. The notion of stimulus-dependence captures that idea. In saying that we can cannot choose what we perceive, I mean to imply that we cannot, under ordinary circumstances, have a perceptual representation generated top-down when the current stimulus is disposed to induce an incongruent representation. Perceptual systems are stimulus dependent in this sense, and they are quasi-modular.

In sum, while I have not offered a definition of perception, I have identified four features that are characteristic of perception. Perception takes place in modality-specific input systems; perception involves the generation of representations, which represent proximal, distal, or relational stimuli; third, perceptions can be consciously experienced; and fourth, perceptions are quasi-modular. In arguing that emotion is a form of perception, I will consider each of these features in turn. If I can establish that emotions exhibit all four features, then, to that extent, emotions are like paradigm instances of perception. I don't want to insist that each of these features is necessary for qualifying as a case of perception, but collectively they strike me as a plausible set of sufficient conditions. No one condition is sufficient on its own to establish that emotions are perceptions. Perhaps a proper subset of these conditions would suffice, but I will remain neutral about that question here. I will argue that emotions exhibit all four features, and thus deserve to be called perceptions. This is not intended as a conceptual claim. I mean to argue that it is an empirical fact that emotions share features that can be empirically observed in paradigm instances of perception. Getting mad is very much like seeing red.

II. Emotions Are Modality-Specific

I think emotions qualify as states of modality-specific input systems. They are interoceptive; emotions are states in the sensory systems that respond to changes in the body. I will defend the interoception thesis in this section. To remain neutral about the question of whether emotions are *perceptions* of the body, as opposed to merely being states that happen to occur in a sensory system, I will adopt a distinction between registration and representation. I will say that a response within a perceptual system that reliably occurs in response to a stimulus *registers* that stimulus. To *represent* rather than merely registering, the state would have to have the function of being caused by the stimulus. A mental state represents that which it has the function of reliably detecting (cf. Dretske 1988). Correlatively, to qualify as a perception of a stimulus, the state would have to represent it. States of sensory systems that register stimuli can be called "perceptual states" simply in virtue of being modality-specific, but to grant them the title "perceptions" we might demand that they also represent the stimuli that cause them. It will be the burden of this section to show that emotions are perceptual states, but the burden of the next section to show that they represent.

The link between emotions and interoception was most influentially explored by William James (1884) and Carl Lange (1885). On more traditional folk psychological theories, emotions were presumed to cause various bodily changes, such as crying or trembling or fleeing. For James and Lange, this gets things back to front. Emotions are the effects of bodily changes, not the causes. Crying makes us sad, or, more accurately, the feeling of sadness is the feeling of a range of bodily responses that includes crying. On this view, emotions arise in the following way. We encounter a stimulus or have a thought that is (as the result of evolution or learning) disposed to trigger a pattern of changes in our bodies; when those changes occur, they are registered in brain systems that are sensitive to somatic states; these neuronal responses are experienced as feelings, and those feelings are what we call emotions. Lange focuses on vascular changes, but James, following Darwin, argues that each emotion is associated with a complex range of bodily changes and emotions feel different as a result of the different bodily patterns that they register. When frightened, we tremble, and breathing becomes strained. When angry, our muscles tighten, our brows lower, and blood rushes to our face and extremities. When overjoyed, our hearts race, our breathing becomes relaxed, and our arms widen receptively. Our circulatory systems, respiratory systems, facial expressions, and bodily movements are all correlated with emotions. When inferring causation from correlation, we tend to think that emotions are the causes of these varied bodily changes, rather than the effects, but James reverses the order of events. The brain contains interoceptive systems that are linked to the body by a vast network of nerve fibres. Like the rods and cones in our eyes, these nerves serve as transducers converting physical changes into electrochemical signals that are sent into the brain. The interoceptive systems that register patterned changes in the body are the neural substrates of emotions on the James-Lange view. Emotions are interoceptive states that register patterned changes in the body. Call this the registration thesis.

Both James and Lange defend the registration thesis by means of a thought experiment. They ask us to imagine having an emotion without having any changes in the body. Imagine terror, for example, without any spine-tingling, trembling, or constrained breathing. Imagine that your body is completely relaxed. James and Lange think it will be obvious that there is nothing in this placid bodily state that could be recognized as terror. Subtract the bodily perturbation, and the emotion goes as well. This suggests that emotions are interoceptive states.

This argument rests on introspective intuitions, which may not be shared by everyone. Lange comments that it is easy to deceive yourself into thinking that you can have an intense emotional experience in the absence of any somatic feelings. Somatic feelings are often not recognized as such. When we have a twinge or muscle tension or a subtle imbalance in our vestibular systems, we do not always recognize the cause. So the appeal to introspection will not persuade everyone that James and Lange are right. We need other sources of evidence. In recent years, there has been a growing body of empirical evidence in support of the registration thesis (for reviews, see Damasio 1994; Prinz 2004). Here I mention just a few lines of evidence.

First, there is now a large body of evidence suggesting that emotions can be induced by changing states of the body. One method is to use drugs that act on the autonomic nervous system. When people are injected with adrenalin, they report having experiences that feel like emotions (Marañon 1924). Another method uses feedback from the body. When we make facial expressions (Strack et al. 1988), or change our posture (Stepper and Strack 1993), or change our breathing pattern (Philippot et al. 2002), we often experience a corresponding emotion. Smile and you will feel happy; scowl and you will feel mad. This is just what the registration thesis predicts.

Further evidence for the registration thesis comes from neuroimaging. There have now been hundreds of studies of brain activity during emotion episodes. Again and again, there studies implicate the same structures (Phan et al. 2004; Wiens 2005). The structures that get discussed most frequently are the amygdala, which is primarily believed to be involved in the induction of emotions, and the cingulate and insular cortices, which are implicated in the emotions themselves. The amygdala is essentially an association area that links perceptions or thoughts to bodily responses. When an emotionally significant event is perceived or contemplated, the amygdala sends signs to brain structures that regulate changes in the endochrine system, the autonomic nervous system, and in systems that control stereotyped behavioural responses (LeDoux 1996). Both the cingulate and the insula are involved in the regulation and response to changes in the body. Both of these complex brain areas are implicated in interoception (Critchley et al. 2004; Wiens 2005). The fact that emotions reliably correlate with activity in these brain areas, and do not systematically correlate with activity in other areas, provides support for James and Lange's suggestion that emotions are interoceptive states.

The evidence from bodily feedback suggests that bodily changes can be sufficient for emotions, and the evidence from neuroimaging suggests that emotions co-occur with, and may ordinarily be constituted by states in brain systems that register bodily changes. This is strong evidence in favour of the registration thesis that was expounded by James and Lange. But critics of this tradition may complain that, while perceptions of the body are sufficient for emotions, they are not necessary. They may argue that some emotions arise in the absence of bodily changes and perceptions thereof. In response, defenders of the registration thesis could either concede the some emotions are disembodied, as it were, or they could dig in their heels and argue that all emotions are perceptions of bodily states. I think a qualified version of heel-digging is defensible. Let me introduce two qualifications:

First, emotions can be attributed as states or as traits. As an example of an emotion trait, consider the sentence, "Scottie is afraid of heights." This statement is true of Scottie even when Scottie isn't experiencing the state of fear. Emotion traits are not perceptions of bodily changes. But, I think a person can be truly attributed an emotion trait only if he or she is disposed to have the corresponding state (Scottie is afraid of heights if and only if heights instill fear in him), and emotion states, I claim, are always perceptions of bodily changes. I defend this claim in more detail elsewhere (Prinz 2004).

Second, emotions sometimes seem to arise before we've had time to perceive bodily changes (Cannon 1927), and they can even arise in individuals who have limited capacity to perceive bodily changes due to spinal cord injuries (Chwalisz et al. 1988). These points are usually presented as an objection to the James-Lange approach, but, as Damasio (1999) points out, there is an easy response. For James and Lange, emotions are interoceptive states – states in brain systems that normally register changes in the body. Presumably such states can arise even in the absence of actual bodily changes. Just as we can visually imagine an object without seeing it, we can imagine bodily changes without those changes taking place. It is extremely plausible that, when we encounter familiar emotion elicitors, our interoceptive systems become active before the body has had time to change. The brain anticipates what the body will do. Thus, the claim that emotions are interoceptive states is compatible with the claim that emotions can occur before bodily changes and when bodily changes are imperceptible due to spinal injury. This may appear *ad hoc*, but it's not. There is evidence that when bodily changes are executed endogenously, as when we move our limbs, motor and somatosensory systems generate a "forward model" that predicts what the executed bodily changes will be like (Wolpert and Flanagan 2001). When acting, we generate images of our actions before they have even occurred. The present suggestion is that interceptive systems use forward models as well. This proposal requires a slight refinement of the registration thesis. Emotions, I will say, are states of interoceptive systems that either register or *anticipate* changes in the body. In cases where emotions involve interoceptive states that merely anticipate bodily changes rather than registering them, emotions are more like perceptual *images* than perceptions. But this qualification does not vitiate the claim that emotion is, in general, a form of perception. If it did, we would have to deny that vision is a form of perception. After all, we can form visual imagery, and we often generate visual images in anticipation of the objects that we are about to see (Kosslyn 1994). When watching a moving ball, we may spontaneously use imagery to anticipate its trajectory; likewise, when responding to an impending threat, we may spontaneously anticipate how our bodies will feel once the fear response has been fully activated.

In sum, I think a strong case can be made for James and Lange's proposal that emotions are interoceptive states that (normally) serve to register changes in the body. The registration thesis is consistent with evidence from psychology and neuroscience. The research on bodily feedback suggests that body changes can cause emotions, and neuroimaging results show that emotions supervene on brain structures that register changes in the body. Taking these finding at face value, we should conclude that emotions are interoceptive states.

Given the evidence, opponents of this view have the burden of proof. I am convinced that James and Lange were right.

If emotions are interoceptive states, then emotions are perceptual states because interoceptive systems are perceptual systems; interoception is one of our senses. But are emotions perceptions? To qualify as perceptions, emotions must be perceptions *of* something. Is having an emotion perceiving anything? If so, what?

III. Emotions Are Representations

So far, I have been very cautious about terminology. I said that emotions are perceptual states, not that they are perceptions. In particular, I have not said that emotions allow us to perceive anything. To defend that claim, I must establish that emotions represent something. Perceptions are representations. On the face of it, this might look like a trivial step from the evidence that I have been presenting. After all, I have been arguing that emotions register patterned changes in the body. Can't I just switch terminology and say that emotions represent such changes? Aren't emotions perceptions of bodily changes? Well, perhaps not. In this section I want to argue that, while emotions register bodily changes, they don't represent them. Indeed, this conclusion is important because, if emotions were representations of bodily states, they couldn't be distinguished from itches, twinges, or chills. Emotions have semantic properties that distinguish them from garden variety bodily perceptions. Let me explain.

According to the theory of representation mentioned in section II, representation requires that two conditions be met. A mental state represents that which it has the function of reliably detecting (for a defence, see Dretske 1988; Prinz 2000). The reliable detection condition is causal. Under ordinary conditions, mental representations are causally activated when we contact their referents. When we see red, our red representations are tokened, and when we see water our water representations are tokened. But many different things can cause a mental state to activate. Hearing the word "rose" may cause a red image to activate, and a long trek in the desert may lead us to token a representation of water. If mental representations referred to all of their causes, red would refer to the word "rose" and our water concepts would refer to the arid desert. To avoid this unwanted consequence, we should following leading theories in psychosemantics and say that mental representations represent only those of their many causes that they have the function of detecting. In this context, "function" can be cashed out in terms of causal history. We can ask, how was the mental representation in question acquired in the course of learning or natural selection. If a mental representation was passed on through natural selection as a result of our ancestors successfully detecting red things, then it represents red. If a mental representation was learned as a consequence of being presented with samples of water, then it is a water representation.

Assuming this psychosemantic theory is correct, we can ask, what do emotions have the function of detecting? I have already suggested that emotions detect patterned changes in the body. These things reliably cause emotions to occur. But do they have the function of detecting such changes? Let's assume, for these purposes, that our emotions are the product of natural selection. I think this is true of some emotions and others are learned by deploying evolved emotions in new contexts. Focusing on evolved emotions, we can ask, did our capacity to detect patterned bodily changes get passed onto us in virtue of the fact that they co-varied with those bodily changes, or for some other reason? Like any question about our evolutionary history, this is difficult to answer, but I think we can safely speculate by considering the current function of emotions. Emotions are, if the registration theory is right, reliable indicators of body states. They carry the information that our hearts are beating and our lungs are contracting. The body does need to monitor such bodily states in order to regulate the basic biological functions necessary for life. But information about our viscera is not essential to the functional role of *emotions* in regulating behaviour. Emotions help us choose behavioural responses that cope with external situations, not with internal organs. But how do they do that?

The trick is to use the body as an indicator of how we are faring in the world. Think about how smoke alarms work. They are wired to emit a sound when smoke is near. Likewise, we are wired to enter into patterned bodily states when matters of concern arise. Evolution has set things up so that we enter into a distinctive bodily pattern when we encounter certain dangerous things (loud sudden noises, predators, sudden loss of support), another bodily pattern when we encounter certain threatening things (a glare, theft, or attack from a conspecific), and a third pattern when we encounter certain losses (the death or disappearance of an conspecific with whom we have a close relationship). For each biologically basic emotion, there is a distinctive bodily pattern and a distinctive set of eliciting conditions. Each set of eliciting conditions instantiates a specific kind of organism-environment relation that bears on well-being (danger, threat, loss, and so on). Call these relations "concerns." Because we are wired in this way, our bodily patterns *and the brain states that register them* are reliably caused by concerns. Quite plausibly, it is in virtue of detecting these concerns, and not the bodily states themselves, that our body-pattern detectors got passed down from our ancestors.

Think of it this way. There is good evolutionary reason why we should be able to register local changes in the body, such as a racing heart or constricted breath. Bodily homeostasis requires feedback from the organs regulated by the central nervous system. But why do we need to register *patterns* of bodily change? Why do we need brain states that register a racing heart *together with* strained breathing? Homeostasis may not require that. So it is an evolutionary puzzle why we would be able to detect patterns of bodily change. The puzzle is solved if we imagine that these patterns ordinarily occur in special circumstances. If the heart races together with strained breathing under situations that were dangerous to our ancestors, then the brain could use this information to register danger, and, more specifically, it could use that signal to tell action-selecting systems to search for response strategies that are useful for avoiding danger. The body, like the tone in the smoke alarm, signals that there is something we need to cope with in our environment.

What I am suggesting is that a neural response to a patterned bodily change causally covaries with two different things. The response covaries with the bodily change in question but also with a concern, such as danger, threat, or loss. The neural response detects both of these things, but it represents only the one that it has the function of detecting — the one that it was selected for detecting. It seems very plausible that neural responses to patterned bodily changes have the function of detecting concerns. Such neural responses register bodily changes, but they thereby represent concerns such as danger, threat, and loss.

This conclusion may seem to be at odds with the thesis that emotion is a kind of perception. It seems reasonable, on the face of it, to say that neural states in our interoceptive systems are perceptions of bodily changes, but bizarre to say that they are perceptions of danger, threat, and loss. Those concerns seem too abstract and too disparate in form to be perceived. After all, dangers don't share any morphological properties in common. They don't look alike. There is no obvious set of appearances uniting all and only dangers. In paradigm cases of perception, we assume that the perceived property is a superficial appearance and that the perceptual representation of that property resembles it, in some respect. We think that a visual perception of a circle consists in a perceptual representation that is circular. Emotions don't resemble the concerns that I have been considering, nor could they. Those concerns are instantiated by concrete objects and events that are too variable in form.

The worry is easily addressed once we realize that the resemblance theory of perception is false — even in paradigm cases. Assume, for example, that colours are secondary qualities. Assume that red is the power to cause a certain experience in us. Two things follow from this. First, the property of being red is morphologically heterogeneous. The physical entities that have the power to cause red experiences in us are highly varied. They have nothing intrinsic in common in virtue of which they might be grouped together. Their unity lies in the effect they have on us. Second, our perceptual representations of red do not resemble what they represent. Red is represented as a specific phenomenal quality. There is nothing out there that is intrinsically red. The world, without us, is colourless. So red experiences do not resemble what they represent. Some people deny that red is a secondary quality. I don't want to take a stand on that debate. The point is that perceptual representations can represent complex relational properties that have no intrinsic morphological unity, and they can represent without resembling their referents. If this is even a *possibility* in the case of red, we should not rule out the possibility that emotions represent abstract relational properties such as danger, threat, or loss.

I conclude that emotions do represent concerns. It will take a little more work, however, to show that they are *perceptions* of concerns. I will come to this point in the final section, but first a detour through consciousness.

IV. Emotions Are Perceptually Conscious

The fact that emotions feel like something is a tip-off to the fact that they are perceptual. After all, every other phenomenally conscious state seems to be perceptual in nature. We have visual experiences, auditory experiences, olfactory experiences, tactile experiences, and so on. Beyond the experiences associated with each sense modality, there seem to be no phenomenal qualities. As remarked above, even conscious thoughts seem to come to us in the form of mental images of what those thoughts denote or images of the words we would use to express them. Subtract away all conscious perceptual representations and we have nothing left in consciousness at all. This is a controversial position, but I see no compelling example of a conscious quality that cannot be pinned on a particular sensory system. If emotions are conscious, they must be sensory.

But what are conscious emotions like? How should we describe their qualitative character? I have just been arguing that emotions represent abstract relational properties, such as danger and loss. Should we say that fear feels dangerous? In a certain sense, this way of talking is completely appropriate. Fear is a way of detecting danger, and consequently dangerous things cause fear in us. If danger feels like anything at all, it feels like fear. We can say, "I feel a sense of impending danger" or "that looks hazardous," meaning that some situation has induced in us a feeling of fear. But the feeling of fear can also be described in another way. If you attend to the phenomenology of fear, you will notice that the characteristic qualities of the experience are somatic. Muscles tighten, the body arches back or cowers, hairs stand on end, eyes widen, blood vessels become constricted, the heart races, and breath shortens. As James argued, these bodily changes seem to exhaust the feeling of fear.

If this story about the qualities of emotional experience is right, then emotional consciousness is a species of perceptual consciousness. This is a satisfying discovery because it lends itself to a unified theory of conscious experience. Most of our conscious episodes are *obviously* perceptual. At any given moment, we are seeing things, hearing things, touching things, and perhaps smelling and tasting things. Arguably, the sum total of conscious qualities at any given moment can be entirely explained in perceptual terms. Even the conscious experience of thinking can be characterized perceptually. Most typically, conscious thoughts are verbalized. As you mull over a philosophical hypothesis, you describe it to yourself in silent speech. The experience of thinking is the experience of hearing sentences in your head. Of course, thoughts are also sometimes accompanied by other forms of imagery; we may visualize the things that sentences describe. All this, I submit, can be explained in sensory terms (Prinz, 2007). But, in addition to silent speech and visual images, our conscious thoughts and experiences are also often accompanied by conscious emotions. If emotional consciousness could not be explained in perceptual terms, we would be stuck with the odd conclusion that all consciousness is perceptual except emotional consciousness. This would be an inelegant outcome. All conscious states share something in common, namely the fact that they have phenomenal qualities. It would be nice to have a unified theory of phenomenal qualities. If all consciousness were perceptual, a unified theory might be possible, but, if emotional consciousness were not a form of perceptual consciousness, then we might have to develop two theories of consciousness – one for perception and the other for emotion. Fortunately, I think emotional consciousness is perceptual. Indeed, the very fact that emotions are conscious suggests that they belong to the class of perceptions, since consciousness seems to be restricted to perceptual states. The James-Lange approach to emotional consciousness is both intuitively plausible and theoretically advantageous. It allows us accommodate emotional consciousness within a unified account.

I think we can go one step further. It can be shown that at least one plausible theory of perceptual consciousness can be extended to apply to emotions. The theory I have in mind was first advanced by Ray Jackendoff (1987). Jackendoff begins with the observation that the senses are hierarchically organized. Low-level sensory systems respond to very discrete local features of an incoming stimulus, without integrating those features into a unified whole. In vision, low-level systems register edges, but not whole shapes. In hearing, the low-level captures discrete tones, but not melodies. Another stage of processing is required. Intermediate-level perceptual systems take these local features and integrate them: edges become contours, and tones become tunes. The intermediate-level delivers coherent representations, rather than a buzzing confusion, but it is not the final level of perceptual processing. The intermediate level retains information about stimulus properties that is highly specific. If you see a chair, the intermediate level encodes its specific orientation with respect to your vantage-point. If you hear a word or a song, the intermediate level encodes information about its pitch and other acoustic properties. In order to achieve categorical recognition of a stimulus, it is often necessary to abstract away from such specific information. We need to be able to recognize a chair from many angles, and we need to be able to know what song is being played or what word is being uttered, not just the unique qualities of the performance or speech sounds we are hearing. High-level perceptual systems abstract away from specific features and facilitate recognition. A chair representation at the high level may be vantage-point invariant, and a high-level representation of a word may be invariant across the variable qualities of different speakers' voices. Given this organization, Jackendoff asks, where is consciousness? The answer should be obvious. When we see an object, we experience it from a point of view; when we hear a sound, we experience its unique acoustic profile. Consciousness resides at the intermediate level.

Can this story apply to emotions? Jackendoff (1987) implies that it cannot. After arguing that the account applies readily to the familiar senses, he makes no effort to argue that emotions are perceptual, much less that they are organized hierarchically. Instead, he characterizes emotions as 'markers' that colour the quality of visual, auditory, and other sensory experiences. This is puzzling for a reason mentioned earlier. Emotions obviously feel like something, and it would be odd to think that they get their qualitative character in a different way than other mental states that feel like something. It would be more parsimonious if we could explain emotional consciousness in the same way that we explain perceptual consciousness.

Elsewhere I have argued that Jackendoff's theory of perceptual consciousness can be extended to apply to emotions (Prinz 2004, 2005). Emotions, I have argued, are states in interoceptive systems, and interoceptive systems, like other perceptual systems, are probably hierarchically organized. There has been surprisingly little research on the organization of interoceptive systems, but there are principled reasons for postulating the following hierarchy. Interoceptive systems must register changes in each of the various bodily systems, including circulatory, digestive, respiratory, muscular, and endocrinal changes. Each of these systems may have its own three-level hierarchy in the brain. In respiration, for example, the low-level may register each breath, the intermediate-level may register the specific quality of our breathing pattern, and the high-level may categorize these patterns (e.g., as strained or deep or relaxed). In addition to these processing hierarchies for each bodily system, the brain presumably has some way of recognizing when different bodily systems are working in concert; the brain can recognize patterns of activity across different bodily systems. This, too, may involve a hierarchy: first bodily changes in individual bodily systems are registered; then patterns across different systems are registered; and finally, the brain abstracts away from the specific details of a pattern to categorize it as a pattern of a specific type. These hierarchies are not separate. We can think of the pathway that looks for patterns as containing the pathways that monitor each bodily system. The pattern-detecting pathway monitors these bodily pathways and registers when different bodily states co-occur.

Now where do emotions fit in this picture? If emotions are interoceptive states that register patterns of bodily change, then emotions can be identified with the simultaneous and integrated occurrence of perceptions in pathways that register changes in specific bodily systems. Emotion categories (fear, sadness, anger, and so on) are probably applied when we abstract away from details about the specific way in which we are currently breathing or tensing our muscles. In each episode of fear, for example, our bodies will be configured somewhat differently, so to recognize fear as such, we may need to abstract away from those differences. Fear recognition occurs at a high level. But what about fear experience – the qualitative character of fear? Intuitively, fear experience is located at the intermediate level. When you experience fear, the quality is determined by specific features of your current bodily state. If you cower in a corner it will feel different than if you arch backwards. If you freeze, it will feel different from fleeing. If your breathing stops for a moment, that will feel different than if your merely suffer from shortness of breath. Each of these differences affects the character of a fear experience on any given occasion.

Thus, emotions seem to arise at the intermediate level of two hierarchies. They comprise intermediate-level representations in each of the pathways that monitor bodily systems, and they occur at an intermediate level of a pathway that registers patterns of bodily change. One can think of emotional experiences as integrated, co-occurring, intermediate-level representations in pathways that register bodily changes. The experience of fear is an experience of a heart racing in a specific way along with a specific rate of breathing and a specific level of muscle tension, and so on. Emotions are experienced as bound episodes of specific changes throughout the body.

This proposal locates emotional consciousness at an intermediate level of perceptual processing. If I am right, then emotional consciousness is a case of perceptual consciousness, and perceptual consciousness can be explained in the same way across sense modalities. This lends support to the thesis that emotions are perceptions.

V. Emotions Are Quasi-Modular

So far I have argued that emotions are states in our interceptive systems that represent abstract concerns and become conscious in just the way that paradigm instances of perceptual states do. Perhaps this is enough for concluding that emotions are perceptions. But opponents of that thesis might quibble. Emotions seem to interact with cognitive states in a way that makes them seem quite different from ordinary perceptions. We often have emotional responses as the result of a cognitive process. We think about a situation, and our cognitive assessments determine our emotional response. In paradigm cases of perception, there is no role for intermediating thoughts. We see the world and then judge, rather than the other way around. This apparent contrast between emotions and perceptions ties into the idea of stimulus dependence, which I introduced in my definition of quasi-modularity. To approach this objection, I will argue that emotions are quasi-modular. I will begin with the first four features of quasi-modularity and work up to the fifth condition, which is stimulus dependence. I will argue that the alleged contrast between perception and emotion is not sufficiently great to deny the thesis that emotion is a form of perception.

The first condition on quasi-modularity is functional specialization. Quasi-modules serve specific functions. It should be perfectly obvious that this is true in the case of emotions. Emotions are designed to provide information about our relation to the world. They represent concerns, and they do so in a way that captures our attention and influences our behaviour. By drawing attention to concerns, emotions disrupt our ongoing plans and force us to adopt coping strategies. Fear, for example, draws our attention to a danger, and thereby forces us to decide whether to engage in avoidance behaviour. There is, in other words, a characteristic functional role for the emotions. Emotions are triggered by inputs that bear on well-being and they send outputs to centres involved in planning and action-guidance.

The second attribute of quasi-modules is that they break down in characteristic ways. Compare emotion and vision. Damage to low-level visual areas can cause blindness because visual information cannot get into the system if these structures are compromised. Likewise, damage to the centres that allow bodily information to get into the central nervous system leads to a reduction in emotional experience (Chwalisz et al. 1988). In both cases, however, there can be a residual capacity for experience through mental imagery. When the primary visual cortex is destroyed, visual images can occur, and when the spinal cord is damaged, emotions can be experienced through bodily imagery.

Damage to intermediate-level visual areas leads to blindness as well because the intermediate level of vision is the locus on conscious experience. Similarly, emotional experience can be diminished or eliminated by damaging portions of the anterior cingulated cortex, in a condition called *akinetic mutism* (Damasio and Van Hoesen 1983). The anterior cingulate probably isn't a low-level interoceptive area; it receives inputs from other medial cortical areas like the insula. This suggests that the anterior cingulate is the locus (or a locus) of intermediate-level emotion processing.

Finally, damage to centres associated with high-level vision do not eliminate visual experience, but they prevent a person from interpreting their visual states – a syndrome called *associative agnosia*. Likewise, there is an emotional condition called *alexithymia* in which a person has emotions but fails to identify them correctly. Such individuals may misindentify their emotions, or mistake emotional responses for mere bodily aches and twinges (somatization). Poor emotion recognition has been associated with reduced or abnormal function in rostral areas of the anterior cingulate and structures in the medial frontal cortex (Lane et al. 1997; Berthoz et al. 2002). These structures may contain the correlates of high-level emotion processing. In sum, emotions can malfunction in characteristic ways, and these breakdowns mirror the kinds of disorders found in vision and other sense modalities.

The third characteristic of quasi-modules is automaticity. I don't think that perceptual systems are entirely automatic or always automatic. When we form visual images, or engage in visual search, we exercise a considerable amount of control over our visual systems. But, the visual system *can* function automatically, as when a visual state is triggered bottom-up without effort or intervention. Visual pop-out effects are a clear case of this. Likewise, emotions can be triggered automatically. If someone were to suddenly pull the chair from under you, you would experience fear, and that fear would require no effort or control. Likewise, seeing someone cry can induce sadness, and getting cut off by another car on the highway can trigger rage.

The fourth characteristic of quasi-modules is innateness. Quasi-modules can certainly contain many learned rules and representations. In vision, we store memories of previously perceived objects and scenes, and we develop visual skills through practice (e.g., chicken-sexing or interpreting ambiguous images). But vision capitalizes on a stock of innate rules and representations. There are species-typical, biologically prepared mechanisms for detecting colours and shapes. Visual contrast and constancy effects, motion perception, and depth perception all trade on innate rules and representations. Emotions are equally dependent on innate rules and representations. We have innate mechanisms for perceiving changes in the body, and, as mentioned earlier, specific bodily patterns are innately disposed to be triggered by specific stimuli. For example, looming objects and loud sudden noises trigger the bodily response that we experience as fear.

Turn now to the final characteristic of quasi-modularity: stimulus-dependence. At first, it might seem a trivial matter to show that emotions are stimulus-dependent. If the body is perturbed in a particular way, we will register that perturbation. The stimulus drives the response. But, granting this sense in which emotions are stimulus-driven, there is another sense in which emotions seem quite unlike paradigm cases of perception. Under ordinary circumstances, emotions are not induced by directly altering the body. Rather, there is a prior mental event – a perception or a judgment pertaining to one's current circumstances. For example, fear might be elicited by seeing a venomous spider or by judging that there is a prowler in the house. These mental events trigger a perturbation in the body, which then generates the emotion. Qua response to body change, emotions seem to be stimulus-driven, but qua prior perception or judgment, their induction seems suspiciously endogenous. Emotions seem to require one step too many to qualify as perceptual. When we see something, there is no other sensory state between the stimulus that we see and the resultant visual perception. In the case of emotions, there is an intermediary. A danger out there must be perceived by some sense other than interoception before it can trigger the bodily response that causes the emotion. In this respect, ordinary cases of emotion elicitation are indirect. Does this show that they are not stimulus-dependent?

I think not. Even if we grant that the link between an emotion and its eliciting condition is indirect, we must admit that, under many circumstances, the link is nevertheless driven bottom-up. We see the spider; it causes a visual experience, which then causes the emotion. The emotion is not chosen. It is triggered by the stimulus. In these cases, at least, emotional response has a passivity that is highly characteristic of perceptual responses. Emotions are often just as stimulus-dependent as paradigm cases of perception.

Emotions also exhibit what I called perceptual trumping in section I. Consider a situation in which an emotion has been triggered bottom-up by a prior perception or judgment. Once the emotion has been triggered, it conveys relational information. Fear represents danger, for example. We can, after an emotion has been elicited, form a belief that conflicts with the content of the emotion. After fear is elicited, we can form the belief that we are not in danger. When this happens, the emotion does not simply evaporate. Darwin tells an anecdote about being startled by a puff adder, which lunged at him from behind a glass cage. Darwin knew he was safe, but he experienced fear. While watching horror films, we experience the same phenomenon. Likewise, music can make us feel sad even when we know there has been no loss in our lives, and tickling can induce delight even though none of our goals have been satisfied. Emotions are recalcitrant. They cannot simply be overridden by contrary beliefs. In these cases, emotions are like optical illusions: they persist even when we know that they are misrepresenting the actual situation. This confirms my contention that emotions are stimulus-dependent, and their dependence seems to be very much like the kind of dependence we see in paradigm cases of perception. So, I think the fact that emotions are indirectly linked to their eliciting stimuli should not distract us from the fact that they behave in ways that are just like quasi-modular perceptual states. Trumping is a symptom of stimulus-dependence. In sum, then, emotions have all the marks of quasi-modularity.

VI. Conclusion

I began this discussion with four properties that characterize paradigm cases of perception. Perception takes place in modality-specific input systems; perceptions represent things; perceptions can be consciously experienced; and perceptions are quasi-modular. I suggested that anything exhibiting all four of these characteristics deserves to be called a case of perception. The bulk of this discussion has been dedicated to showing that emotions exhibit all four characteristics, and it is therefore appropriate to think of emotions as a form of perception. There is a sense in which emotions allow us to perceive matters of concern, and they do so by registering changes in the body. This conclusion has implications for theories of emotion, and it also has implications for other theoretical domains in which emotions have been implicated. For example, it is sometimes suggested that moral judgments are emotional in nature. If that is right, and if emotions are perceptions, then we can make literal sense of the phrase "moral perception." Just as we can perceive danger and loss, we may be able to perceive right and wrong. I leave that possible implication for another occasion.

References

Berthoz, S., E. Artiges, P.-F. Van de Moortele, J.-B. Poline, S. Rouquette, S. M. Consoli, and J.L. Martinot. 2002. Effect of impaired recognition and expression of emotions on frontocingulate cortices: An fMRI study of men with alexithymia. *American Journal of Psychiatry* 159: 961–67.

Cannon, W. B. 1927. The James-Lange theory of emotion: A critical examination and an alternative theory. *American Journal of Psychology* 39: 106–24.

Chwalisz, K., E. Diener, and D. Gallagher. 1988. Autonomic arousal feedback and emotional experience: Evidence from the spinal cord injured. *Journal of Personality and Social Psychology* 54: 820–28.

Critchley, H. D., S. Wiens, P. Rotshtein, A. Öhman, and R. J. Dolan. 2004. Neural systems supporting interoceptive awareness. *Nature Neuroscience* 7: 189–95.

Damasio, A. R. 1994. *Descartes' Error: Emotion, Reason and the Human Brain.* New York: Gossett/Putnam.

Damasio, A. R. 1999. *The Feeling of What Happens: Body and Emotion in the Making of Consciousness.* New York: Harcourt Brace.

Damasio, A. R., and G. W. Van Hoesen. 1983. Emotional disturbances associated with focal lesions of the limbic frontal lobe. In *Neuropsychology of Human Emotion*, ed. K. M. Heilman and P. Satz. (85–110) New York: Guilford Press.

Dretske, F. 1988. *Explaining Behavior.* Cambridge (Mass.): MIT Press.

Fodor, J. 1983. *The Modularity of Mind.* Cambridge (Mass.): MIT Press.

Jackendoff, R. 1987. *Consciousness and the Computational Mind.* Cambridge (Mass.): MIT Press.

James, W. 1884. What is an emotion? *Mind* 9: 188–205.

Kosslyn, S. M. 1994. *Image and Brain: The Resolution of the Imagery Debate.* Cambridge (Mass.): MIT Press.

Lane, R. D., G. L. Ahern, G. E. Schwartz, and A. W. Kaszniak. 1997. Is alexithymia the emotional equivalent of blindsight? *Biological Psychiatry* 42: 834–44.

Lange, C. G. 1885. *Om Sindsbevaegelser: Et Psyko-fysiologisk Studie.* Kjbenhavn: Jacob Lunds. Reprinted in *The Emotions*, ed. C. G. Lange and W. James, trans. I. A. Haupt. Baltimore: Williams and Wilkins, 1922.

LeDoux, J. E. 1996. *The Emotional Brain.* New York: Simon and Schuster.

Marañon, G. 1924. Contribution à l'étude de l'action émotive de l'adrenaline. *Revue française d'endocrinologie* 2: 301–25.

McGurk, H., and J. MacDonald. 1976. Hearing lips and seeing voices. *Nature* 264: 746–48.

Phan, K. L., T. D. Wager, S. F. Taylor, and I. Liberzon. 2004. Functional neuroimaging studies of human emotions. *CNS Spectrums* 9: 258–67.

Philippot, P., C. Chapelle, and S. Blairy. 2002. Respiratory feedback in the generation of emotion. *Cognition and Emotion* 16: 605–627.

Prinz, J. J. 2000. The duality of content. *Philosophical Studies* 100: 1–34.

Prinz, J. J. 2004. *Gut Reactions: A Perceptual Theory of Emotion.* New York: Oxford University Press.

Prinz, J. J. 2005. Are emotions feelings? *Journal of Consciousness Studies* 12(8–10): 9–25.

Prinz, J. J. 2006. Is the mind really modular? In *Contemporary Debates in Cognitive Science,* ed. R. Stainton. (22-36) Oxford: Blackwell.

Prinz, J. J. 2007. All consciousness is perceptual. In *Contemporary Debates in Philosophy of Mind,* ed. B. McLaughlin and J. Cohen. (335-357) Oxford: Blackwell.

Stepper, S., and F. Strack. 1993. Proprioceptive determinants of affective and nonaffective feelings. *Journal of Personality and Social Psychology* 64: 211–20.

Strack, F., L. L. Martin, and S. Stepper. 1988. Inhibiting and facilitating conditions of the human smile: A nonobtrusive test of the facial feedback hypothesis. *Journal of Personality and Social Psychology* 54: 768–77.

Wiens, S. 2005. Interoception in emotional experience. *Current Opinion in Neurology* 18: 442–47.

Wolpert, D. M., and J. R. Flanagan. 2001. Motor prediction. *Current Biology* 11: R729–R732.

CANADIAN JOURNAL OF PHILOSOPHY
Supplementary Volume 32

Two Views of Emotional Perception: Some Empirical Suggestions[1]

ANDREW SNEDDON

I. Perception and Modularity

One stream in contemporary philosophical and psychological study of the emotions argues that they are perceptual capacities (e.g., Prinz 2004).[2] For instance, Jesse Prinz has recently defended the view that emotions are perceptions of bodily changes and, via these, of "core relational themes" (2004, 224–25). Core relational themes are, roughly, relations an individual has to his/her environment that pertain to that individual's welfare (2004, 15–16). The present project is to compare and contrast two possible models of emotional perception. The central difference between these models is the notion of modularity that they use, and the corresponding overall view of the nature of the mind. I will suggest some empirical tests that might adjudicate between these different kinds of emotional modularity, and hence between these two models of emotional perception. I will conclude with some remarks about the extent of the relevance of this issue.

So, suppose that emotions are perceptual capacities. How would one go about conceiving of and studying such capacities? A natural way to proceed is to use other perceptual capacities as a model: identify important characteristics of uncontroversial perceptual capacities, then see whether emotions have identical or similar features. This is

---

1 This paper was written with the assistance of the Social Sciences and Humanities Research Council of Canada (SSHRC).

2 Ronald de Sousa (1987) considers this sort of view, but Jesse Prinz argues that his variety does not count as a true perceptual theory (Prinz 2004, 223).

Prinz's method (2004, 221–22, and throughout the same chapter). One of the characteristic features of ordinary perceptual capacities, and the only one which will concern us here, is their modularity. Prinz argues that emotions share the characteristics of classical, Fodorian modularity (more or less; both he and Fodor 1983 acknowledge that modularity can be a matter of degree; Prinz 2004, 232–36). This means that they share a very important feature with uncontroversially perceptual capacities, such as vision. Thus an important part of the overall case for emotions as perceptual capacities is in place.

This view of perceptual modularity is connected to a particular overall view of the structure of the mind. Prinz gives us an explicit statement of this view:

> The mind is divided into different kinds of information-processing systems. There are perceptual systems that provide inputs, action and motor systems that provide output, and, perhaps, higher cognitive systems that engage in reasoning, planning, problem solving, and other mental operations that mediate between inputs and outputs when we move above the level of reflex response. (2004, 221)

If emotions are perceptual capacities, then they fall into the input part of this view of the mind. They provide information to, in all likelihood, both the action-production systems and higher cognition.

Susan Hurley has called this view of the mind into question. She calls it the "classical sandwich" view of the mind (1998, 20–21): higher cognition is the filling between the input and output layers that have more direct contact with the environment.[3] Hurley describes this view of the mind as being structured with *vertical* modules. The metaphor of verticality is used to capture the constitutional independence of modules in this view of the mind. On this view, higher cognitive processes and action-production systems are both *constitutively distinct* from all perceptual capacities. Classical, Fodorian modules have their natural home in this vertically modular, classical sandwich view of the mind. If emotion is a classically modular perceptual capacity, then it too is constitutively distinct from the modules that realize higher cognition and output.

---

3 For diagrammatic representation, see Hurley (1998), 407.

Hurley argues that this view of the mind, and specifically its vertical modularity, has been called into question by neuroscience. Instead of a mind composed of constitutively distinct vertical modules, Hurley argues that neuroscience reveals a mind structured by *horizontal* modules. Horizontal modules are content-specific and task-specific systems that " [loop] dynamically through internal sensory and motor processes as well as through the environment." (Hurley 1998, 21; see 408 for discussion) These systems are "modular" in virtue of their content- and task-specific functionality. However, they are importantly different from vertical modules. First, each module is constituted by *both* input and output functions. Functioning *within* each module can include feedback from relatively more downstream to relatively more upstream stages of processing. Second, there is no modular layer that, by itself, constitutes higher cognitive functioning. Instead, this is something that emerges from the interplay of the specific perception-action layers.

If Hurley is correct that recent findings from neuroscience point towards a horizontally modular mind rather than a classically vertically modular one, then the task of modelling emotional perception on other perceptual capacities is complicated. In one sense, the task of describing the features of perceptual capacities has to be done more in a case-by-case manner than it had seemed before: maybe some modalities are classically modular, while others are horizontally modular. However, in another sense, just a little horizontal modularity seems to pose a large problem for vertically modular views of perception. Horizontal modularity of any kind seems to call into question the overall view of the mind in which vertical modularity has its natural home. Hurley claims that it challenges the status of the classical sandwich as a general conceptual framework for thinking about the mind. With regard to emotion research, Hurley's suggestion complicates the matter of assessing such views of emotional perception as the one offered by Prinz. How then should we proceed?

Although vertically and horizontally modular accounts of perception and the mind share such features as domain-specificity, they differ in ways that allow for empirical testing. Such testing might provide direct evidence for one of these views of the modularity of emotional perception. In section III, I offer two suggestions for such testing. Before doing this, more attention has to be given to vertically and horizontally modular models of emotional perception. The resulting refinements will give us a better view both of what might be empirically tested and of how such testing could be conducted.

II. Refinements

The topic is the views of modularity associated with two different accounts of perception, in general, and of emotional perception, in particular. That is, the topic is the *structure* of emotions, and in particular of the kinds of processing that realize emotions. I take it that a particularly important way to study this topic is to study the neural processes that implement such processing. Hence the refinements I shall attend to have to do with neurobiology and vertical and horizontal modularity.

II.i. Vertical Modularity

In a consideration of possible objections to the view that emotions have a classically modular structure, Prinz distinguishes two different sorts of pathway that constitute emotional processing (2004, 234–36):

1) First, there are *initiation* pathways. These may be thought of as the input routes to the emotional module. Their general job is to receive input from a variety of sources, and then to prepare this input in a manner appropriate to the remainder of the emotional processing. As an example, Prinz discusses the role of the amygdala in the processing of fear, disgust, and sadness: "The amygdala receives inputs from a variety of different brain regions and initiates a pattern of bodily outputs, which then give rise to these emotions" (2004, 234).

An important feature of the initiation pathway is what Prinz calls *calibration files*. Calibration files are sets of representations linked to particular bodily responses. Prinz holds that such files allow us to modify emotions via judgments. The establishment of new calibration files allows us to modify emotions (more specifically, embodied appraisals) to apply to things other than those to which they evolved to apply to (2004, 99–100).

2) Second, there are *emotion response* pathways. Crucially, Prinz holds that this is where the actual emotions take place. Strictly speak-

ing, on this view the initiation pathways are distinct from the modules of emotional perception. This means that the features of classical modularity apply to the response pathways alone. Take domain-specificity as an example: Prinz claims that the amygdala is not domain-specific, but the response-pathways that receive information from the amygdala about objects of fear, disgust, or sadness are (2004, 234).

Accordingly, emotional processing has the following structure (Prinz 2004, 235):

Initiation Pathway   Response Pathway

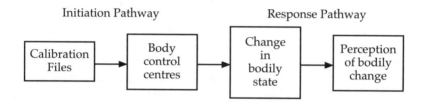

Although it is important to distinguish initiation and response pathways, we have reason to question the details of this picture of emotional processing. In particular, recent research calls into question the confinement of the amygdala to input preparation. Richard Davidson and William Irwin (1999, 15) claim that the amygdala is important for both the perception and production of negative emotion. In a recent summary, Elizabeth Phelps claims that research shows that the amygdala has a critical role in both the acquisition and expression of fear-learning (2004, 1005 and throughout). Glenn Schafe and Joseph LeDoux give the amydala a central role in both input and output pathways in fear-conditioning (2004, 987–89). In particular, they claim that the relations between the various parts of the amygdala are essential for fear-expression (2004, 989). Even more important are the studies on emotion reappraisal that I will discuss in section III. Overall, the working assumption in studies of the neurophysiology of fear seems not to be that the amygdala is solely part of an input pathway to a fear module, but that it could be more intrinsically woven into the processes that realize fear itself. Even if all of this does not constitute conclusive support for inclusion of the amygdala in the response pathway of fear, I take it to show that the evidence from neuroscience does not currently support a rigid bound-ary between the functioning of the amygdala and, in this case, the neural processes that realize fear.[4]

II.ii. Horizontal Modularity

Hurley defends a position she describes in terms of two-level inter-dependence. The levels in question are the personal one, at which we ascribe perceptions and actions, and the subpersonal one that we characterize in terms of input and output processes. One of Hurley's principal concerns is that the classical sandwich picture of the mind simplistically maps personal and subpersonal levels onto each other. Hence distinctions found at the personal level that are described in terms of perceptual content and the content of intentions respectively are taken to be functions of distinctions in input and output respectively. Hurley argues in a variety of ways that both distinctions and invariants in personal-level content can be a function of *relations between* input and output. In such cases, there is no one-to-one mapping of personal-level distinctions to subpersonal-level distinctions. Hence the alternative view of the mind has, so far, here been described in terms of horizontal modules constituted by feedback relations that cut across the subpersonal boundaries between input and output. And higher cognitive processes have been alluded to as emerging from the interplay of horizontal modules, rather than depending on central subpersonal processes distinct from both input and output systems.

However, another theme from Hurley modifies this stark contrast with the classical sandwich view of the mind. This is her commitment to empirical study of the processes that realize mentality. Accordingly, she thinks that it is an empirical issue whether a given kind of mental processing is realized by classical, vertical modules or by horizontal ones with both input and output functioning. Due

---

4 The amygdala is a complex structure, giving us the possibility that some parts are for emotional input only, while others are not. Whether this is the case, or whether all amygdala sub-structures resist rigid assignment to a particular job, has to be determined on *a posteriori* grounds. However, the complexity of the amydala implies that defenders of vertical modularity can pursue more fine-grained accounts of emotional input processing if evidence suggests that the amygdala has some constitutive role in the realization of emotions proper.

to this commitment, she seems to be committed to the existence of more and less centralized processes. For instance, much of her case depends on arguing that certain studies in neuroscience show, e.g., the dependence of perceptual content on output systems. She considers an objection to her case that claims that perceptual content depends on input and central processing, but not output (Hurley 1998, 383–84). If Hurley were really committed to there only being input and output systems, then she could dismiss this objection as relying on a class of neural processes that do not exist. But this is not her reply; instead, she acknowledges the possibility of centralized processing but denies that the line of thought in the objection can deliver a principled distinction across sensory and action modalities between central and peripheral processing. She also thinks that such an objection already admits her point, which is that personal-level content can depend on relations between different sorts of sub-personal processing rather than simply mapping onto a single kind of subpersonal processing.

All of this calls for a refinement of our view of horizontal modularity. Instead of there being just one kind, now there are two broad kinds to consider:

1. *Full Horizontal Modularity*: This is horizontal modularity as originally described: domain-specific modules constituted by both input and output processing, and hence cutting across the full width of the mind.

2. *Abbreviated Horizontal Modularity*: This is horizontal modularity that does not cut across the full width of the mind from input to output, but that does cut across some of the vertical boundaries that are characteristic of the classical sandwich view of the mind. Given the tripartite division of the classical sandwich view, there are two possible kinds of abbreviated horizontal modules:
    - Input-Central processing modules—relations between input processing and more centralized processing subserve some specific sort of personal level perceptual content.[5]

---

5 Incidentally, finding this would show that the kind of information processing in question is not informationally encapsulated. Informational encapsulation is a particularly important feature of classic, vertical modules (Karmiloff-Smith 1992, 2).

- Central processing-Output modules—relations between more central processing and output processing subserve some specific sort of personal level intentional content.

Both versions of horizontal modularity are relevant to my empirical suggestions, to which we now turn.

III. Empirical Suggestions

Given the differences in structure between vertical and horizontal modules, we should be able to design tests to determine which view, if either, fits perception, in general, and specific sorts of emotional perception, in particular. I have two suggestions for such testing.

III.i. Empathic Emotional Recognition

An important part of Hurley's case concerns neurons and neuron populations that play roles in both perception and action. So-called "mirror neurons" have been discovered both in monkeys and in humans (Prinz discusses this briefly: 2004, 229; see Rizzolatti et al. 1996; Keysers et al. 2003; Gallese et al. 2004). These neurons are activated both when observing another monkey perform an action of a particular kind and when performing the same kind of action oneself.

Can similar cases be found for emotion? The sort of phenomenon to look for is *perception* of emotion and related behaviour in others that is processed with at least some of the same neural circuitry as the *production* of the same emotion or emotional behaviour. A promising starting point is Robert Gordon's model for the general psychological capacity of empathy. Broadly taken, empathy involves sharing the feelings of others. When I feel what you feel, I am empathizing with you. This is also referred to as "emotional contagion" – feelings are catching, in that exposure of one person to another person displaying certain feelings often produces the same feelings in the observing person. However, it is reasonable to differentiate between different sorts of empathy (see de Vignemont and Singer 2006, and especially Singer 2006, for recent psychological work that attends to different sorts of empathy). For present purposes, full empathy or emotional contagion is not the issue. Instead, the relevant phenomenon to search for is what I shall call "empathic emotional recognition": perception of emotions in others without experiencing those emotions oneself, but which involves the same neural basis as the experience of those emotions. The role of the same neuron populations in both the production and recognition of emotions is what makes this broadly "empathic." Gordon's work is a promising starting point because he models empathy in terms of simulation. In general, simulation consists in "off-line" use of one's own cognitive apparatus to take the perspective of another person. Off-line processing means that the cognitive processes in question are detached from the normal routes leading to practical decision-making and action for oneself. One is using them not for oneself, but to understand the perspective of another, so they do not need to be plugged into these practical processes. Simulation of the feelings of another would require the use of the neural circuitry that realizes the feelings in question for oneself, but detached from normal processes delivering emotional experience and related conduct (Gordon 1995).

Here are two more detailed versions of the kind of empirical test suggested by this line of thought:

i. Specify, even roughly, the neural processing of a certain emotion. With this information in hand, see whether the same neural circuitry is implicated in recognition of this emotion in other people.

ii. Specify, even roughly, the neural processing of a certain emotion *plus* some sort of typical response. With this information in hand, see whether the same neural circuitry is implicated in recognition of this emotion *plus* response in other people.

The first test requires that we are able to recognize emotions in other people detached at least from typical responses, and maybe from all expressions. This may be impossible; I leave this to be determined *a posteriori*. The second test does not require this. If the results for (i) vindicated the simulation model of empathic emotional recognition, then we would have empirical support for abbreviated horizontal modularity for the emotion in question. This kind of test supports abbreviated horizontal modularity because action is not implicated in what is recognized. All that would have been discovered was that the same neural circuitry was involved in experiencing and perceiving a particular emotion. By contrast, (ii) would provide evidence of full horizontal modularity. The reason is that this test would show that the same neural circuitry is implicated in both the perception of the combination of a particular emotion and an associated response and in the production of the combination of the first-person experience of the same emotion and the first-person performance of the same response.

Fear provides a promising test case. The reason is that there are already well-developed methodologies for studying both the experience of fear and the expression of fear responses. For example, recognition of objects or states of affairs that are threatening, and that hence call for a fear response, are accompanied by a distinctive eye movement known as the startle eyeblink. Recent studies of fear have combined subjective reports of emotion, measurements of the startle eyeblink, and fMRI scanning (e.g., Ochsner et al. 2002, Schaefer et al. 2002). Accordingly, here is a first pass at modifying this methodology to study the form of modularity of fear: Subjects could be divided into two groups: a "fear group" subjected to fear stimuli and an "observing group," which would observe the first group. Specifically, the observing group would watch the faces of the fear group. Startle eyeblink could be used as an objective measure of fear response in the fear group.[6] It, and other facial expressions, would be the behavioural evidence of fear for the observing group. fMRI scanning would be performed on both groups. If the scans revealed significant overlap of neural processing in both the fear group and the observing group, we would have evidence of, arguably, full horizontal modularity of fear-processing.

In fact, studies of the neural processing of fear and of recognition of facial expressions of fear in others suggest this sort of overlap of neural processing. As mentioned before, the amygdala has been shown to be an important part of the neural foundations of fear-learning and

---

6 The working assumption here is that veridical expressions of fear are desirable for this test, and that the startle eyeblink is an objective measure of such veridicality. If such veridical expressions are not a necessary feature of this means of testing emotional modularity, then measurements of startle eyeblink magnitude are not necessary.

experience. PET and fMRI studies have also shown greater amygdala activity when people observe fear facial expressions than when they see facial expressions of other emotions. Davidson and Irwin (1999, 15), in a review of such studies, note that this goes even for faces that are not consciously noticed. This suggests that the perceiving subject is not actually experiencing fear as a result of perceiving the faces. This seems to amount to off-line activity of an important part of the neural basis of the experience of fear.[7] In other words, empathic emotional recognition seems to have been found for facial expressions of fear.

To find the general pattern of empathic emotional recognition for a particular emotion such as fear, it would be desirable to study an array of behaviours, not just facial expressions and certainly not just the startle eyeblink. It is not difficult to devise a wide array of stimuli for the observing group – actors and photographs/films are readily available. However, it is difficult to devise procedures to generate real fear and the particular desired fear behaviours, as opposed to the simulated ones that actors would produce. Consequently, this methodology might be confined to a fairly limited range of fear behaviour, and hence the information it provides might be quite limited. Other emotions might be more easily operationalizable.[8]

III.ii. Noninstrumental Content Dependence

Here is a more fully developed empirical suggestion for assessing whether vertical or horizontal modularity characterizes emotions. The crucial issue is how the content of experience is related to the subpersonal processes that realize it. In the classical sandwich view of the mind, personal-level content is mapped onto subpersonal-level processes in a one-to-one fashion. This limits the ways that subpersonal output processes can influence personal-level perceptual content. On the vertical view of perceptual modules, the only way output or central processing can affect perceptual content is *instrumentally*,

---

7 Studies cited in Davidson and Irwin (1999) include: Morris et al. (1996); Morris et al. (1998); Breiter et al. (1996); Phillips et al. (1997); and Whalen et al. (1998).

8 There is reason to think that empathic emotional recognition has been found also in the case of disgust: see Wicker et al. (2003). Space limitations prevent discussion here.

i.e., by bringing about changes in input to perceptual mechanisms. The reason for this is that perception and action mechanisms, as well as central cognitive processing, are conceived of as constitutively distinct on this view. Such instrumental dependence is also possible on the horizontal view, but there is another possible kind of content dependence in this case. Since action and perception are constitutively interwoven on this view, it is possible for there to be *noninstrumental* dependence of perceptual content on output processing. This is revealed by changes in perceptual content even when input to perceptual mechanisms is held constant. Since such variation cannot be explained in terms of variation in input, feedback *within* the module from variation in other kinds of subpersonal processing to perception must be invoked instead. If noninstrumental content-dependence can be found for emotional experience, then we would have evidence for horizontal modularity and against vertical modularity.

Hurley argues that evidence from studies from neurophysiology, marshalled in thought experiments based on such studies, shows that noninstrumental content-dependence can be found for visual perception.[9] The present task is to devise studies that would do a similar sort of testing for emotional perception. The crucial thing to do is to determine whether changes in emotional perceptual content can be brought about even when the input to emotional processing is held constant. If this is possible, then we have evidence that at least certain emotions are horizontally modular. If it turns out that this is not possible for certain emotions, then we have failed to find an important kind of empirical support for the horizontal modularity of these emotions.

For present purposes, abbreviated horizontal modularity will be the focus. The reason is that, over the past decade, much work has been done on the regulation of emotions. Broadly put, emotion regulation consists in the use of attention or some cognitive strategy to alter one's emotions (Phelps 2004, 1007). If extant work on emotional regulation shows that emotional perceptual content can depend on relatively more central processing without changes in input, then we have empirical evidence inconsistent with vertical modularity but

---

9 See her discussion of Ivo Kohler's well-known study involving blue-yellow tinted glasses, and her adaptation of this work into a thought experiment (Hurley 1998, 287–92).

consistent with both abbreviated horizontal modularity of emotion and the absence of modularity.

In one study (Schaefer et al. 2002), subjects were asked to view photos of two kinds: negative and neutral. Following exposure to the photos, there was a short delay period, after which subjects were asked how they felt. During both the viewing and delay periods, subjects were asked either to respond passively to the pictures – to let the emotional process that they triggered happen without any conscious intervention – or to maintain the emotion that the photo triggered. Functional magnetic resonance imaging (fMRI) was used to see what was going on in subjects' brains while viewing the pictures, either responding passively or maintaining their emotion, and reporting their feelings. The results: subjects asked to maintain their emotions reported stronger negative feelings in response to the negative pictures. The fMRI imaging revealed prolonged amygdala activity in maintain trials compared to the passive response trials (2002, 913). Overall, this study provides evidence both that subjects can consciously regulate their emotions and that this is done, for negative emotions and at least in part, by affecting the activity of the amygdala.

In a similar study (Ochsner et al. 2002), subjects were shown negative pictures for a period of four seconds, followed by another four-second period. During the second period, an instruction appeared in the viewing field. Subjects were given one of two instructions:

1. *Attend*, which required subjects to pay attention to the emotions triggered by the pictures without trying to change them, or
2. *Reappraise*, which required subjects to try to diminish negative emotions triggered by the pictures (Ochsner et al. 2002, 1217).

Eyeblink startle tests had already confirmed that subjects could diminish their negative emotions through cognitive reappraisal: subjects reappraising their emotions had a smaller startle eyeblink magnitude than subjects not doing this (Ochsner et al. 2002, 1216). In this subsequent part of the study, fMRI was used to discern the neural mechanisms of such reappraisal. In reappraise trials, as compared to the attend trials, there was increased activity in the dorsal and ventral regions of the left lateral prefrontal cortex (LPFC) and the dorsal medial prefrontal cortex (MPFC); the LPFC appears to be more important. There was greater amygdala activity in the attend trials than in the reappraise trials (Ochsner et al. 2002, 1220); there was also greater activity in medial orbito frontal cortex (MOFC). Interestingly, there was a significant correlation between increased LPFC activity and decreased amygdala activity, and vice versa. This suggests that the neural mechanisms for regulation of negative emotions have, as important components, connections leading from the LPFC and MPFC to the amygdala and/or MOFC. Apparently, emotion is regulated via LPFC and MPFC suppression of activity in the amygdala and/or MOFC. Even further, connections between the LPFC and the amygdala appear to be particularly important.

What does all of this mean for the project of assessing whether vertical or horizontal modularity is an apt model of the structure of emotional perception? Well, these studies suggest that the content of emotional experience can be affected by relatively more central processes. More specifically, Schaefer et al. note that the initial activity of the amygdala is not affected by reception of the regulation instruction prior to exposure to the picture (2002, 915). It is later activity that the instruction affects. This is consistent with the role of feedback mechanisms in horizontal modules as Hurley describes them. What might be happening is that information initially processed by the amygdala is used by parts of the brain, such as the LPFC and MPFC, which realize regulation of emotion, such that subsequent amygdala activity is affected after feedback. This is speculative, but something like this is necessary for abbreviated horizontal modularity. More work needs to be done here.

Even so, showing these things to be the case would not suffice to provide empirical support for abbreviated horizontal modularity. For this, at least a couple of things remain to be shown:

First, that the amygdala is part of the response pathway of the relevant emotions, not just part of the initiation pathway, as Prinz holds.[10] If it turns out that the amygdala is relegated to the initiation pathways for these emotions, then we will not have evidence for abbreviated horizontal modularity. The reason is that it would seem

---

10 I focus on the amygdala because it is examined by both studies, whereas only Ochsner et al. discuss the MOFC. The same thing would have to be shown for the MOFC also.

that regulation of negative emotions was working only by affecting the input to the relevant processing. This would constitute *instrumental* dependence of emotional content on relatively more central processing. But *noninstrumental* content dependence is required for abbreviated horizontal modularity, and this requires the possibility of central processing affecting emotions without changing the input to these emotions.

Relatedly, that, even if the amygdala is part of the response pathway for the emotions in question, the regulation of the relevant emotions is accomplished while input to the amygdala (or MOFC) is constant. These studies did give this issue some attention: Ochsner at al. instructed subjects reappraising not to look away, nor to distract themselves with extraneous thoughts (2002, 1225). Likewise, Schaefer et al. instructed subjects not to look away (2002, 918). However, this hardly seems adequate. If, as seems plausible, emotional processing can take thoughts as input, then instructions not to look away nor to think about extraneous things cannot guarantee constant input. More stringent measures are needed to ensure that input to emotional processing really is constant while cognitive regulation of emotions is attempted. Here are two broad possibilities (which may well outstrip current technological capacities):

1. Very close monitoring of input, to see whether there are significant differences between, e.g., attend and reappraise trials.
2. Electrical or chemical regulation of input so that the experimental protocol controls its variation and constancy.

Even if input to, for example, the amygdala can be held constant, more subtle issues remain. Consider Prinz's division between initiation and response pathways. Calibration files constitute part of the initiation pathway. These files allow flexibility in patterns of emotional response, which is determined by judgments – i.e., by cognitive control mechanisms. In the face of constant input to the initiation pathway, changes to the calibration files would facilitate changes to the information sent to the response pathway. Although input is, in such a case, constant in one sense, it is not constant in another. Accordingly, we can distinguish between two kinds of noninstrumental content-dependence:

1. *Weak* noninstrumental content-dependence: effects on content are brought about by changes to the calibration files without changes to the input to the initiation pathway.
2. *Strong* noninstrumental content-dependence: effects on content are brought about by changes to the response pathway without either direct changes to input or indirect changes via modification of the calibration files.

Obviously, instrumental content-dependence alone means that horizontal modularity lacks empirical support. Finding strong noninstrumental content-dependence would provide evidence consistent with abbreviated horizontal modularity. What about weak noninstrumental content-dependence? The significance of this depends upon one's view of recalibration and input. If, on a vertically modular view, recalibration must happen through the same input channels as normal processing, then weak noninstrumental content-dependence is consistent only with horizontal modularity. But if a vertically modular view recognizes recalibration via non-input pathways, then weak noninstrumental content-dependence is consistent with both vertical and horizontal modularity. Given a tendency to assume the general view of the mind in which vertical modules have their natural home, discovering a state of affairs that calls for abstaining from judging between vertical and horizontal modularity would still be interesting, even if inconclusive.

Can the present studies shed much light on the likelihood of finding either weak or strong noninstrumental content-dependence? More research seems to be needed on just what the input pathways to the amygdala are. Once we are clearer about the input pathways, this information can be compared with the routes by which emotional regulation occurs. Ochsner et al. speculate about three routes by which the LPFC might modulate the activity of the amygdala (2002, 1223–24):

1. Directly. This is unlikely due to the fact that there seem to be few direct connections between these regions.
2. Via the MOFC. This is also unlikely since the correlation between LPFC activity and MOFC activity was not as significant as that between LPFC activity and activity in the amygdala.
3. Via the occipital and parietal regions.

Overall, Ochsner et al. think more research is needed on this issue. If it turns out that the routes by which the LPFC affects the amygdala are much the same as the general input pathways to the amygdala, then we would have empirical support for either vertical modularity or, perhaps, weak horizontal modularity. But if the routes by which the LPFC affects activity in the amygdala differ from the normal input routes, then we would have evidence consistent with weak or even strong horizontal modularity of the relevant emotion.

IV. What's at Stake?

Let's take a step back and assess what's at stake here. It is natural to think that the kind of modularity characteristic of emotion and other perceptual modalities is a relatively local issue, of importance only to people researching the mechanics of the mind. I think this under-estimates the range of this topic. The starting point of this discussion was a description of two general pictures of the mind. Each of the two types of modularity has its home in one, but not the other, of these pictures of the mind. Hence empirical studies that shed light on the structure of emotional modules should provide evidence for one but not for the other of these overall pictures.

Vertical modularity belongs to a picture of the mind and brain as essentially an information processor. Information comes in at certain points, gets manipulated, then gets passed on, gets manipulated some more, etc. Types of information processing are discretely isolated from each other. The kind of information processing most familiar to us – the processing characteristic of higher cognitive processes – is not just discretely separated from the mechanics of other kinds of processing, but from the world beyond the physical boundaries of the person as well. By contrast, horizontal modularity belongs to a picture of the brain and mind as instruments for participation in this wide world. Not only are the boundaries between perception, action, and higher cognition much more porous on this view, so are the boundaries between person and world. Hurley thinks that the processes by which, e.g., output functions affect input functions need not be contained within the physical boundaries of the organism (1998, 332). "Horizontal modules are essentially 'situated'. Each dynamic layer is a system that is distributed across a perceiving and acting organism and relevant parts of its environment (perhaps including other organisms ...)" (1998, 408). In short, vertical modularity lends itself to internalism about mental content and mental processes, and horizontal modularity lends itself to externalism about both of these things.[11]

Once we broaden our attention to include the concerns of various debates over internalism and externalism, new possibilities for empirical research related to the mechanisms of emotion present themselves. I will explore just one here. Think about the phenomena briefly examined in this paper: negative emotions, reactions to facial expressions, empathy, connections between emotion, action, and higher cognition. Explaining the nature and mechanics of these phenomena seems likely to illuminate the nature and mechanisms of significant aspects of social interaction, including moral understanding. If emotional modules turn out to be vertically modular, then we have an empirical basis for thinking of social and moral cognition in terms of calculative information-processing divorced from an agent's physical and social context. That is, we would have empirically principled grounds for dividing agents from their world. If emotional modules turn out instead to be horizontally modular, then we would have an empirical basis for rejecting such division of agent from context. Instead, we would have a platform on which to model social and moral cognition in terms of cognitive systems stretching beyond the physical bounds of the agent.[12]

Consider a feature of moral cognition that has been getting a lot of recent attention. Gilbert Harman (1999) and John Doris (1998, 2002) have emphasized the importance of findings in social psychology to moral philosophy. In particular, they think that what is known as *situationism* has relevance to our understanding of moral cognition in general and to thought about the psychology of the virtues in particular. Social psychology seems to show that seemingly insignificant features of situations can have quite significant effects on behaviour. Both

---

11 For discussion of different sorts of externalism, with emphasis on designing psychological hypotheses, see Sneddon (forthcoming).

12 I take the idea of thinking of externalism in terms of systems in which an agent participates from Rob Wilson (2001, 2004).

psychologists and philosophers differ on how to explain such cases. Since some seem to involve emotional mechanisms, getting clear on the kind of modularity characteristic of emotions promises to shed light on the mechanisms of such situationist phenomena.

Here is a striking example, discussed at some length by Doris: experimenters arranged to have a passer-by drop a load of papers in front of people leaving a particular phone booth. Sometimes there was a coin in the phone change slot, sometimes it was empty. The point was to assess whether finding a coin had any effect on the tendency of the users of the phone booth to help the passer-by with the dropped papers. The results:

	Helped	No Help
Coin	14	2
No Coin	1	24

(Doris 1998, 504)

The researchers speculate that the difference in behaviour could have been caused by effects on affective states: finding the coin put people in a relatively better mood, and this translated, in the short term, into a willingness to help strangers (Doris 2002, 30).[13] Besides such prosocial behaviour, Doris lists a range of phenomena to which mood has been empirically shown to be relevant (2002, 30). This strongly suggests that examining the mechanisms of such affective states could illuminate an important variety of behaviours.

Suppose that the mechanisms of such affective states are just emotional mechanisms. If emotions are vertically modular, then cases such as the coin in the payphone phenomenon require the following sort of mechanisms:

---

13 Christian Miller (2003) places the Isen and Levin dime study in a wider context of attempts to replicate the results. Overall, replication was achieved in some studies – clearly in Levin and Isen (1975), less clearly in Batson et al. (1979) – and not in others – Blevins and Murphy (1974), Weyant and Clark (1977). Even so, Doris reports that overall, more than one thousand studies have produced "situationist" results about helping behaviour alone (2002, 34).

1. Input mechanisms by which emotions are produced;
2. Relatively more central mechanisms by which the emotions and associated information are passed on to become not just relevant but decisive with regard to the production of action. This might involve effects on the processing responsible for general understanding of the agent and the world.

These have to occur without conscious awareness (or at least the possibility of the lack of conscious awareness) of the links between finding the dime and subsequent behaviour.

On the other hand, if emotions are horizontally modular, then this sort of case calls out for different mechanisms. It is more difficult to speculate about just what these might be, but here are some possibilities:

3. Emotional input-output mechanisms that fairly directly connect environmental information to action.
4. Emotional input-output mechanisms by which, in general, agents participate in the systems that subserve social and moral cognition.
5. Mechanisms by which the processing of a particular horizontal module becomes decisive in the production of behaviour, given that other horizontal modules are also active.
6. Mechanisms by which the deliverances of some horizontal modules are available for conscious attention while others are not.

I'm sure more could easily be added to these preliminary lists. The present point is that seemingly local work on the structure of emotions could well have implications for how we think of moral cognition, in general, and for the study of specific aspects of moral cognition, in particular.

References

Batson, C. D., J. S. Coke, F. Chard, D. Smith, and A. Talisaferro. 1979. Generality of the 'glow of goodwill': Effects of mood on helping and information acquisition. *Social Psychology Quarterly* 42(2): 176–79.

Blevins, G., and T. Murphy. 1974. Feeling good and helping: Further phone booth findings. *Psychological Reports* 34: 326.

Breiter, H. C., N. L. Etcoff, P. J. Whalen, W. A. Kennedy, S. L. Rauch, R. L. Buckner, M. M. Strauss, S. E. Hyman, and B. R. Rosen. 1996. Response and habituation of the human amygdala during visual processing of facial expression. *Neuron* 17: 875–87.

Davidson, R. J., and W. Irwin. 1999. The functional neuroanatomy of emotion and affective style. *Trends in Cognitive Sciences* 3(1): 11–21.

de Sousa, R. 1987. *The Rationality of Emotion.* Cambridge (Mass.): MIT Press.

de Vignemont, F., and T. Singer. 2006. The empathic brain: How, when and why? *Trends in Cognitive Sciences* 10(10): 435–41.

Doris, J. 1998. Persons, situations, and virtue ethics. *Nous* 32(4): 504–30.

Doris, J. 2002. *Lack of Character.* Cambridge: Cambridge University Press.

Fodor, J. 1983. *The Modularity of Mind.* Cambridge (Mass.): MIT Press.

Gallese, V., C. Keysers, and G. Rizzolatti. 2004. A unifying view of the basis of social cognition. *Trends in Cognitive Sciences* 8(9): 396–403.

Gordon, R. 1995. Sympathy, simulation, and the impartial spectator. *Ethics* 105(4): 727–42.

Harman, G. 1999. Moral philosophy meets social psychology. *Proceedings of the Aristotelian Society* 99: 315–32.

Hurley, S. L. 1998. *Consciousness in Action.* Cambridge (Mass.): Harvard University Press.

Karmiloff-Smith, A. 1992. *Beyond Modularity.* Cambridge (Mass.): MIT Press.

Keysers, C., E. Kohler, M. A. Umiltà, L. Nanetti, L. Fogassi, and V. Gallese. 2003. Audiovisual mirror neurons and action recognition. *Experimental Brain Research* 153: 628–36.

Levin, P., and A. Isen. 1975. Further studies on the effect of feeling good on helping. *Sociometry* 38: 141–47

Miller, C. 2003. Social psychology and virtue ethics. *Journal of Ethics* 7: 365–92.

Morris J. S. C. D. Frith, D. I. Perrett, D. Rowland, A. W. Young, A. J. Calder, R. J. Dolan. 1996. A differential neural response in the human amygdala to fearful and happy facial expressions. *Nature* 383: 812–15.

Morris, J. S., K. J. Friston, C. Buchel, C. D. Frith, A. W. Young, A. J. Calder, and R. J. Dolan. 1998. A neuromodulatory role for the human amygdala in processing emotional facial expressions. *Brain* 121: 42–57.

Ochsner, K. N, S. A. Bunge, J. J. Gross, and J.D.E. Gabriele. 2002. Rethinking feelings: An fMRI study of the cognitive regulation of emotion. *Journal of Cognitive Neuroscience* 14(8): 1215–1229.

Phelps, E. 2004. The human amygdala and awareness: Interactions between emotion and cognition. In *The Cognitive Neurosciences, III*, ed. M. Gazzaniga, 1005–1016. Cambridge (Mass.): MIT Press.

Phillips, M. L., A. W. Young, C. Senior, M. Brammer, C. Andrew, A. J. Calder, E. T. Bullmore, D. I. Perrett, D. Rowland, S. C. Williams, J. A. Gray, and A. S. David. 1997. A specific neural substrate for perceiving facial expressions of disgust. *Nature* 389: 495–98.

Prinz, J. 2004. *Gut Reactions: A Perceptual Theory of Emotion*. Oxford: Oxford University Press.

Rizzolatti, G., L. Fadiga, V. Gallese, and L. Fogassi. 1996. Premotor cortex and the recognition of motor actions. *Cognitive Brain Research* 3: 131–41.

Schafe, G. E., and J. E. LeDoux. 2004. The neural basis of fear. In *The Cognitive Neurosciences, III*, ed. M. Gazzaniga, 987–1004. Cambridge (Mass.): MIT Press.

Schaefer, S. M., D. C. Jackson, R. J. Davidson, D. Y. Kimberg, and S. L. Thompson-Schill. 2002. Modulation of amygdalar activity by the conscious regulation of negative emotion. *Journal of Cognitive Neuroscience* 14(6): 913–21.

Singer, T. 2006. The neural basis and ontogeny of empathy and mind reading: Review of literature and implications for future research. *Neuroscience and Biobehavioral Reviews* 30: 855–63.

Sneddon, A. Forthcoming. The depths and shallows of psychological externalism. *Philosophical Studies*. Published online on March 6, 2007: http://www.springerlink.com/content/38k27p3010550173/

Weyant, J., and R. Clark. 1977. Dimes and helping: The other side of the coin. *Personality and Social Psychology Bulletin* 3: 107–10.

Whalen, P. J., S. L. Rauch, N. L. Etcoff, S. C. McInerny, M. B. Lee, and M. A. Jenike. 1998. Masked presentations of emotional facial expressions modulate amygdala activity without explicit knowledge. *Journal of Neuroscience* 18: 411–18.

Wicker, B., C. Keysers, J. Plailly, J.-P. Royet, V. Gallese, and G. Rizzolatti. 2003. Both of us disgusted in *my* insula: The common neural basis of seeing and feeling disgust. *Neuron* 40: 655–64.

Wilson, R. A. 2001. Two views of realization. *Philosophical Studies* 104(1): 1–31.

Wilson, R. A. 2004. *Boundaries of the Mind: The Individual in the Fragile Sciences*. New York: Cambridge University Press.

CANADIAN JOURNAL OF PHILOSOPHY
Supplementary Volume 32

Assembling the Emotions

VINCENT BERGERON AND MOHAN MATTHEN[1]

Endogenous depression is highly correlated with low levels of serotonin in the central nervous system. Does this imply or suggest that this sort of depression *just is* this neurochemical deficit? Scorning such an inference, Antonio Damasio writes:

> If feeling happy or sad ... corresponds in part to the cognitive modes under which your thoughts are operating, then the explanation also requires that the chemical acts on the circuits which generate and manipulate [such thoughts]. Which means that reducing depression to a statement about the availability of serotonin or norepinephrine in general – a popular statement in the days and age of Prozac – is unacceptably rude (1995, 161).

Damasio's thought is that depression is *essentially* a modification of how we perceive the world, reason about it, and make decisions about how to act in it – in other words, that it is essentially cognitive. A reduced level of serotonin might cause the said modification, but no adequate account of depression would identify the malady with its cause. A proper account would minimally need to say how cognitive processing is affected by a reduced level of serotonin. (On this, see also Castrén 2005.) Damasio's broader point is that the emotions must

---

1 This paper brings together and extends themes from the work of each author. Most of section II originates from Bergeron's work on modularity for his doctoral dissertation. The material on the feeling of presence in visual experience in section III derives from Matthen (2005), chap. 13. We worked collaboratively on the remainder of the paper, and on the writing of it. We thank an anonymous referee and especially the editors for insightful and useful comments.

receive cognitive or intentional – as opposed to merely affective or behavioural – characterizations.

In this paper, we identify (section I) a problem with cognitive characterizations of the emotions, facts which suggest that they must be non-cognitive affective states. We suggest (section II) that this problem is an instance of certain obstacles that make it difficult to come up with cognitive characterizations in neuropsychological theorizing. This leads us to the constructive part of the paper (sections III–IV), in which we suggest how the problem might be solved.

I. Cognitive Accounts of the Emotions: A Puzzle

The following puzzle arises from certain recent discoveries about the localization of emotion in the brain reported by Damasio himself.

Damasio reports that emotional response is destroyed in patients who suffer lesions of the ventromedial portion of the prefrontal cortex; these patients seem not to care about themselves as normal people do. Patients whose brain is thus damaged also suffer from a strange decline in decisiveness – they seem unable to formulate a plan of action and carry it through to execution. However, when only this portion of the brain is damaged, it appears that many forms of rational processing are spared, including those which lead to the social and moral assessment of hypothetical scenarios. Thus, it appears, the lack of decisiveness is associated not with the inability to assess a situation, but from a disengagement of emotion. Conversely, there are many lesions of dorsolateral prefrontal cortex that result in deficits of rational processing but not necessarily in flatness or lack of emotional response (Milner 1964). In summary:

	Emotional Affect/ Decisiveness	Rational Assessment of Social/Moral Scenarios
(Some) ventromedial lesions	Impaired	Spared (also memory and "frontal lobe" cognition)
(Some) dorsolateral lesions	Spared	Impaired

This pattern of impairments seems to show that emotional affect is separate from social cognition. But if this is so, what *cognitive* function is left over for emotion, over and above the rational assessment of social and moral scenarios? This is a puzzle because the cognitive role that the best recent philosophical accounts have assigned to emotion *is* precisely the assessment of such scenarios (cf. de Sousa 1987). Nor can one hold that emotion is a *parallel* or independent system for such assessment, since emotional arousal normally requires prior assessment. That is, you have to figure out by rational assessment that you have been slighted, or wronged, or helped before you can feel mortified, or indignant, or grateful – patients with ventromedial lesions retain at least a reduced capacity to figure such things out, but they do not get emotionally aroused by them. What exactly are they missing then, other than affect or mood?

Traditionally, affect is not thought to have cognitive content – considered as affect, sadness may *accompany* the belief that things are bad, but *qua* affect it has no propositional content. So the evidence just cited seems to show that Damasio is simply wrong to insist that emotion must be cognitively characterized. And this flies in the face of the most convincing philosophical approaches to emotion as well. It would be good to save cognitive content for emotion. But how? One more puzzle: What is the connection between the impairment of emotional affect and the reduction in decisiveness? Are emotion and decision associated merely because a certain affect or mood is required to mediate rational assessment and action? Or is there a cognitive connection?

In this paper, we attempt to throw light on these questions by a consideration of modularity as it occurs in certain other areas of cognition, particularly vision. We shall try to show that certain cognitive modules particularize an experience by providing the subject with a *feeling* concerning how she herself is located in a scene. We suggest that emotional feelings are analogous in this respect.

II. Some Methodological Issues

Before we embark on our main line of argument concerning emotion, we review some methodological issues that surround the cognitive characterization of modules.

II.i. Modules and Dissociations

Patterns of dissociation such as the one displayed in the table given above are generally regarded as providing evidence for the existence of *modules*. A module is a functional unit that is specialized for the performance of some cognitive task. Certain cognitive tasks are performed as parts of the integrated functioning of the mind. When such integrated functioning is knocked out, all associated operations are disabled – witness patients whose intellectual capacities are damaged very widely by strokes or Alzheimer's syndrome. Dissociations between tasks show that they are *not* integrated with one another, but rather separated or modularized.

A cognitive task *A* is said to be dissociated from *B* when at least some individuals are observed who show a significant deficit with respect to *A* in the absence of a corresponding deficit in *B*. *A* and *B* are said to be *doubly* dissociated when, in addition, we observe individuals in whom *B* is significantly impaired without a corresponding deficit with regard to *A*. Neuroscientists generally hold that dissociations are signs of separateness. If *A* is observed to fail when *B* does not, then one may infer that *A* involves some process *M* that *B* does not involve, or at least that there is some process that *A* more significantly draws on than *B* does. When this process *M* is obstructed, it is argued, *A* fails and *B* does not. In the case of a double dissociation, the inference is stronger, namely that *A* and *B* each involves (or significantly draws on) some process that the other does not. (See Shallice 1988 for a detailed discussion of this methodology.) Where the process in question is a cognitive process, then, dissociations provide evidence of the existence of what are known as *modules*.

The double dissociation summarized in the table above indicates that the emotions and rational social assessment each involves some module not involved in the other.

II.ii. Modularity: Cognitive vs. Anatomical

When Jerry Fodor (1983) introduced the notion of a module, he was thinking of functional units that perform a particular data-processing job. He thought of modules in terms of transformational and inferential rules that characterize the computation performed by that module

– let's call these the *cognitive basis* of the module. In Fodor's conception, the cognitive basis of each module is innately specified; it cannot avail itself of new information. Moreover, it is *informationally encapsulated*; that is, it has restricted access to information available elsewhere in the system. Further, its cognitive basis has non-universal application; in other words, it is *domain-specific* (though the exact sense in which it is so needs clarification, as we shall see in our discussion of face-perception in II.v below). Let us call a unit of this sort a *cognitive module*.

Cognitive neuroscientists are interested in cognitive modules that are, in addition, anatomically localized – in *anatomical modules*, as we shall call them, i.e., in Fodor-style cognitive modules that reside in a bounded region of the brain. The reason is that lesions, single-neuron recordings, and brain-scans, the neuroscientist's main tools, detect activity in discrete areas of the brain, and so are powerless to reveal cognitive modules that are not anatomically localized (Coltheart 2001, Bergeron 2007). The kind of modularity that is in question for the emotions is anatomical, not merely cognitive or functional.

Now, a dissociation between tasks *A* and *B* does not imply that *A* and *B* are completely separate, only that one involves a process that is not involved, or only marginally involved, in the other – not that all neuroscientists are scrupulous about this. Similarly, a double dissociation does not imply that two tasks are completely separate, just that each involves a process that the other does not – this is compatible with there being overlap between the two tasks. Interpreted cautiously, therefore, anatomical dissociations give us some hints as to the anatomical location of some cognitive process that is involved in one but not the other cognitive task. It is very important to state it this way: it implies that anatomically based dissociations may rest not on the cognitive basis for the entire observed deficit, but on some subprocess. In particular, patients with ventromedial lesions may not lack the entire apparatus of emotional response, but only some necessary part thereof.

Damasio's general approach can be taken to accord with the above statement: he does not take the absence of emotion in otherwise rational patients to be a sign that emotion and rationality are completely separate. Rather, he searches for some cognitive element that is involved in emotion, but not in the assessment of social situations.

The puzzle posed in the previous section is that since social assessment seems to exhaust the cognitive content commonly ascribed to emotions, there does not seem to be room for any such element, even if it is clearly recognized to be only a part of the emotional circuitry in the brain.

II.iii. Merely Cognitive Dissociations

Evidence for dissociations may simply be cognitive. The unsurprising double dissociation between sight and hearing is of this type: most blind people can hear, and most deaf people can see. From this we can infer what we already knew, namely that vision involves some process that is not involved in audition and vice versa. Of course, there is plenty of anatomical evidence as well for the divergence of vision and audition – our point is just that the above argument does not appeal to evidence of this type.

More substantive and surprising cognitive dissociations have recently been discovered in developmental studies. For example, it has been found that infants are able to differentiate large set-sizes on the basis of gross ratio, when that ratio is large enough, but not when it is small (Xu et al. 2005). For example, they are able to differentiate between 8-membered sets and 16-membered sets, or between 16-membered sets and 32-membered sets, but not between 8-membered sets and 12-membered sets or 16-membered sets and 24-membered sets. Adults show analogous limitations on their ability to discriminate set-size for large sets. However, adults are able to differentiate *small* sets even when the ratios are small – they can differentiate between 3-membered sets and 4-membered sets, for instance. By contrast, babies' failure to discriminate low-ratio sets extends to small-numbered sets as well. This shows that in the case of small sets, adults are using some process that is unavailable to babies. Presumably, this process is connected with counting, while infants can only use ratio-estimation. Thus, infants lack some crucial element of counting.

This data on size estimation says nothing whatsoever about anatomical modularity. The argument just mentioned is purely psychological: it relies from the start on a cognitive characterization and does not imply anything about anatomical localization.

II.iv. Lesion Studies and Anatomical Dissociation

As far as anatomical modularity is concerned, evidence for the localization of cognitive activity is required in addition to evidence for dissociation. Such evidence is traditionally found in lesion studies, which are concerned with cognitive loss following disease or injury involving localizable areas of the brain, or deliberate ablation of a portion of a subject's brain. More recently, such evidence has also been sought in various indicators of brain activity: electrophysiological measurements, fMRI and PET scans.

Beginning, then, with lesion studies, we note that these may involve large samples or only isolated individuals. The classic method involving large samples was to collate dozens or even hundreds of reports of cognitive deficits suffered by equivalent lesions caused by bullet wounds suffered in war (Kleist 1934 is the classic review) and insults endured during psychosurgery or brain surgery to relieve epilepsy. As far as psychosurgery was concerned, certain dissociations were surgical wards because the number of patients with frontal lobectomies is (or rather, once was) surprisingly large: Brenda Milner at the Montreal Neurological Institute did studies involving more than one hundred such patients, with all sorts of different areas removed, one group with one set of lesions being used as a control for experiments on another with another.

These studies of large groups of injured humans led, however, to no very conclusive results. In part, this is because the damage from both the bullet wounds and the surgery were circumstantial and indiscriminate. It's not as if small regions of the brain were precisely ablated in these cases, and so it was impossible to control for damage to precise areas of the brain. Nor did the cognitive tests employed in these studies reveal precisely characterizable deficits – perhaps there were no such deficits suffered in common by all of these patients; perhaps the tests employed were not very sophisticated. The large numbers of patients studied led, paradoxically, to confusion. Since no two of these patients had exactly the same lesion, and because the cognitive deficit could not be characterized specifically enough, generalizations over large samples came only at the cost of extreme vagueness. In the case of the Montreal Neurological Institute studies of frontal lobectomies, this kind of confusion even led, around 1960, to scepticism about whether the frontal lobes were associated with *any* cognitive activity, and to a loss of confidence in earlier studies (such as Paul Broca's classic study, described below).

Another kind of problem encountered in large sample studies is that it is difficult to match up the cognitive activity of a given area across species. We learn *something* about human cognition from animal studies. For instance, we know that animals that are frontally lobectomized have certain problems in switching between simple task-oriented inferential strategies. Presumably, this has some relevance to why frontally lobectomized humans have difficulties with the Wisconsin Card Sorting Test, which requires the subject to switch sorting criteria mid-task. Still, it is obvious that the kinds of data-processing involved are much more complex in humans than they are in animals. Thus, though we might like to pull the animals into the same class as humans for the purposes of establishing a systematic double dissociation, it is difficult to characterize this dissociation in sufficiently informative cognitive terms. By the same token, though it might be clear that humans suffer deficits with regard to emotion as a result of damage to the frontal lobes, it is difficult to correlate these with the cognitive and behavioural deficits that chimps suffer under the same anatomical insults.

Some lesion studies involve deficits observed in just a few patients, or even only one, where we are dealing with a single lesion and, often fortuitously, with an easily characterized cognitive deficit. David Milner and Mel Goodale's postulation of two visual systems was initially based on a double dissociation in just two patients, one who displayed optic ataxia, the ability to recognize shapes accompanied by an inability to manipulate them, and another who displayed visual agnosia, the opposite dissociation (Milner and Goodale 1995). Similarly, the postulation of a speech production module in Broca's area was based on a single patient, Tan, and the discovery of a motion detection module in the mediotemporal cortex by Zihl et al. (1983) was also based on a single patient. And despite her access to neurosurgical wards in Montreal, Brenda Milner's (Scoville and Milner 1957) stunning demonstration of a dissociation, brought about by the surgical bilateral ablation of the hippocampus and surrounding areas, between what are now called *episodic* and *semantic* memory on the one hand, and other forms of procedural learning on the other, was based on a single famous patient, HM.

With small sample sets, there is obviously no need for a single description that fits a whole lot of cases. But even with them, it is still often unclear how one is to characterize the cognitive deficit suffered by these brain-damaged patients. Certain aspects of the deficit can be extremely striking, after all, and this tends to bias the investigator. At first, indeed, the modular deficit is not even noticed. HM was profoundly amnesic and has remained so for more than fifty years. One might have been tempted to characterize his deficit in just this way and leave it at that. However, Brenda Milner was able to teach him certain out-of-the-way sensorimotor skills, such as how to trace a shape while looking only at its mirror image. This showed that HM had not lost procedural memory. In a similarly fortuitous manner, Elizabeth Warrington and Lawrence Weiskrantz discovered that amnesic patients could be classically conditioned, and, as Endel Tulving (inspired by Warrington and Weiskrantz) discovered somewhat later, they could also be primed by prior exposure to words or images. These discoveries were often, as we said, fortuitous: the experimenter just decided to try something out and it worked. But this points to a difficulty on the other side of the dissociation. Could it not be that the characterization of the more specialized deficit is similarly incomplete? Thus, one recent critic has said: "The emphasis in this earlier work tended, probably necessarily because of our limited knowledge at the time of both anatomy and behaviour, to be on rather open-ended searches for a behavioural deficit, ideally achieving a double dissociation of lesion and deficit" (Latto 2004).

To summarize, then, the trouble with the use of dissociations in the search for anatomical modules is that the evidence is restricted to deficits of performance. Such deficits have as yet to be cognitively characterized. It has often proven hard to find appropriate cognitive characterizations to link up with the performance deficit that we find associated with a particular part of the brain.

II.v. Neuroimaging and Modularity

The development of brain scanning techniques such as fMRI would seem to hold considerable promise for addressing some of the limitations of earlier research into anatomical modules. For now it seems possible to observe more or less directly which areas of the brain are active when certain cognitive tasks are actually being performed. However, the difficulties of inferring cognitive processes from performance remain. We observe, moreover, that certain persistent fallacies continue to foul the search for anatomical modules.

Consider the discussion relating to the supposed module for face recognition. (For further discussion, see Bergeron 2007). Lesions in a relatively small area of the brain, the fusiform gyrus, lead to a marked decline in the ability to recognize faces – the condition known as *prosopagnosia* – though other visual abilities, including most other visual object-recognition abilities, are spared. Further, the reverse dissociation has also been observed (Rumiati and Humphreys 1997). Thus, there seems to be a double dissociation between face recognition and object recognition, and the fusiform gyrus seems to be implicated on the face side. This postulate is supported by a marked increase of metabolic activity in this area, as revealed in fMRI studies, when a face is perceived. This extends even to cases where the stimulus itself is unchanged, as in face-vase reversals, etc., and cases where the face is simply a cartoon, or is presented upside down, and so on (Kanwisher 2003) – in all of these cases, activation of the fusiform gyrus correlates with subjective awareness as of a face. Cumulatively, this evidence makes it quite likely that there is an area in the fusiform gyrus that is intimately involved both in the identification of faces as faces and the discrimination of faces from one another. Nancy Kanwisher calls this the Fusiform Face Area (FFA).

Is it legitimate to say, as Kanwisher et al. (1997) have, that FFA constitutes a "module specialized for face perception"? We would argue that the answer is "yes," but that one has to be careful about what exactly one means by this. Here are some important clarifications.

1. Neuroscience can be taken to have shown that some cognitive modules involved in face-discrimination are localized and do not extend widely across the brain. This does not mean, of course, that all data-processes relevant to face perception are confined to these regions of the brain. Some may involve the interaction of many widely distributed modules passing data back and forth.

2. When Kanwisher talks about a "module specialized for face perception," therefore, she should *not* be taken to imply that face perception is localized in FFA. In fact, she emphasizes a number of

other areas that are sensitive to faces. For example, she acknowledges (2003) that direction of gaze seems to be registered in the superior temporal sulcus, and the amygdala reacts to emotional expression.

3. It is thus likely that the human experience of faces arises from the output of more than one module. FFA is clearly one of these. A double dissociation between some aspect of face perception and of, say, body perception will not show that there is no overlap between these processes. What it shows is that there is in each process an area of non-overlap with the other. In other words, it may only show that some module that is necessary for face perception is not shared with body perception, and vice versa.

Now, it has been argued by Isabel Gauthier et al. (1999, 2000) that the FFA is not face-specific, on the grounds that it is active when experts on other objects – cars, birds – are engaged in identifying these objects. This, however, does not show that FFA is domain-general, as Gauthier suggests it is. Certainly, Gauthier would be right to say that FFA is able to perform tasks other than face perception. But this is compatible with the idea that it is specialized for face perception – one can, after all, use a wrench, which is specialized for grasping and twisting, as a hammer.

Gauthier's findings are compatible with the claim that FFA is the site of a sub-process specialized for face recognition, but recruited for other purposes as well. In other words, it might be that face recognition skills, innate though they are, are transferable to other tasks. It is intriguing in this connection that cross-domain application is only true of *experts*, i.e., car-enthusiasts, ornithologists, and the like. This suggests that these individuals might have *become* expert by learning how to recruit the cognitive basis of FFA to their areas. If so, it could still be true that FFA is domain-specific, with the proviso that other domains can be related to this one by the use of analogy. If, as this allows, FFA was selected for its utility in recognizing faces, it would still be reasonable to say, albeit in a sense of biological function, that it is *for* face perception. In other words, it might be that the selective advantage conferred upon human individuals by FFA's activity is that these individuals are able to recognize other humans by their faces. (This hypothesis is supported by the recent finding of Tsao et al. 2006 that a certain area of the macaque cortex, presumably homologous to the fusiform gyrus, "consists almost entirely of face-selective cells." Whatever role this structure may be playing in macaques, the finding shows that it could have been seized upon during human evolution for its evident utility to members of our species in recognizing other humans.) It may be that the utility of this area in the recognition of birds, cars, etc., is secondary in the evolutionary scheme of things. In short, it might be that the Fodorian basis of the cognitive module realized in the FFA concerns faces, though they might come in certain cases to be applied to other objects.

We conclude that though it might be a mistake to say that FFA *performs* face perception – it is (a) not the only area involved and (b) this is not the only thing it does – it might still be correct to say that it is specialized for some cognitive component of face perception, in the sense that it is selected for a function that is designed by evolution to contribute specifically to face perception. This illustrates a general point: the modularity thesis loses its point when the cognitive basis of anatomical modules is specified at too high or abstract a level. In the first place, the kinds of performances that we readily recognize in a psychology lab are often the outputs of several cooperating modules. Secondly, the function for which a module was selected and is specialized might be much more specific than the tasks to which it can be recruited. Methodologically, therefore, it makes sense to search for quite concrete cognitive specifications of modules and to explain their contribution to psychological tasks by the interaction of specific modules.

The nineteenth-century German neurologist Carl Wernicke appeared to be well aware of this. For in his model, higher psychological functions arise from interactions between more basic functions. In this respect, the contrast between Wernicke and Franz Joseph Gall, the founder of phrenology, could not be more stark: a fundamental error of Gall's phrenology was to specify anatomical modules at much too high a level – amativeness, executiveness, veneration, as so on. In Wernicke's system, even language comprehension was assembled from parts shared by other cognitive functions.

Fodor (1983) claimed that modular functions were not assembled from other modules. For Fodor this follows from the informational encapsulation of each module; nevertheless, this is peripheral to his purposes, and in our opinion it is extremely important to drop encapsulation as a characterization of modules and to admit both the possibility of cooperative processes that involve more than one module and the possibility that a single module might participate in several such cooperative processes (see also Coltheart 1999). Though one might continue to hold, with Fodor, that the results of modular processes are encapsulated with respect to what Fodor called "central processing," i.e., voluntary processing at the personal level, it is in our view useful to suppose that they might exchange information with other modules and be a part of larger overlapping data-processing networks.

III. Assembling Visual Experience

So far, we have been discussing how the attribution of cognitive functions to modules can go wrong, thus masking the data-processing inter-relationships between modules. Now we turn to a particular aspect of inter-module convergence in the visual system and in memory. As we shall see, certain experiences contain traces of more than one cognitive module. Sometimes, this is not a result of these modules cooperating in data-processing as such – they need not contribute to any shared cognitive process – but in a kind of complementarity and overlay that is nonetheless of cognitive significance. We suggest that something of this sort might be at work in the emotions.

To vision, then. It is by now a commonplace of cognitive neuroscience that there is more than one visual system. In fact, several data streams emanate from the retina and branch out to different parts of the brain. One of these goes to the superior colliculus, a mid-brain structure, and is there used to control direction of gaze and other involuntary mechanisms relating to vision. Another pathway travels through the lateral geniculate nucleus and on from there to the primary visual cortex. There, this stream divides into two. One of these, the dorsal stream, so called because it travels upwards to the parietal lobe, creates agent-centred spatial maps that subserve voluntary action; the other, known as the ventral stream because it goes downward to the temporal lobe, is responsible for most of the features that are presented as objective properties of objects in conscious vision: colour, form, and texture, as well as faces, places, and bodies (Milner and Goodale 1995).

Now, the details of this division are somewhat contested (Glover 2004). It is clear, nevertheless, that the cortical visual system is divided into two kinds of subsystem. What is generally called ventral stream vision is used to build up a lasting record of the objects in our environment – its job is to provide us with information about the visual features of external objects. On the other hand, the dorsal stream, as well as a number of other subsystems, is concerned with the visual guidance needed for the execution of actions by moving the limbs. This job is primarily agent-centred – it pertains to how the agent will move her body with respect to things around herself. As philosophers, we would be wise to use these functional characterizations to tag the systems and to avoid physiological terminology (such as "dorsal" or "ventral stream"). Accordingly, we employ the following terminology (cf. Matthen 2005, chap. 13). *Descriptive* vision is the capacity to register and record properties, including spatial properties, such as position, that distal objects possess. *Motion-guiding* vision is the visual capacity to represent the position of objects *relative to the perceiver's body* for purposes of guiding bodily motion.

Now, it is often said that only descriptive vision is conscious. And this is generally linked to the fact that it produces representations that can be recalled to the mind at later times. On the other hand, motion-guiding vision is occupied with transient relations between the perceiver's body and objects in the environment. Its determinations are never recalled to the mind – indeed, they decay and fade away in a few seconds – because these precisely controlled relations do not, for all practical purposes, recur. (It is difficult to recreate one's tennis-stroke as if to a ball that was hit to one *yesterday*: motion-guiding vision dealt with the situation when it occurred but did not store its records in a way that would make them accessible later.) Now, some suppose that all consciously presented representations can be recalled to the mind. And so they suppose that the representations created by motion-guiding vision are not conscious. Reasoning like this has been taken to imply that visual *experience* is a product of only descriptive vision. Visual experience gives us knowledge of the objective features of objects, features such as colour, form, texture and the like, and the claim is that these presentations exhaust the content of visual *experience* or "seeing" (cf. Goodale 2001).

This argument, however, cannot be wholly correct. For what would visual experience be like if we *lacked* motion-guiding vision – what is "optic ataxia" like, what does it *feel* like? A partial answer can be obtained by reflection on the fact that motion-guiding vision is primarily concerned with bodily guidance. It is therefore very much concerned with locating external things relative to the perceiver's body. While descriptive vision presents things in terms that centre on external objects – in allocentric terms – motion-guiding vision presents them in egocentric terms. Moreover, motion-guiding vision gives us a feeling that we are able to make contact with and manipulate objects in our immediate vicinity. *Lacking motion-guiding vision, therefore, we would be deficient in egocentrically represented information concerning objects, and we would not feel that we are able to make contact with them or manipulate them.* We would, in other words, receive all the *information* about external things that descriptive vision affords us, but this information would be couched in allocentric terms, and we would consequently lack the sense that we can directly act on perceived objects – reach for them, size our grasp so as to fit them, walk toward them, and so on. In short, we would not feel them to be located relative to ourselves in the way that is implied by the ability to act on them. One would see an object, then, as "Three feet away, which is roughly as far as I can reach," but though this kind of description would help one *think* about and *verbally describe* spatial relations in one's immediate vicinity, it is not in the limb-centred form that would help control one's bodily parts while reaching out to the thing. Earlier, we claimed that our awareness of our capacity to act on external objects is presented as something that pertains to ourselves, not just to the external objects in question.

This egocentric form of experience is missing in pictures. This conclusion is bolstered by considering our experience of objects in a picture. (The discussion that occupies the next few paragraphs summarizes the fuller account in Matthen 2005, 309–318.) Depicted objects engage descriptive vision. This is why we can learn about a thing by looking at an accurate depiction – we know by looking at paintings by Velasquez what Philip II of Spain looked like; we can trace the Hapsburg lip through paintings of successive generations of the family. There is, in the experience of looking at an object realistically depicted in a picture, *some* component that resembles the experience we would have had if we had looked at the same object directly – the picture presents us with certain properties and relations of the object in such a way as to ensure this. However, depicted objects do not engage motion-guiding vision. The kind of information that we get from pictures is not the kind that will allow us to manipulate pictured objects – nor does our experience of pictured objects give us the feeling that they are there to be acted upon by us. The picture itself does, of course: that is, the physical object – the framed canvas – that has the picture on its surface can be reached out to and manipulated. But the objects *in* the picture cannot – you cannot without the learned and practised skill of a mime reach out and appropriately shape your hand to stroke Philip's cheek or grasp his wrist, and you don't feel you can when you are in front of the portrait. Depicted objects do not, consequently, look as if they are spatially related to ourselves. *Where* is the object in that painting? In the space of the picture, not in my space – it doesn't make any sense, even visual sense, to suppose that we can point to depicted objects in the way that we point to real ones, get closer to them by walking towards the picture, grasp their nose or stroke their cheeks by moving one's hands.

There is, then, a difference between a visual experience to which motion-guiding vision contributes and one to which it does not. However, the difference does not lie in those properties that vision attributes to distal objects: any one of these can be replicated by a picture, usually even in the same way. The difference has rather to do with how the spatial relationship between the perceiver and object is presented. To repeat: it does not have to do with the spatial relationship itself, since descriptive vision presents this, albeit allocentrically; rather, it has to do with the egocentric, body-centred form of the presentation. In vision that includes motion-guiding vision, objects are there to be manipulated; in vision that does not involve motion-guiding vision, they are not. Because these visual objects are presented in *full* vision – vision of objects presented to both visual systems – as being related to the perceiver, the perceptual state, moreover, presents itself as being *true*. Neither of these aspects of vision is shared by merely descriptive – pictorial or imagined – visual states. Objects in pictures are not there to be manipulated; depicted scenes are not experienced as real or true. We sum this up by saying that in *full* vision, objects have a *feeling of presence*; in merely descriptive (e.g., pictorial) vision, they do not (cf. Matthen 2005, 304).

The feeling of presence is not awareness of any feature of an object. The very same object, with all of its visually presented features, can be experienced both in a picture and in full vision, but it is only in full vision that it feels present, only when it engages both descriptive and motion-guiding vision. And the feeling of presence does not distinguish one object from another. Everything that you experience in full vision has it, regardless of how it might be discernible from other objects. The feeling of presence is a way of experiencing an object. If *o* is a visually presented object, the feeling of presence involves a certain way of knowing the spatial relationship between *o* and the perceiver; if it is a scene or state-of-affairs, it involves the feeling of actuality or truth.

Interestingly, this relates to a point about episodic memory – the kind of memory in which you recall sensory images from the past as past. There is a difference, often noted by philosophers, between remembering a scene by "reviving a perception" of it and merely recalling a visual image or verbal description. In the first case, episodic memory, the remembering subject is a part of the remembered scene; the second case, semantic memory, is merely descriptive. Episodic memory has an essential connection to the occasion when you were in contact with the object; semantic memory does not. When you remember your grade school teacher telling you that Paris is the capital of France, that is episodic memory; when you remember that Paris is the capital of France, that is semantic memory. The first has an essential reference to an event in which you participated, and perhaps the visual or auditory features of this event; the second is not event-related in any way, and is merely informational. Again, this difference does not trace to what or how much information the memory state contains. A semantic memory can contain as much information as an episodic memory, or even more. Nor is the difference a matter of the episodic memory being like a sensory image and the semantic memory being propositional. An eidetically presented memory – for instance, one's mental image of the Mona Lisa – can have "pictorial form," but still not be presented in a relative-to-the-moment-of-experience or event-based manner. In this case, as with full vision, the difference is the involvement of the subject. The subject is a part of the scene in an episodic, but not a semantic, memory, and it is a consequence of her being a part of the scene that she experiences it in a temporal way relative to the now.

The Capgras delusion is yet another example of the phenomenon we are attempting to highlight. Capgras patients recognize that people they see *resemble* people with whom they are intimate. And they are often right because these people actually *are* the ones in question – the ones they are thought to resemble. However, these patients do not experience the "feeling of familiarity" that normally accompanies seeing a familiar face. Consequently, they are inclined to think that the people around them are impostors. What is the difference between the Capgras experience of a familiar face and the normal experience? Not any object-characterizing visual feature such as colour, shape, or configuration. Not even visual *recognition*, since it is visually evident to these patients whom these people resemble – on a feature-based conception of recognition, then, these patients are not completely deficient. What they lack is a non-informational "feeling" – the feeling of familiarity – a feeling that is as much a characteristic of the perceivers themselves as of the objects they are viewing. Again, this is a self-involving feeling – the face is presented as belonging to somebody that the patient has not encountered before, or to somebody to whom the patient is not intimately related. (Our thanks to the editors for mentioning Capgras' syndrome in this context.)

In each of the cases that we have discussed, we find a non-informational difference between two cognitive states. In these cases, the difference between two informationally similar states lies not in the content of the visual information they present, but in the fact that the information is presented in a way that involves the perceiver or agent herself. Yet these are cognitive differences: they are relevant to how the agent acts on the state.

IV. Modularity and the Emotions

Let us return now to the questions we asked at the beginning. Damasio speculates that

(1)   When there is severe damage to the ventromedial frontal lobe, emotional response is flat.

He further claims that

(2) These patients are unable to act in a normally prudent manner because they are unable to choose among activities that make competing demands on their time and energy.

For example, Damasio recounts an incident in which his patient "Elliot" was offered a choice of two time-slots for his next consultation and continued to debate the choice for more than half an hour until finally the researchers simply had to choose for him. Finally, he claims that

(3) These patients perform normally in a battery of tests designed to gauge their capacity to assess moral and social implications of various courses of action in hypothetical situations.

Suppose that he is correct in all three claims. What sort of conclusions can we draw about the nature of the task performed by the damaged area of the brain?

One diagnostic difficulty with Damasio's own analysis of the situation has to do with his attribution of the problem with decision-making to the flatness of emotional response. He does, as we saw in section I, claim a double dissociation between emotional response and various forms of rational processing: when ventromedial prefrontal cortex is damaged, emotional response is damaged, but situational assessment is spared; when the dorsolateral portion is damaged, either both are damaged or emotional response is spared (sometimes distorted, but this is not relevant). Thus, we are entitled to conclude that there is something in the ventromedial portion that is important to emotional response. But it certainly does not follow that the flatness of emotional response is responsible for the difficulty in making decisions, no more so than that the difficulty in making decisions is responsible for emotional impassivity. For it is possible that there are *two* circuits which overlap in this portion of the brain: one of these might be the decision-making circuit, the other the emotional response circuit. The destruction of this overlapping portion might make both circuits fail, but it does not follow that the failure of one is responsible for the failure of the other. This would indicate that, as with certain other double dissociations we mentioned earlier, the function of this portion of the brain is being specified at too high a functional level. Something very specific might be missing, not something as inclusive and complex as emotional response.

A second difficulty is that the nature of the cognitive deficit is not clear. Recall that anatomical modularity is *cognitive* modularity plus localization in the brain. We have been given evidence to suppose that there is some *performance* deficit in patients with the said brain damage, namely that they are unable to make choices in situations that demand action. But what exactly is the *cognitive* deficit that results in this behaviour? As we saw in section II, it is an endemic problem in attributions of modularity that the answer to such a question may not be obvious.

Damasio's own characterization is puzzling:

> I began to think that the cold-bloodedness of Elliot's reasoning prevented him from assigning different values to different options, and made his decision-making landscape hopelessly flat. It might also be that the same cold-bloodedness made his mental landscape too shifty and unsustained for the time required to make response selections, in other words, a subtle rather than basic defect in working memory which might alter the remainder of the reasoning process required for a decision to emerge. (1995, 51)

Of course, Damasio knows Elliot well, and we do not. But as presented this diagnosis is puzzling. One problem is that as (3) reveals, Elliot has no problem assessing values in a moral landscape. For example, he was given a test devised by Lawrence Kohlberg to assess the development of his moral reasoning.

> Presented with a social situation that poses a conflict between two moral imperatives, the subject is asked to indicate a solution to the dilemma and to provide a detailed ethical justification for that solution. In one such situation, for instance, the subject must decide, and explain, whether or not a character should steal a drug to prevent his wife from dying. (ibid., 48)

Presented with this kind of problem, Elliot apparently displayed little difficulty coming up with viable solutions. For instance, he is able to figure out that stealing a drug is bad, but stealing it to prevent your wife from dying is not so bad. It is not that he is prevented "from assigning different values to different options" as such. It cannot be, then, that his moral or decision-making landscape is intrinsically flat. Nor does any deficit in working memory interfere with his capacity to reason concerning moral options.

We also do not find the following suggestion particularly plausible:

> If it had been "real life," for every option Elliot offered in a given situation there would have been a response from the other side, which would have changed the situation and required an additional set of options from Elliot, which would have led to another response, and in turn to another set of options required from him, and so on. In other words, the ongoing, open-ended, uncertain evolution of real-life situations was missing from the laboratory tasks. (ibid., 49–50)

The question is this. Why would Elliot suffer from cascading moral options when he is dealing with real-life situations, but not when he is dealing with hypothetical ones? Besides, what could the "responses from the other side" have been in the simple case of choosing between two time-slots for a medical interview? In such simple cases, what could the difference be between the cognitive content of thought and reasoning about real-life situations and that pertaining to hypothetical situations? In any case, Damasio himself gives us reason to believe, the problem arises *after* reasoning is done. Elliot says: "And after all this, I still wouldn't know what to do." Or as Damasio says in a revealing aside: "Normal performance in this task demonstrated the existence of social knowledge and access to it, *but said nothing about the process or choice itself.*" The problem does not lie in rational assessment, then, whether of real life or of hypothetical situations, but in the process of making a choice.

What does it take to make a decision? What is "the process of making a choice"? Certainly, it is important for the agent to have access to a range of possible alternatives, and to value them differentially. But is this enough? You may believe that it is better to read Henry James than John Grisham. Notoriously, it does not follow that you will read James rather than Grisham. Traditionally, the problem has been posed as one of weakness of the "will": you may not be able to get yourself to read James, inclination being for the ease of reading

Grisham. This is an example of a problem with your choice-making faculty, though it is not the same as Elliot's. Your problem is that of putting into effect what you know to be best, and what you want for that reason. Elliot's problem is that he has no inclination at all. He doesn't want anything, neither because it is better, nor for any other reason. It is not that he has problems with his reasoning. The problem is that situational assessment does not lead to wants in his case.

Put in this way, one can discern an analogy with visual experience. Recall that visual experience consists of two different kinds of component, a representational component that describes external objects and a "feeling of presence" that (normally) marks the experience as relating to real objects. We argued that this latter component, the feeling of presence, is as much attributed to the perceiver as to the perceived object: it indicates (truly or falsely) the perceiver's ability to manipulate the object in question and is tied up with an egocentric representation of her own position relative to it. Something similar can be said for the case of decision-making. Elliot is able to entertain different valuations of real and hypothetical situations. What he lacks is the "feeling" that these valuations are *his*, that they give *him* a reason to act in a certain way. Reading James may be better than reading Grisham, and you may know it. But it may be that in order that this should result in your actually making the choice to read James, it is not enough that you should know that it is better – it may be necessary in addition that you should *feel* this difference in value, that you should, in other words, place yourself in the world of these values and make them *yours*. Perhaps this is the ability that Elliot lacks. Perhaps this is the function of emotional affect. Emotional affect may not be non-cognitive, in other words, it might be a manner in which situational content is entertained and apprehended. Just as the feeling of presence endows visual content with location in the perceiver's bodily action space, so also emotional affect might endow evaluative content with location in the agent's decision-making "space."

The following observation lends further support to this suggestion. The representational content of a perceptual or motivational state can occur in alethic as well as non-alethic modes. For example, a red sphere can be actually seen or merely imagined. The difference between these two states lies not in their *content*; it is a matter of the propositional operator that is attached to the content, not of the content itself. The propositional operator that is attached to visual content in "full" vision is alethic; the subpersonal visual system is performing the equivalent of asserting the content – this is the often-remarked-on "stative" character of (full) visual perception. (The agent is, of course, free to reject this assertion and to question or reject the deliverances of full vision.) It is because it is "asserted" in this manner that the state can be adjudged true or false – scenes that we see in pictures or visually imagine are not so adjudged and do not possess the phenomenology of assertion. In other words, the operator attached to the same content in visual imaging is non-alethic. This difference is clearly cognitive – it makes for the difference between a truth-assessable state and one that is not so assessable, and also for the difference between a state that presents itself as essentially involving a relationship between the perceiver and the object and one that does not so present itself. But the cognitive difference is not one of *content*, at least as far as properties attributed to the object of perception are concerned. It is a difference of how the content is entertained.

There is a similar distinction to be made in the case of emotion. One can think in great detail of a scenario that would generate anger; for example, one can imagine being imprisoned under some anti-terrorist legislation simply because one subscribed to the wrong faith. However imagining this scenario and realizing everything wrong with it does not amount to being angry. To be angry, one has to have certain feelings as well. The point is this: just as one is in a state of seeing X when one has a visual image of X *and* experiences the feeling of presence, so also one is in a state of being angry when one contemplates the above scenario *and* experiences the feelings of anger. These feelings cannot be experienced when one is simply imagining that one is angry: to experience them when contemplating such a scenario is simply to be angry. The claim we are making is that feeling angry is a manner of entertaining the wrongness of the scenario in question. It is a mark of a subpersonal system readying the agent to act in a way that gives effect to the values in question. In this sense, it marks a subpersonal commitment to the values. (Again, it is possible for the agent to resist this kind of commitment.) Damasio's "Elliot" might be capable of contemplating scenarios and attaching values to them, but his subpersonal systems do not commit to these values. As a consequence, he finds it difficult to commit to them himself.

There is an important difference between the visual feeling of presence and the operator that we are using to interpret emotional affect. We suggested earlier that the difference between seeing a red sphere and merely imagining it is that, when one sees it, one feels that one has the capacity to manipulate it – and that such a capacity would be a relation between the perceiver and the object of perception. This feeling marks a particular visual state (truly or falsely) as one of actual interaction with the environment, as distinguished from an internally generated image. In the case of emotion, the attitude is not one of assertion but of commitment. Thus, it is not the actuality or even the personal relevance of the values that are in question, but the readiness to act on them immediately.

If we are right, an emotional response consists of two components, just as Damasio suggests (see section I above). One component is purely cognitive: it consists in entertaining a scenario with values. The second consists of what one might call a state of moral deixis, which figuratively speaking locates oneself in the world of values so entertained. This, we suggest, is the feeling associated with emotion. Just as the feeling of presence makes a visual presentation an act of seeing, so also emotional feeling makes a situational evaluation motivationally relevant. This theory fits well with the more sensible cognitive theories of emotions that have been advanced recently – it fits for example with de Sousa's, which gives a role to affect, but not with Sartre's, which does not. (There is one respect in which our view contradicts de Sousa, however: he thinks that emotional affect is part of the cognitive module that assesses situations – we do not.) Our view has, however, two novel consequences.

The first is that it allows for a non-descriptive component of emotional states. A theory like de Sousa's suffers, we believe, from a slight embarrassment in that it attributes cognitive content to the state of arousal that is part of emotion – to what we have been calling *feelings* of anger. However, it is notoriously a problem with such views that such feelings and their neurophysiological accompaniments are far too undifferentiated and generic to carry detailed content (cf. Cannon 1927, Schachter and Singer 1962). People do not in fact have much capacity to differentiate between the feeling associated with anger, say, and that associated with fear: any feeling that goes with these emotions is likely associated with a generalized state of arousal, and not any specific emotion. We would like to point out that it is entirely explicable on our view how arousal can be generic and undifferentiated without compromising the detail of the accompanying scenario. We said earlier that the feeling of presence does not differentiate different kinds of objects in a scene. Similarly, emotional response simply makes different assessments have presence in the agent's own decision-making landscape. They do not differentiate the evaluations themselves. On the other hand, our analysis is compatible with other differences in brain activity accompanying different emotions. Indeed, it is very much indicated by our hypothesis that lesions of ventromedial prefrontal cortex would correlate with some essential component of emotional response, but not to the whole of emotional response.

A second novel consequence of our view follows from our claim that emotional feeling has a morally deictic quality. To feel anger or gratitude is, on our view, to entertain a particular scenario with attached values and for a subpersonal action system to commit to acting on those values. If this is correct, then it is in some sense deficient to have an emotional experience but with no attached scenario. Thus, it is in some sense deficient to feel angry or sad or happy, but in virtue of no attached scenario. This, of course, is a proposition that has often been asserted on intuitive or theoretical grounds. The novelty of our approach is that we are denying the completeness of ungrounded emotional states on logical, rather than merely normative, grounds. On the view that we have advanced, feeling anger but not about something, is akin to issuing a mark of assertion but with no proposition attached, or stating commitment but to no stated value. These are *logically* incomplete performances. Analogously, our theory grounds the incompleteness of objectless anger on the incompleteness of its logical form. Similarly, it is odd when rational assessment of a situation *conflicts* with emotional response. Our analysis suggests that there is a theoretical conflict in this case: two opposite analyses, only one of which is engaging emotion.

Appendix: An Unresolved Complication

Damasio et al. (2000) detailed differences in brain activity with respect to recalled emotional response – happiness, sadness, anger, fear. These authors suggest that the differences relate to the bodily expression of emotion – preparation for action, etc. On the other hand, the studies did not involve *present* emotion, but memories thereof. If this is correct, the differences indicate a certain visceral level of preparation for bodily expression combined with the non-activation or suppression of actual action. Significantly, the study involved relatively few changes to the activity in the amygdala and ventromedial prefrontal cortex, and this supports our line of thought. On the other hand, they clearly involved affect. The authors remark: "It is possible that the amygdala is less engaged by recalled stimulus images. Also, our data collection was skewed toward the feeling phase of the emotion-feeling cycle, rather than to its induction" (*ibid.*, 1053). These remarks suggest that perhaps Eliot's deficit was even more specific than indicated by our hypothesis and that the relationship between *affect* and positioning in the agent's decision-making landscape is itself a complex activity. It is obviously not possible for us to address these speculations more fully here. We thank the editors for querying us about the relevance of this study.

References

Bergeron, V. 2007 Anatomical and functional modularity in cognitive science: Shifting the focus. *Philosophical Psychology* 20: 175-95.

Cannon, W. 1927. The James-Lange theory of emotions: A critical examination and alternative theory. *American Journal of Psychology* 39: 106–24.

Castrén, E. 2005. Is mood chemistry? *Nature Reviews Neuroscience* 6: 241–46.

Coltheart, M. 1999. Modularity and cognition. *Trends in Cognitive Sciences* 3: 115–20.

Coltheart, M. 2001. Assumptions and methods in cognitive neuropsychology. In *The Handbook of Cognitive Neuropsychology*, ed. B. Rapp, 3–21. New York: Psychology Press.

Damasio, A. 1995. *Descartes' Error: Emotion, Reason, and the Human Brain*. New York: Putnam.

Damasio, A. R., T. J. Grabowski, A. Bechara, H. Damasio, L. L. B. Ponto and Richard D. Haichwa. 2000. Subcortical and cortical brain activity during the feeling of self-generated emotions. *Nature Neuroscience* 3: 1049–1056.

de Sousa, R. 1987. *The Rationality of Emotion*. Cambridge (Mass.): MIT Press.

Fodor, J. A. 1983. *The Modularity of Mind*. Cambridge (Mass): MIT Press.

Gauthier, I., M. J. Tarr, A. W. Anderson, P. Skudlarski, and J. C. Gore. 1999. Activation of the middle fusiform 'face area' increases with expertise in recognizing novel objects. *Nature Neuroscience* 2(6): 568–73.

Gauthier, I., P. Skudlarski, J. C. Gore, and A. W. Anderson. 2000. Expertise for cars and birds recruits brain areas involved in face recognition. *Nature Neuroscience* 3: 191–97.

Glover, S. 2004. Separate visual representations in the planning and control of action. *Behavioral and Brain Sciences* 27: 3–24.

Goodale, M. A. 2001. Why vision is more than seeing. In *Naturalism, Evolution, and Intentionality*, Canadian Journal of Philosophy supplementary volume 27: 187–214.

Kanwisher, N. 2003. The ventral visual object pathway in humans: Evidence from fMRI. In *The Visual Neurosciences*, ed. L. Chalupa and J. Werner, 1179–89. Cambridge (Mass.): MIT Press.

Kanwisher, N., J. McDermott, and M. M. Chun. 1997. The fusiform face area: A module in human extrastriate cortex specialized for face perception. *Journal of Neuroscience* 17: 4302–4311.

Kleist, K. 1934. Kriegsverletzungen des Gehirns in ihrer Bedeutung für die Hirnlokalisation und Hirnpathologie. In *Handbuch der Aerzlichen Erfahrungen im Weltkriege 1914–18. Vol. 4: Geistes- und Nervenkrankheit*, ed. K. Bonhoefer, 343–1360. Leipzig: Barth.

Latto, R. 2004. Form follows function in visual information processing. *Behavioral and Brain Sciences* 27: 43–44.

Matthen, M. 2005. *Seeing, Doing, and Knowing: A Philosophical Theory of Sense-Perception*. Oxford: Clarendon Press.

Milner, B. 1964. Some effects of frontal lobectomy in Man. In *The Frontal Granular Cortex and Behavior*, ed. J. Warren and K. Akert, 313–31. New York: McGraw-Hill.

Milner, A. D., and M. A. Goodale. 1995. *The Visual Brain in Action*. Oxford: Oxford University Press.

Rumiati, R. I., and G. W. Humphreys. 1997. Visual object agnosia without alexia or prosopagnosia. *Visual Cognition* 4: 207–217.

Schachter, S., and J. E. Singer. 1962. Cognitive, social, and physiological determinants of emotional state. *Psychological Review* 69: 379–99.

Scoville, W. B., and B. Milner. 1957. Loss of recent memory after bilateral hippocampal lesions. *Journal of Neurology, Neurosurgery and Psychiatry* 20: 11–21.

Vincent Bergeron and Mohan Matthen

Shallice, T. 1988. *From Neuropsychology to Mental Structure*. New York: Cambridge University Press.
Tsao, D. Y., R. B. H. Tootell, and M. S. Livingstone. 2006. A cortical region consisting entirely of face-selective cells. *Science* 311: 670–74.
Xu, F., E. S. Spelke, and S. Goddard. 2005. Number sense in human infants. *Developmental Science* 8: 88–101.
Zihl, J., D. von Cramon, and N. Mai. 1983. Selective disturbance of movement vision after bilateral brain damage. *Brain* 106: 313–40.

212

Cognitive Modularity of Emotion

LOUIS C. CHARLAND

I. Perceptual Fixation

In a recent survey of contemporary philosophy of emotion, Ronald de Sousa states that "in recent years ... emotions have once again become the focus of vigorous interest in philosophy, as well as in other branches of cognitive science" (de Sousa 2003, 1). He then goes on to make the important observation that "in view of the proliferation of increasingly fruitful exchanges between researchers of different stripes, it is no longer useful to speak of the philosophy of emotion in isolation from the approaches of other disciplines, particularly psychology, neurology and evolutionary biology" (de Sousa 2003, 1). This last remark is particularly apt in the case of a topic like modularity and emotion, which represents an ideal opportunity for reflecting on the emerging alliance between the philosophy of emotion and emotion science. In addition to being interesting in its own right, the topic also illustrates some of the perils associated with the new alliance, as different academic traditions must adapt to interdisciplinary dialogue.

In what follows, I start by reviewing the staggered history of the concept of modularity in contemporary philosophy of emotion. This is largely a history of isolated pronouncements to the effect that there are interesting examples of modularity in emotion science. It is not always clear whether the purpose of these discussions is simply to defend a particular philosophical theory of emotion or to contribute to emotion science by providing heuristic advice that might help orient theoretical reasoning and experimental practice. Often, it appears to be a mixture of both. Even so, the overall result has been disappointing. Emotion scientists have generally failed to make any concrete experimental use of these philosophical proposals, which represents a lost opportunity for the new alliance. Philosophically, the situation is equally lackluster. The proverbial wheel is repeatedly reinvented and set to roll, with contributors regularly crossing paths without apparently knowing it.

The philosophical history of modularity and emotion contains several common promising ideas echoed by almost all contributors. However, at times it also reveals an unfortunate lack of critical discussion among participants. What is common to all contributors is the idea that there are fast and automatic *perceptual* processes in emotion that are relatively impervious to reasoning and changes in beliefs and desires (Charland 1995b; Clarke 1986; de Sousa 1987; Griffiths 1990, 1997; Hanoch 2005; Prinz 2004). What is often overlooked is the fact that there may also be *cognitive* modular factors in emotion. This last observation contradicts the reliance most philosophers have shown for the original perceptual characterization of modularity proposed by Jerry Fodor (Fodor 1983). What appears to have been missed is the fact that modularity is essentially a *representation-governed* phenomenon (Charland 1995a, 76–77; 1995b, 289–90; 1997, 567). That assumption invites us to consider the possibility that modularity in emotion might sometimes operate on a cognitive level. It also helps us to distinguish modularity, which is a representation-governed affair, from transduction, which is not (Charland 1995b, 296n5).

Let us therefore see what we can learn from the philosophical history of modularity and emotion and use those lessons to bolster the chances for an alternative – but complementary – cognitive proposal. This exercise should also contribute to the intelligibility of current perceptual proposals, which suffer because they fail to consider the representational character of modularity in sufficient detail. The stakes are high. For what is in question is nothing less than whether the explanation of how modularity figures in emotion should be carried out in psychological or physical terms, and when.

II. Representation-Governed Character of Modularity

In the context of an interdisciplinary alliance like the present one, what would a successful history of a topic like modularity and emotion look like? At the very least, there would have to be productive dialogue between the two parties involved – philosophers of emotion and emotion scientists. That has not happened. Apart from one lone exception, philosophical claims about the empirical merits of modularity do not appear to have led to any substantial empirical proposals or discussions.[1] One reason for this lack of response might be pragmatic. Many emotion scientists are simply too busy to read the relevant philosophical literature, to which they may not have easy access. Another reason may be the disconnected state of the philosophical literature on modularity. This last problem is worth pondering.

Consider, first, a recent philosophical discussion of modularity by Jesse Prinz (2004, 232–36). In this admittedly original and incisive contribution, the only reference Prinz makes to previous philosophical work on the topic is to a brief discussion by Paul Griffiths (1997, 91–98).[2] On his side, Griffiths makes no reference at all to the philosophical literature on modularity and emotion. To scientists investigating the topic, this makes it appear as if there is nothing else philosophically important written on the topic. But that is misleading. For there is in fact a wealth of valuable philosophical material on modularity and emotion, much of it relevant to emotion science.[3] Ironically,

---

1 The only exception I know of is Nico Frijda, who explicitly refers to modularity in his article, "The Laws of Emotion" (Frijda 1988).

2 There is a reference to an example in Greenspan (1988) at Prinz (2004, 235), but she never discusses "modularity" as such.

3 The first published version of a modularity hypothesis for emotion appears to be an article entitled, "Emotion: Rationality Without Cognitivism," by Canadian philosopher Stanley G. Clarke (1986). Clarke explicitly draws a connection between Fodor's modularity hypothesis and emotion theory. He explores various results in experimental psychology that seem to confirm the presence of modular factors in emotion, especially the work of Robert Zajonc (1980). Evidence gleamed from Zajonc's experimental work is marshalled in defence of a broadly perceptual theory of emotion. Of special interest is Clarke's suggestion that representation in emotional modularity and perception is probably less than propositional; a promising idea that has other precedents in emotion theory (Charland 1995a, 1995b, 1997; de Sousa 1987; Tappolet 2002). Another substantial philosophical account of the role of modularity in emotion is offered by Ronald de Sousa (de Sousa 1987). Like Clarke, his defence of the modularity hypothesis is broadly situated in the perceptual camp of the philosophy of emotion. De Sousa refines the modular hypothesis considerably, arguing that modularity in emotion is a matter of degree. He argues that, while emotions "mimic" the encapsulation of perception, they are not strictly perceptual. Hence, modularity in emotion is "moderate," a conclusion that seems to open the door to the possibility that there may be cognitive modular factors in emotion. Finally, in a more recent

that material also bears directly on the proposals made by Prinz and Griffiths. To see what has been lost in this unfortunate history of omission, let us return to the point of departure for all philosophical discussions of modularity. This is Jerry Fodor's influential book, *The Modularity of Mind* (Fodor 1983).

Fodor's modularity hypothesis is that some of the *representational* operations of mind might be relatively separate information processing "input systems" or "modules." He argues that there exists a special class of *computational* representational processes in perception that are encapsulated and typically impenetrable and impervious to changes in beliefs and desires. These special-purpose information-processing systems seem "hard-wired" and accordingly differ from the more centralized and flexible general-purpose informational processes of cognition. Importantly, as defined by Fodor, modular processes are *inferential* and defined over *mental representations* (Fodor 1983, 37–42). More specifically, the processes in question are *representation-governed* and, as such, require explanation in psychological terms (Charland 1995a 76–77; 1995b, 289–90; 1997, 566–69). No doubt, perceptual modular processes are physically instantiated. However, physical terms alone are not sufficient for their explanation, which must always include a psychological, mental representational, dimension. Finally, and crucially, the representational inferential processes effected by modules differ from transduction. Transducers encode physical information into representational form, and vice versa (Fodor 1983, 38–42; Pylyshyn 1984, 147–53; see also Charland 1995b, 296n5). But their processes are not representation-governed. Note also that, strictly speaking, transducers do not perform inferences.

Now both Prinz and Griffiths fail to mention these central defining aspects of Fodor's modularity proposal in their discussions. As a result, it is impossible to assess the real merit of their contributions to the topic. This is because too many important detailed questions about the scope and nature of psychological explanation and representation in emotional modularity are left untouched and therefore go unanswered. This seriously lessens the overall intelligibility of their respective proposals.

---

discussion of modularity, Hanoch (2005) explores the implications of emotional modularity for decision-making and the frame problem in cognitive science.

Consider Prinz. Like others before him, he proposes to treat modularity as a "cluster" concept. His point is that not all the defining criteria for modularity need to be present in order for there to be a meaningful application of the concept (Prinz 2004, 232). After a brief but innovative discussion of the relationship between modularity and plasticity, Prinz eventually argues for the very strong conclusion that "emotions are modular in the Fodorian sense" (236). The account of modularity he gives is framed in terms of his "embodied appraisal theory" of emotion (78). This is a perceptual theory of emotion. According to that theory, "emotions are perceptions, and they are used to perceive our relationship to the world" (225). Valence is crucial to Prinz's theory. He argues at length that "emotions are valent embodied appraisals" (178). On the whole, this is supposed to be a representational theory of emotion, where emotions are said to represent core relational themes in the world, while they merely "register" and "detect" inner bodily changes, without describing them (58–59, 67–69). Note that, according to Prinz, "in ordinary cases emotions are not cognitive at all" (50). Among other things, "they are not generated by acts of cognition, and they are not conceptual" (50). This would appear to rule out the possibility that there may be cognitive modular factors *in* "emotion." There are also other problems with Prinz's proposal.

Recall the distinction Prinz makes between representation on the one hand, and registration and detection on the other. That distinction raises an important question. Are registration and detection akin to what Fodor calls "transduction"? If so, that would make the kind of processes involved very different from those associated with Fodorian modules. But then how can Prinz maintain that "emotions are modular in the *Fodorian* sense" (Prinz 2004, 236; emphasis added). At the very least, the omission of any discussion of how Fodorian transduction relates to emotional modularity obscures the theoretical meaning and significance of Prinz's modularity proposal. Since the matter is so central, it is a pity Prinz was unable to build on earlier discussions on the topic, where the distinction between modules and transducers is explicitly raised and discussed (Charland 1995b; 1997; de Sousa 1987). Unfortunately, as it stands, Prinz's claim that emotions are Fodorian modules appears to contradict his claim that registration and detection, which occur *in* emotion, are *not* representational.

There is a further problem with Prinz's claim that emotions are Fodorian modules. It revolves around the notion of representation. Prinz resorts to Dretske-style semantics to ground his account of emotional representation (Prinz 2004, 52–55). However, while this theory may provide an interesting account of the intentional and semantic content of representation in emotion, it is unclear how it is supposed to capture and account for the *symbol-processing* computational character of representation in Fodorian modularity. Again, it is hard to see how Prinz can consistently maintain that emotions are Fodorian modules (Prinz 2004, 236).

Another recent defence of the claim that there is modularity in emotion is proposed by Paul Griffiths. He suggests that some basic emotional responses might be modular in Fodor's sense (Griffiths 1997, 90–96). Evidence for this claim is taken from the work of Paul Ekman, a leading defender of the view that there are basic emotions (Ekman 1992). For additional examples of emotional modularity, Griffiths turns to the work of Robert Zajonc (1980). In this case, the argument is that the fast, usually subliminal, affective responses described by Zajonc constitute plausible examples of Fodorian modularity (Griffiths 1997, 24–27, 95–97). Now Griffiths is not the only philosopher to argue that Ekman's "affect programs" provide a plausible example of modularity in emotion (Charland 1995b). Neither is he the only philosopher to highlight the relevance of the work of Zajonc to this question (Clarke 1986; Charland 1995b, 1997). What is worth noting is that these other discussions all consider the computational representational aspects of Fodor's modularity framework, which Griffiths does not. As a result, it is very difficult to assess the real merit of his contributions to the topic. Is this really Fodorian modularity? It is impossible to tell.

In his account of modularity and emotion, Griffiths does not discuss the computational and representational dimensions of Fodor's modularity proposal. Of special importance in this case is Fodor's distinction between: (a) *modules*, which are perceptual representation-governed computational mechanisms; (b) *transducers*, which are physical mechanisms that are not representation-governed; and (c), *central processors*, which are cognitive representation-governed mechanisms. Now these distinctions are directly relevant Griffiths' proposal, even though he does not mention them. The problem with this omission becomes immediately apparent when Griffiths compares modules to reflexes. Following Fodor, he states that modules are analogous to reflexes (Griffiths 1997, 94; Fodor 1983, 71–72). However, unlike Fodor, he fails to stress that "modules are also *computational* in a way that reflexes are not" (Fodor 1983, 71–72; emphasis added). The qualification is crucial. For as emphasized by other philosophical commentators on the topic, Fodorian modules are representation-governed computational mechanisms (Charland 1995a; 1995b; 1997; Clarke 1986; de Sousa 1987, 152–53). This means that the explanation of modular processes must appeal to semantically interpreted representational categories and representational principles defined over such categories.

Thus, modules *require* explanation in terms of representations and semantic-level principles (Charland 1995b, 290). This makes modules very different from transducers, which are physical mechanisms for which a physical explanation suffices (Charland 1995b, 290; de Sousa 1987, 152). Now, do reflexes involve representation? Arguably, many like the knee-jerk reflex do not. Hence, in one respect, reflexes are not at all like modules. What Griffiths fails to appreciate is that the central point at issue in the reflex analogy is where mental representation starts and stops in the explanation of an information-processing task or mechanism. As we have seen, Fodor draws a sharp line between what is psychological and representation-governed and what is physical and not representation-governed. Unfortunately, because Griffiths fails to consider this point, his discussion of modularity is fraught with ambiguity. It is therefore impossible to assess the exact philosophical meaning and significance of his modularity proposal and its supporting examples. We simply do not know where to locate the interface between transduction, modularity, and cognition. Nor do we know where representation starts and stops or when it is completely irrelevant. This is unfortunate, since in outline Griffiths' interpretation of how Fodorian modularity relates to emotion is both original and important (Charland 1995b, 298n13).

Apparently, both Prinz and Griffiths consider modularity to be an exclusively perceptual affair and that certainly is part of the spirit of the original Fodorian conception of modularity. However, because they both overlook and fail to clarify how Fodor's distinction between transduction and modularity relates to their respective proposals, their suggestions are theoretically ambiguous. Neither Prinz nor Griffiths gives us a sufficiently authentic interpretation of how exactly Fodorian modularity might apply to emotion since both fail to respect the computational spirit of Fodor's distinction between the representational and representation-governed character of modular processes, and the non-representational nature of transduction. But that distinction is absolutely central to Fodorian modularity. Since Prinz's and Griffith's proposals are theoretically ambiguous and unclear on this question, so is the experimental value of their proposals. Sadly, despite so much promise, the perceptual project for modularity in emotion appears to be at a standstill.

These disappointing results invite the question whether there might be other prospects for modularity worth exploring. The representation-governed character of Fodorian modularity offers a clue where to look for new empirical vistas. The clue points directly to the cognitive dimensions of emotion. Let us then try to make progress in this area, while perceptual defendants of modularity refine their case.

III. Depression as a Cognitive Module

Fodorian modular processes are representation-governed. They are also informationally encapsulated and cognitively impenetrable (Fodor 1983, 52–55, 71–73, 133). These two criteria play an especially prominent role in many philosophical discussions of modularity and emotion. Fodor actually offers several criteria for modularity (Fodor 1983, 41–42, 73). Philosophical authors differ in how many of these criteria they cite and discuss. In what follows, it is primarily only encapsulation and penetrability that will be at issue. The narrow selection is legitimate since the point is not so much whether Fodor's model is exactly right, but whether it leads to interesting testable theoretical and empirical questions (Charland 1997, 567). This is part of what Prinz means by his suggestion that modularity is a cluster concept (Prinz 2004, 232).

Informational encapsulation can be understood as a matter of what kinds of representations a system has access to in effecting its computations (Charland 1997, 567). Cognitive penetrability can be understood as a matter of whether or not a system's operations are susceptible to alteration in light of an organism's changing beliefs and desires (Charland 1997, 567). Now, as Prinz correctly notes, "modularity is consistent with some degree of plasticity" (Prinz 2004, 234). That means it is compatible with some degree of emotional change. Thus, emotional change and learning can modify how emotional modules develop into modules, and how they come and cease to function as modules. That modularity can come and go in this way does not constitute evidence there can be no modularity in emotion. It is simply part of the richness of the concept. Depression is a good example of an emotional disorder where such a transition takes place. While we may not presently understand how exactly the pathologies that underlie depression come to constrain thoughts and feelings in the way they do, once those thoughts and feelings get constrained in the manner that is considered characteristic of depression, the result is something that looks very much like a module. However, this kind of modularity may operate at different levels.

Depression is often considered to be a mood disorder, a disorder in feeling or "affect." In that respect, it provides an interesting example of modularity in the *feeling* dimension of emotion (Charland 1995b). However, depression is also often considered to be a cognitive disorder, a disorder in thinking. In that respect, it provides an interesting example of modularity in the *cognitive* dimension of emotion (Charland 1995a). This is not the place to adjudicate between these two alternative views, which are in any case probably compatible. It is sufficient for our purposes that both represent plausible options in the relevant literature. That said, in what follows it is the *cognitive* aspects of depression that will concern us.

Examined from a cognitive point of view, depression provides an interesting example of what cognitive modularity in emotion might look like. As noted above, while the processes responsible for the onset and recovery from depression may exhibit some degree of plasticity, there are periods – sometimes lengthy ones – when depression assumes the character of a cognitive module. A good theoretical formulation and defence of this hypothesis can be found in Aaron Beck's well-known cognitive theory of depression.

As the title of one of his major works indicates, Beck is interested in "Cognitive Therapy and the Emotional Disorders" (Beck 1976). One such "emotional disorder" is depression (Beck 1979).[4] Beck's

---

4 De Sousa (1987) refers to depression as an emotion. Certainly for Beck (1967), it is a cognitive emotional phenomenon; one of the "emotional disorders" (Beck 1979). See also (Shorter 2005, 78).

cognitive theory of depression "postulates three specific concepts to explain the psychological substrate of depression: (1) the cognitive triad, (2) schemas, and (3) cognitive errors (faulty information processing)" (Beck 1979, 10). The cognitive triad is really the heart of Beck's theory. It consists of: (1) a patient's negative view of his or her self; (2) a general tendency to interpret present circumstances negatively; and (3) a negative view of the future (11). The main hypothesis of the theory is that in depression this triad gets "hardwired" into the cognitive architecture of an individual's cognitive system. This results in a representational restructuring of that system's functioning: notably, the deployment of distinctly depressive kinds of interpretive schemas and various related modes of faulty reasoning (Beck 1967, 282–87; 1979, 14–15). According to Beck, one of the chief consequences of the wiring of this depressive-axiomatic triad into an individual's cognitive system is an idiosyncratic constriction and distortion in that individual's cognitive field. If Beck is correct, then there is a very literal sense in which the depressed individual ends up suffering the burdens of an immured and hopeless world. Echoing Wittgenstein, there is a very real sense in which the world of the sad man is different from that of the happy one.

So, according to Beck, depression is sometimes best characterized as a disorder in information processing of a representational sort. Diagnosis, prognosis, and treatment all involve trying to explain the thoughts and behaviour of depressed patients. That in turn requires adverting to a specialized nomological class of depressive cognitive principles and a corresponding specialized domain of cognitive representational mental states. Beck calls the representational states involved in depression "depressive cognitions" (Beck 1967, 232, 237). In effect, what these depressive cognitions and the principles that govern them amount to is a distinct, specialized, informationally encapsulated cognitive representational subsystem that is not easily cognitively penetrable.

Thus, in its cognitive aspects, depression would appear to constitute a plausible and interesting example of what might count as a cognitive emotional module. Another class of examples can be constructed from the literature on "cognitive appraisal" theories of emotion (Greenberg and Safran 1987). In that literature, primary cognitive appraisals that operate very much in the manner of modules are said to underlie the "dramatic plots" and "schemas" that define the distinct representation-governed character of basic emotions (Lazarus 1991; Lazarus and Lazarus 1993; Scherer et al. 2001). The fact that many emotions have a "cognitive structure" that can be computationally modeled provides another interesting example of what cognitive modularity in emotion might look like. For example, the philosopher Robert M. Gordon has developed a computer program designed to mimic the inferences that are typical of fear (Gordon 1987). It exploits the inferential laws and principles that cognitively define the "logic" of fear. On this kind of view, each emotion is defined by its own special "logic" or characteristic patterns of cognitive appraisal. Without that "logic," the project of computationally modelling the workings of emotion would be impossible. Yet this is something that can obviously be done (Gadanho and Hallam 2001; Minsky 2006).

No doubt, there are numerous ways to explore the logic of the inferential processes in emotion and depression. What is interesting about the Fodorian modularity hypothesis in its application to depression, and more widely to emotion and emotional pathology, is that it offers a bold and falsifiable conjecture about *how* to understand these inferential processes; notably, in a *representational computational symbol-processing* way. The aim of this article is not to dismiss other alternatives, but to develop this particular one as a working hypothesis. Of course, whether or not and to what degree the processes and underlying mechanisms in these examples are truly informationally encapsulated and cognitively impenetrable is an interesting empirical question. Are the modules in question "virtual" or are they "hard wired" into neurophysiological processes and mechanisms? First we must formulate and ask such questions in order to investigate. The point is that these are interesting questions to ask, and they follow from adopting a more or less strict Fodorian modularity perspective as a working hypothesis.

The distinction between transduction and modularity is especially relevant to our project. It is a core defining feature of Fodor's overall model of the organization of mind, and it needs to be investigated in the domain of emotion and emotional disorders. It may of course turn out that there are better ways to investigate these phenomena. In that case, the empirical refutation of the relevant claims would mark a scientific advance. Still, that does not negate the fact – and it is a fact

– that, in their cognitive dimensions, the emotions can be computationally modelled along the representation-governed lines that Fodor suggests for perception.

Admittedly, at first sight, it might appear difficult to consistently make sense of the idea that depression and other emotional phenomena might at times function like cognitive modules of a strict Fodorian sort. First of all, Fodorian modularity has essentially to do with perception and not cognition. In response to this objection, it can be noted that the project of extending Fodorian modularity to cognition is already underway, with some measure of success, at least if gauged by the number of such discussions (Carruthers 2003). Therefore, this problem need not detain us. A more serious objection lies on the emotion side of the equation. This is that emotions are often thought of as essentially perceptual in nature, meaning that they cannot possibly be cognitive modules. However, it is by no means agreed that emotions are perceptual. In fact, there exist a plethora of cognitive theories of emotion which in some important respects lend themselves nicely to a modularity perspective. Hence, insofar as emotions are cognitive phenomena – and many emotion theorists believe they are – there is no a priori reason to exclude them from the reaches of a more cognitive variety of Fodorian modularity.

But there are other problems. One is that emotions often exhibit cognitive penetrability, since they change in light of fluctuations in beliefs and desires. That would appear to imply that emotions are poor candidates for Fodorian modules, which by definition are impenetrable to such changes. But here the facts ask that we be nuanced. Many cognitive theorists of emotion agree that emotions are governed by a special logic of their own, where each paradigmatic case of emotion has its own special defining script or dramatic plot (Lazarus 1991), or its own defining inferential "cognitive structure" (Gordon 1987). In that respect, emotions satisfy both the representational and representation-governed requirements of Fodorian modularity: they are inferential computational cognitive structures or programs of a representational sort. Viewed in that way, the various regularities and inferential schemas associated with different emotions can be logically captured and explained by alluding to propositional, or perhaps in some cases sub-propositional, conceptual representational terms (Charland 1995b). How and to what extent the representational contents of these putative emotion modules items are "shallow" or "non-conceptual" is a matter to be investigated. And of course how to define "cognition" is another matter that it is impossible to settle without looking at specific proposals case by case. Yet certainly there is no a priori reason to suppose that representation in emotion cannot be mixed; that is, both "conceptual" and "non-conceptual," or both "propositional" and "sub-propositional."

Finally, there is the question of cognitive penetrability. One suggestion here may be that impenetrability to beliefs and desires is simply a variable feature of emotion, which may be turned on or off. Likewise with encapsulation. For example, in learning and other conditions, emotions exhibit penetrability. However, there are cases where just the opposite is true; for example, when emotional planning and responses are frozen by pathology (Charland 2006). Thus, emotional phobias and neuroses may be considered examples of emotional modules. The purpose of cognitive therapy in this case is to restore flexibility and normal penetrability to the emotional system. In such cases it is also possible to envision a role for encapsulation. This is because in emotional pathology, various aspects of emotions and their associated processes can become closed to the influence of outside information, or artificially limited to only certain kinds of inputs. The argument advanced here is that a helpful way to approach these examples of emotional pathology is through the intermediary of modularity. Such pathologies are possible because the emotional system is susceptible to modularity. Thus we see pathologies of anger, fear, jealousy, and even love, which it is the purpose of therapy to undo. There are important resemblances here with depression, our opening example of an emotional disturbance that exhibits modularity.

IV. Conclusion

The philosophical case for perceptual modularity in emotion appears to be progressing, perhaps, but very slowly. Further dialogue and critical discussion are needed before more promising philosophical proposals can be delivered to emotion scientists for empirical elaboration and testing. One area of investigation that especially requires attention is the hypothesis that modularity is a representation-governed phenomenon. That suggestion has not been adequately dealt with in the philosophical literature on modularity, leading to ambiguities that make it difficult to assess the merit of some recent contributions to the topic. At the same time, the putative representation-governed character of modularity invites us to consider other possible applications of the modularity concept in emotion.

One promising cognitive application of the modularity concept in emotion is depression. Another is the suggestion that there may be cognitive modular aspects in the appraisal and response mechanisms that govern the working of basic emotions (Charland 1995b; Griffiths 1990, 1997). Finally, there is also the fact that many emotions seem to have a core cognitive structure that can be computational modelled (Gordon 1987). In each of these cases, careful attention must be paid to which factors in emotional functioning count as modular, and when. We must be especially careful to guard against the true but banal suggestion that there are sometimes fast and automatic processes in emotion that are relatively impermeable to cognitive control. Evidently, this is a wheel it is easy to reinvent. It is also easy to think we are making progress as we spin our philosophical wheels in mid-air. Let us therefore endeavour to work more closely together and keep our philosophical inquiries close to the rough ground!

References

Beck, A. T. 1967. *Depression: Clinical, Experimental, and Theoretical Aspects.* New York: Harper & Row.

Beck, A. T. 1976. *Cognitive Theory and the Emotional Disorders.* New York: Meridian.

Beck, A. T. 1979. *Cognitive Theory of Depression.* New York: Guilford Press.

Carruthers, P. 2003. The mind is a system of modules shaped by natural selection. In *Contemporary Debates in the Philosophy of Science,* ed. C. Hitchcock, 293–311. Oxford: Blackwell.

Charland, L. C. 1995a. Emotion as a natural kind: Towards a computational foundation for emotion theory. *Philosophical Psychology* 8(1): 59–84.

Charland, L. C. 1995b. Feeling and representing: Computational theory and the modularity of affect. *Synthese* 105: 273–301.

Charland, L. C. 1997. Reconciling cognitive and perceptual theories of emotion: A representational proposal. *Philosophy of Science* 64: 555–79.

Charland, L. C. 2006. La psychopathologie et le statut d'espèce naturelle de l'émotion. *Philosophiques* 3(1): 217–30.

Clarke, S. G. 1986. Emotions: Rationality without cognitivism. *Dialogue* 25: 663–74.

de Sousa, R. 1987. *The Rationality of Emotion.* Cambridge (Mass.): MIT Press.

de Sousa, R. 2003. Emotion. *The Stanford Encyclopedia of Philosophy* (Spring 2003 ed.), ed. E. N. Zalta. http://plato.stanford.edu/archives/spr2003/entries/emotion.

Ekman, P. 1992. Are there basic emotions? *Psychological Review* 99(3): 550–53.

Fodor, J. 1983. *The Modularity of Mind.* Cambridge (Mass.): MIT Press.

Frijda, N. 1988. The laws of emotion. *American Psychologist* 1: 115–34.

Gadanho, S. C., and J. Hallam. 2001. Robot learning driven by emotions. *Adaptive Behavior* 9(1): 42–64.

Gordon, R. M. 1987. *The Cognitive Structure of Emotion.* Cambridge: Cambridge University Press.

Greenberg, L. S., and J. D. Safran. 1987. *Emotion in Psychotherapy: Affect, Cognition, and the Process of Change.* New York: Guilford Press.

Greenspan, P. 1988. *Emotions and Reasons: An Inquiry into Emotional Justification.* New York: Routledge, Chapman and Hall.

Griffiths, P. E. 1990. Modularity and the psychoevolutionary theory of emotion. *Biology and Philosophy* 5(2): 175–96.

Griffiths, P. E. 1997. *What Emotions Really Are: The Problem of Psychological Categories.* Chicago: University of Chicago Press.

Hanoch, Y. 2005. One theory to fit them all: The search hypothesis for emotion revisited. *British Journal for the Philosophy of Science* 56: 135–45.

Lazarus, R. 1991. *Emotion and Adaptation.* Oxford: Oxford University Press.

Lazarus, R., and B. Lazarus. 1993. *Passion and Reason: Making Sense of Our Emotions.* Oxford: Oxford University Press.

Minsky, M. 2006. *The Emotion Machine: Commonsense Thinking, Artificial Intelligence, and the Future of the Human Mind.* New York: Simon & Shuster.

Prinz, J. 2004. *Gut Reactions: A Perceptual Theory of Emotion.* Oxford: Oxford University Press.

Pylyshyn, Z. W. 1984. *Computation and Cognition: Toward a Foundation for Cognitive Science.* Cambridge (Mass.): MIT Press.

Scherer, K., A. Schorr, and T. Johnstone. 2001. *Appraisal Processes in Emotion.* Oxford: Oxford University Press.

Shorter, E. 2005. *Historical Dictionary of Psychiatry*. Oxford: Oxford University Press.

Tappolet, C. 2002. Long term emotions and emotional experiences in the explanation of action. *European Review of Philosophy* 5.

Zajonc, R. B. 1980. Feeling and thinking: Preferences need no inferences. *American Psychologist* 35: 151–75.

4. The Modularity of Particular Emotion Types

CANADIAN JOURNAL OF PHILOSOPHY
Supplementary Volume 32

Shame and Other Cases of Modularity without Modules[1]

RUWEN OGIEN

On the surface, self-centred emotions like shame or pride are related to subtle understandings of one's own identity and relevant objects (Taylor 1985; Ben Ze'ev 2000). Changes of beliefs about these objects often result in changes in the related emotions.

If I am very proud that, on the first of April, I won the Jacques Chirac Prize for moral philosophy and then realize that it was just an April Fool's joke, my pride will probably vanish. I will probably be ashamed that I believed it. Cases like this support the idea that having beliefs is a necessary condition for feeling pride or shame.

If this is true and if we endorse Jerry Fodor's views about modularity, it follows that shame can't be modular because, according to these views, no beliefs or other central mental processes are supposed to be involved in the operation of modules (Fodor 1983). Further, contempt, derision, or avoidance are supposed to be typical causes of shame, but they may trigger other emotions as well: hatred, anger, self-pity, or sadness, etc. Shame is supposed to result in withdrawal behaviour, hiding, disappearing, or even suicide in the most depressing cases, but it may as well result in attempts to reconstruct or improve oneself or in aggression against others, etc. (Elster 1999). Due to its disjunctive form, the scenario of complex emotions like shame is not totally predictable.

---

1 Many thanks to Christine Tappolet, Luc Faucher and two anonymous referees for their helpful remarks on the first draft of this paper, and many other thanks to Lithe Sebesta for her very generous help in its final editing.

Again, if this is true, and if we endorse Jerry Fodor's views about modularity, it follows that shame can't be modular because, according to these views, modularity implies automaticity, that is, a predictable response of the kind we have in reflex reactions (Fodor 1983, 52–64).

In the specialized literature, we find standard objections to these stories, supporting the view that shame and other emotions of this kind could be modular after all. Some of these objections are empirical. For example, it seems that very young children can be ashamed or exhibit symptoms of shame (Deigh 1992). If this is true, then it is not the case that shame demands subtle understanding of one's identity and clear consciousness of possible objects. Another empirical objection reminds us that typical expressions of shame like blushing are beyond our control. Other objections are of a more conceptual nature. Some suggest that representations governing shame do not deserve the name "judgment," which sounds too conscious and considered. It would be more appropriate to call them "appraisals" or "proto-representations," for instance (Griffiths 2003). Others tell us that the relation between shame and its typical causes and its typical behaviour is such that it rules out the possibility of different scenarios. What we call "shame" is just what is triggered by a specific cause, say the feeling that we have failed to live up to an ideal, and it results in specific behavioural tendencies, such as hiding or disappearing. Whatever does not fit this pattern can't be called "shame."[2]

I think that these standard empirical and conceptual objections are not irrelevant and may support the view that at least some forms or some aspects of shame are modular, even on Fodor's conception of modularity. I could add that I have personally tried to defend some of them (Ogien 2002), in order to reject the mainstream intellectualist view of the distinction between guilt and shame, advocated by John Rawls (1990), among many others.

In this paper I explore a totally different route and raise non-standard objections to the idea that shame could not possibly be modular.

---

2 It could be claimed, also, that if fear or shame produces many kinds of different actions, it is because different kinds of things are covered under these names. It could be that there are modules of fear or shame, but more fine-grained than common language would have us believe. I owe this objection to Christine Tappolet and Luc Faucher.

These objections aren't based on what can be called the "phenomenology of shame" (though I will say something on the subject) but on the *epistemology of modularity*.

I will borrow from the debate between supporters of Fodorian modularity and defenders of other, broader or less demanding, conceptions of modularity. What I have in mind here are conceptions advocated by evolutionary psychologists like Steven Pinker (1997) and evolutionary anthropologists like Scott Atran (2001), Dan Sperber (1996, 2002), Lawrence A. Hirschfeld (1994), Leda Cosmides and John Tooby (1989, 1992), according to which modules are not encapsulated processors, categorically sealed off from information that could be relevant to them, but functional subsystems dedicated to specific tasks, and coming in different shapes with different properties, *depending on the task.*

According to these conceptions, what is needed for something to qualify as "modular" is mainly *domain-specificity;* that is, being sensitive to a limited range of stimuli and exhibiting a limited range of responses.

Within this theoretical framework, something can be both conceptual *and* modular. Overused examples in the specialized literature are folk biology, folk physics, and folk psychology, or the so-called "cheater-detection module," which is supposed to be a cognitive mechanism specially dedicated to the perception of certain forms of social exchange.

Within this theoretical framework, something can be unpredictable or not highly predictable *and* modular. Modules, as functional subsystems, can simply limit the range of possible responses without dictating them.

Within this theoretical framework, nothing would prevent us from claiming that, even if some central mental processes are involved in shame, and even if the scenario of shame is not linear, it does not follow that shame cannot be modular.

Among the many benefits of analyzing shame along these lines is that it helps us see why it is not contradictory to believe, as some philosophers do, that shame and other emotions of the same kind can be both modular and likely to be controlled or educated (Goldie 2000).

If shame, guilt, or pride, etc., do not follow a linear pattern, displaying strict regularity or automaticity as well as strict predictability, as far as the relations between their cognitive antecedents and their action tendencies are concerned, it does not seem impossible to select and reinforce one route over another in the disjunctive scenario of these emotions, by explaining, advising, approving or disapproving, threatening, or rewarding.

In raising these different points, I have no intention to advertise for evolutionary psychology, about which I am quite skeptical, for reasons I will present later. I just want to stress that in the debate over the modularity of emotions we have more than one option open to us. We don't have to debate only within the Fodorian framework.

My plan is as follows: I start with a characterization of shame intended to underline its cognitive features and its openness, as far as its causal history is concerned. Then, I limit myself to two questions:

1. If shame necessarily involves beliefs, does that rule out the possibility of it being modular?
2. If shame does not display strict regularity or predictability, as far as the relations between its cognitive antecedents and its action tendencies are concerned, does that rule out the possibility of it being modular?

To both these questions, my answer will be "no." Nevertheless, my general conclusion will not be as straightforward as it may seem. What I am claiming, after all, is that there are different answers to whether complex self-centred emotions like shame or pride can depend on the global properties of belief systems and still be modular, or can be non-automatic and still be modular, and that this depends on the theory of modularity to which one is committed. From Fodor's point of view, they cannot; from Pinker's (and some others') they can.

I am not sure that such a relative conclusion is as informative as one could expect, though it seems to me of some interest in clarifying the present state of the debate. In fact, this paper serves a very basic and limited conceptual point. Before any attempt to check empirically whether shame is modular or not, we must make clear what we mean by "shame" and by "modular." Let's start with "shame."

I. Shame

For Jon Elster, Aristotle's account of emotions is still valuable, not only for what it says about the place of emotions in Greek political life, but for the light it throws on the emotions in general (Elster 1999, 52). Aristotle anticipated modern thinking about emotions by classifying them according to six dimensions or features that are still considered characteristic.

In Aristotle's taxonomy, each emotion has its specific conditions of arousal, its specific cognitive antecedents, its specific valence (that is, its specific balance of pleasure and pain), its specific intentional objects, its specific physiological expressions, and its specific action tendencies. Characterizing a specific emotion amounts to listing all these specific features. I will concentrate on cognitive antecedents and action tendencies.

In Aristotle's writings, anger, for example, is supposed to be triggered by an undeserved slight and, in turn, to trigger the desire for revenge. More abstractly, anger is supposed to be induced or caused by our perception that someone has intentionally and unjustly frustrated some of our desires. But anger can also be triggered by non-intentional wish-frustration. One can be angry because one feels poor, weak, or sick, or in other undesirable states that have not necessarily been maliciously induced by some other person. Other causes of anger are stronger than just intentional or non-intentional wish-frustration. Anger can be caused by the perception of undeserved attempts to shame or humiliate, whether directed towards us or others. Being exposed to these slights in front of persons we admire or who admire us, or in front of rivals, is a typical condition of arousal of anger. Now, all this may as well cause shame or humiliation or hatred. So, even if it is possible to point to some typical causes and effects of anger, the causes of anger are in fact multiple, they are more or less effective, their operation depends on certain dispositions and environmental conditions, and they are not systematically accompanied by the same effects.

On shame, Aristotle is not as clear, nor as complete, and Elster has tried to fill the gaps in order to draw a picture along the same lines by borrowing heavily from what I would call the "standard view of the distinction between shame and guilt," as it has been developed in contemporary writings in philosophy and psychology, by Gabriele

Taylor (1985), John Rawls (1990), Bernard Williams (1993), and Allan Gibbard (1990), among many others (Morris 1976, 1987; Barrett et al. 1993; D'Arms and Jacobson 1994; Wollheim 1999).

On this basis, Elster assumes the following (1999, 145–64):

1. Shame is triggered by derision, avoidance, the contemptuous or disgusted disapproval by others of something one has done. By contrast, in guilt, the disapproval is supposed to take the form of anger, resentment, indignation and not of derision, avoidance, contempt, or disgust.

2. There is supposed to be an internal relation between the antecedent and the response. In shame the disapproval takes the form of contempt, disgust, avoidance, derision, and it attaches to the totality of the person rather than to the act; in guilt, the disapproval takes the form of anger or indignation and it attaches to the act only. In other words, because of its specific antecedents, shame is supposed to be global rather than behavioural, and guilt, behavioural rather than global. Here is how Elster expresses this: "In shame one thinks of oneself as a bad person, not simply as someone who did a bad thing" (1999, 151). To paraphrase Elster, one could add: "In guilt, one thinks of oneself as someone who did a bad thing, not as a bad person."

3. Another point stressed in the standard view endorsed by Elster is that shame needs, as guilt does not need, the presence of others. In guilt, we face the inner voice of our own consciousness, whereas in shame we have to face the contemptuous or sarcastic eyes of the other.

4. Finally, as far as typical causes and conditions are concerned, and again according to the standard view endorsed by Elster, shame is supposed to be triggered by the feeling that one did not live up to one's ideals, whereas guilt is induced by the feeling that one has not respected important social or moral rules.

What about action tendencies now?

5. According to the standard view, the basic action tendency of shame is to hide, to run away, to shrink, to avoid being seen. Elster stresses that if one cannot run away, suicide may be the

only solution. Here, as in other parts of his analysis, he shows an interesting psychological tendency to dramatize the personal impact of shame. More importantly, Elster notes that there are many other possible reactions to shame than to hide or to commit suicide (Elster 1999, 153). Quoting Bernard Williams, he mentions the possibility that shame induces attempts to reconstruct or improve oneself (Williams 1993).[3] Quoting a psychologist, Elster mentions the possibility that shame induces aggression. The mechanism would be the following: "By putting another down, one may attempt defensively to repair and in comparison to raise up one's shattered sense of self-worth" (Elster 1999, 153). By contrast, the basic action tendency of guilt is to face the wrong done, not to run away from it, or a tendency to make repairs: to undo the wrong one has caused, to confess, preferably to the person one has harmed. But guilt might as well result in an impulse to harm oneself, so as to match the harm one has done to others, and in some magical way to take the sting out of it. If the latter is true, the contrast between shame and guilt would appear weaker than is usually presented.

In general, I think that we should remain skeptical about the standard philosophical criteria that are supposed to clarify the contrast between shame and guilt. Take for example these two sentences:

"I am ashamed that I opened my girlfriend's diary and read a few pages from it."

"I am ashamed that I followed my girlfriend to check whom she was meeting."

It seems to me that both these sentences, which could have been borrowed from Marcel Proust (in spirit, if not in form), make sense. And it also seems to me that in both cases, it is appropriate to say "I am ashamed" and not "I feel guilty," while it does not follow that I think of myself as a "bad person." Why couldn't I say that I am ashamed

---

3 For the record, this action tendency is supposed to be crucial for evolutionary reasons in Allan Gibbard's account of shame (1990).

that I did a bad thing, period, without drawing any global conclusion about the kind of person that I am? Why couldn't I say that my shame was induced by the thought that I had broken an important social or moral rule and not that I failed to live up to my ideals? Why couldn't I say that in cases like these, I can be ashamed without being seen by another person?

These simple examples show, or so it seems to me, that shame does not need global inferences about the kind of person one is, that shame can be triggered by the breaking of moral rules and not necessarily by the thought of not living up to one's ideals, and that being seen is not a necessary condition of shame.

If this is right, we may ask whether the standard philosophical criteria for opposing shame and guilt are as good as they are supposed to be.

Anyhow, as far as modularity is concerned, these not untypical examples show that complex social behaviour, such as consciousness of breaking important moral or social rules and detection of complex social exchanges like relations of avoidance or contempt, are among the typical conditions of shame. It is because the notion of shame seems to presuppose a capacity to detect certain kinds of social exchange (like avoidance or contempt) that the debate about the existence of so-called "cheater-detection-modules" will be crucial to my account.

The discussion of action tendencies in the standard view is also highly questionable, but for other reasons. According to the standard view, guilt induces confession and reparation, and shame induces hiding or personal reformation. Actually, the status of these sorts of statements is not clear. They can be understood either as conceptual or as empirical, that is, either as defining features of shame or guilt or as probable outcomes given certain initial conditions, shame being then a kind of dependent or intermediary variable in a causal model.

It is hard to tell how Elster's statements should be viewed. For instance, he presents a list of possible empirical action tendencies induced by shame, and ends by telling us that the impulse to run away is the primary action tendency of shame. Again, what is the nature of this statement? Is it an empirical statement about the most probable outcome of shame or a conceptual statement about a defining feature of shame?

In any case, in the second part of my paper, I will focus on the empirical reading of the statement because what I am interested in is the predictability of shame. If, as I have suggested, shame and other emotions are to be understood as modular, they must be considered as automatic outcomes given certain initial conditions, or as dependent or intermediary variables in a causal model.

So is shame automatically associated with a typical cognitive antecedent? Does it result automatically in typical action tendencies?

There are several reasons, using an empirical reading of Elster, to believe this is not the case. His discussion shows that in not untypical cases, the scenario of shame is not predictable.

I have discussed the meaning of "shame" as opposed to "guilt." I focused on its cognitive components and its unpredictability.

Now, does the possibility that some forms of shame at least are partly conceptual and that the scenario of shame is not perfectly predictable rule out the idea that shame could be modular?

At first glance – and from Fodor's point of view – it seems to be the case. Shame, as I have described it, can't possibly be modular. But Fodor's view is not the only one we find on the market about modularity. What are the alternative accounts?

II. Conceptuality and Modularity

Many philosophers who try to understand the structure and functions of our emotions have adopted what could be called a "minimal cognitive framework."[4]

By this I mean an account of our emotions that contrasts them with sensations, on the grounds that emotions, and not sensations, are intentional and rationally assessable. It makes sense to ask what our emotion of fear is about, whether it is *about* spiders, or snakes, or stepmothers. But it does not make sense to ask what our sensation of pain is about, whether it is *about* the stomach or the liver. What makes sense, rather, is to ask *where* we feel pain, whether *in* the stomach or *in* the liver. It makes sense to ask whether our fear of very little spiders is

---

4 For this point, I am indebted to Christine Tappolet, The Irrationality of Emotions (unpublished). See also Ronald de Sousa (1987); Jesse Prinz (2003); D'Arms and Jacobson (2003); and John Deigh (2004).

reasonable (for giant spiders the question makes less sense), but not if our tooth pain is "reasonable."

Of course, some philosophers would deny that emotions are necessarily intentional or rationally assessable. Since the question whether emotions are a natural kind, with clear-cut borders and core common features, is still open, it is not surprising that one can find a thing that is currently called an "emotion" and that is not intentional (Faucher 1999).

The overused example is anxiety. Moods like depression or elation are also often offered as examples. But, by and large, philosophers have adopted this minimal cognitive framework for emotions. It does not mean, of course, that they all agree about the structure and functions of emotions. They wouldn't be philosophers if they did. They just unite, more or less, about intentionality and rational assessment. About many others subjects, they divide.

The most important or interesting divide seems to be between conceptualists and non-conceptualists, a division that is orthogonal to the cognitivist/non-cognitivist division.

On the one side, for non-conceptualists, one can sense danger without having the concept of danger, and one's fear might resist one's best judgment that there is no danger. This brings emotion close to perception while keeping it apart from sensations. Leaning on examples borrowed from the literature on perceptual illusions, with, on the front line, the famous Müller-Lyer experiment, they claim that emotions have non-conceptual content, that they are as independent from beliefs as these perceptual illusions.

Conceptualists, on the other hand, are, one could say, more demanding. For them, in order to perceive something as dangerous, one needs to have a minimal conceptual grasp of what a danger is. To be able to specify fear among other members of the family of emotions to which fear belongs, such as horror and disgust, one needs to have some concept of what differentiates them.

Formally, conceptualists suggest that a proper account of emotional states should represent them as propositional attitudes expressed by complex sentences containing a "that" clause, as in "I am proud *that* I did not speak too much at this dinner" or "I am ashamed *that* I spoke too much at this dinner," rather than as sentences with noun phrases as direct objects as in "Bianca fears spiders."

I will not enter into the details of the debate between conceptualists and non-conceptualists.[5] I am merely interested in restating that in the philosophy of emotions the great divide is not between cognitivists and non-cognitivists since most of those who are interested in emotions take them to be intentional and rationally assessable, and therefore are cognitivists in this minimal sense. It is between conceptualists and non-conceptualists.

I am interested in this second divide because, in most cases, those who conceive of emotions as non-conceptual are also those who are ready to buy the idea that they are modular. Put another way, for non-conceptualists, "the modularity of emotions" might just be another name for "the non-conceptual character of emotions."

My main point will be that this equivalence does not hold. Something can be conceptual or partly conceptual *and* modular. There can be conceptual modules, on certain accounts of modularity at least.

The best available example of this idea is called (in the specialized literature) the "cheater-detection module." It is supposed to be more conceptual than perceptual, but as domain-specific as a natural perceptual mechanism.

I will insist on the case of the cheater-detection module and not on other cases of supposed conceptual modules like folk physics or folk psychology because shame seems to require, in some not untypical cases, as I stressed in its description, detection of certain forms of social exchange, say, attempts to put down or humiliate, relations of avoidance, or contempt. And the debate around the possibility of a cheater-detection module is precisely about the possibility of calling "modular" our capacity to detect specific forms of social exchanges.

III. Could Shame Possibly Be a "Conceptual Module"?

Those who believe that we are naturally endowed with a "cheater-detection module" are usually inclined to claim that it has been scientifically established by Wason's famous experiment, the "card-selection task," as it is usually called. In spite of Fodor's sarcastic remarks

---

5 See, for example, John Deigh (1994) for criticisms of the propositional analysis of emotions and other typical conceptualist devices.

about the overexploitation of this test by evolutionary psychologists and Dan Sperber's sharp criticisms of its methodology, it is still considered the best proof that domain-specific conceptual capacities, reasoning mechanisms or modules do really exist (Botterill and Carruthers 1999; Garfield 1994; Fodor 2000; Cosmides 1989; Cosmides and Tooby 1992; Sperber et al. 1995).

I won't present the test in its technicalities (Botterill and Carruthers 1999 is quite good on this account). I will simply try to extract its essential idea.

In fact, the "cheater-detection module" hypothesis can be understood as a tool against Fodor's view of the human mind. Fodor believes that we can't have thinking or reasoning modules, that is, thinking or reasoning domain-specific mechanisms. This is exactly what some evolutionary psychologists deny. Why?

The story is quite long and complicated. I will try to make it as short and simple as possible.

Those who are interested in natural reasoning know that there is a considerable body of evidence that shows that people perform poorly on many reasoning tasks. It seems that we are specially weak in reasoning about probabilities. What the Wason card-selection task shows, supposedly, is that we are quite bad at conditional reasoning as well. In the test, subjects are presented four cards which are said to have letters on one side and numbers on the other side but of which they can only see one face. Two of the cards show letters A and B, and two others, numbers 5 and 8. Subjects are asked: "Indicate which cards you need to turn over in order to decide whether it is true, for these cards, that if there is an A on one side of the card, then there is a 5 on the other. You should select only those cards which it is essential to turn over." In some interpretations, the test is supposed to check our capacity to apply in everyday thinking the rule "a conditional is false just in case the antecedent is true and the consequent false." We should only pick cards according to the rule. But even if we know the rule, we have great difficulties applying it. About 75 to 90 per cent of the subjects fail to make the correct selection. Most people pick the card showing A and the card showing 5, or only the card showing A. But the correct selection is the card showing A and the card showing 8, because only these cards "are potential falsifiers of the conditional 'If there an A on one side of the card, then there is a 5 on the other'"

(Botterill and Carruthers 1999, 109–110). So don't feel bad if you failed, or didn't even get what exactly the test is about!

The most interesting element is that changing some details of the task can dramatically improve the performances. When presented with what is called a "deontic" or "normative conditional" like "If anyone is drinking alcohol, then they must be over 18 years of age," subjects perform a lot better. Up to 75 per cent of the subjects give the right answer.

In order to explain this dramatic improvement in performance, evolutionary psychologists Leda Cosmides and John Tooby (1992) have postulated that we have a specialized cognitive mechanism for normative conditionals of the form "If you have received the benefits, you must pay the costs" or "If you have paid the costs, you should receive the benefits" and nothing of the kind for descriptive conditionals.

This reasoning mechanism is domain-specific: it is triggered by awareness of social behaviour only. It functions rapidly, automatically. It is probably hard-wired. It is called a "cheater-detection module" because it is supposed to help us spot "free riders," people who take the benefits without paying the costs. This capacity to detect cheaters rapidly and automatically is said to be critical for species like ours, which are so dependent on social cooperation.

The important point, for what concerns us, is that, according to Cosmides and Tooby, the cheater-detection module functions exactly like a perceptual module, but is not peripheral: it belongs, in Fodor's terms, to the central system.

Of course, many objections have been raised against this speculation. Some have tried to show that it is possible to explain why we are better at normative conditionals without postulating such a domain-specific cognitive capacity.

But again, what concerns and interests us is this speculative conclusion, and more precisely the hypothesis that domain-specific reasoning mechanisms exist. Reasoning shouldn't be thought of as a general, uniform, capacity. We are better in the specific domain of conditional normative reasoning than in the domain of conditional descriptive reasoning.

What does Fodor think of all this? Well, part of his *The Mind Doesn't Work That Way* (2000) concerns speculations about cognitive modules in general and the "cheater-detection module," in particular.

According to Fodor, there is no such thing as a "cheater-detection module," because, in order to detect a cheater, we have to be able to tell social exchanges from other forms of behaviour, and, in order to do this, some central mental processes must be involved, about which we know nothing at this stage.

In a recent exchange with Steven Pinker, he expresses this idea in his well-known and not-too-moderate style: "Nobody has any idea of what kind of cerebration is required to figuring out which distal stimulations are social exchanges" (Fodor 2005).

But for Pinker, Fodor's reasons for this categorical rejection are unclear. According to him, it is untrue that we have absolutely no idea about what happens when one recognizes a social exchange. In general, "people automatically interpret certain patterns of moving dots on a screen as agents that seek to help or to hurt others" (Pinker 2005a, 17). And he adds: "Of course spatio-temporal categories are not the only or even the primary way that people recognize cognitive domains such as social exchange" (Pinker 2005a, 17). He suggests that part of the input of a subsystem like perception of social exchange comes from the output of another subsystem. "Perhaps the social exchange system is fed by an intuitive psychology that infers people's goals from their behavior" (Pinker 2005a, 17). And this is possible because a subsystem like perception of social exchange is not "categorically sealed off from information that could be relevant to it" (Pinker 2005a, 16).

From this, it may be farfetched, but not totally absurd, to infer that we are naturally endowed with a simple capacity to tell social exchanges from other distal stimulations, and nothing seems to prevent us from calling this domain-specific capacity "cognitive," especially when, according to Fodor, we have just two classes, the perceptual and the cognitive, and when calling this capacity "purely perceptual" would be unattractive. It should be added that here "cognitive" means more than "intentional" and "rationally assessable." We are in the conceptual/non-conceptual area of debate.

In short, we have at least one module belonging to the central system, the cheater-detection module, and this may count as a straight refutation of Fodor's view.

As expected, Fodor rejects the "moving dots argument" (as we may call it) as an expression of brute empiricism, a propensity to reduce categories like social interactions to perceptions and perceptions to sensations (Fodor 2005). He notes sarcastically that it "is a lovely example of how a commitment to local or heuristic models of cognitive processing leads to endorse superficial solutions for deep problems." Then he asks: "How much of your routine behavior *vis-à-vis* your conspecifics (or *vis-à-vis* your pets come to think of it) do you actually suppose could be recognized as social interactions by a machine that knows about them nothing except dots in motion? (Think of phoning to your optometrist to make an appointment for some time early next week. Which way do the dots move when you do that?)." But since Fodor is not such a bad guy, he recommends to those who, like Pinker, have this empiricist propensity to reduce categories like social interactions to perceptions of dots and perceptions of dots to sensations of dots, to read a little of Henry James (Fodor 2005, 28)!

Fodor, of course, has a point here, but only within the frame of his own conception of modularity. He asks: why argue that recognition of social exchange could be thought of as modular if spatio-temporal categories are *not* the only or even the primary way that people recognize cognitive domains such as social exchange; that is, if part of the input of a system like perception of social exchange comes from the output of another system, say intuitive psychology?

In other words, if the detector of social exchanges is not an informationally encapsulated processor, why call it a "module"?

The fact is that there are marked differences between Pinker's "soft" conception of modularity (which leaves room for cognitive modules) and Fodor's "strong" version (which does not). But they are not totally unrelated. Fodor himself has shown how they relate. According to him, we should firmly separate the empirical thesis that cognitive mechanisms are typically modular, and that encapsulated domain-specific processors are really in the brain, from the metaphysical claim that they are typically functionally individuated (as opposed to neurologically individuated). What he denies is only the empirical thesis. He claims that Pinker and many other evolutionary psychologists are left with an unwelcome choice of alternatives: either they jump from the metaphysical thesis about functional individuation to the empirical conclusion about really existing encapsulated processors in the brain, or they are left with no empirical explanation of their existence, of the kind we have if we are able to say something about their physical basis. What they get is just a scheme, a flowchart, a model, a formal speculative description.

Finally, one could say that, according to Fodor, evolutionary psychologists are confused or incoherent. They believe in *modularity without modules*.

The unanswered question in Fodor's discussion is whether we can actually get *more* than modularity without modules. He takes it for granted that the perceptual system is realistically modular, that is modular *with* modules and that the cognitive system can only be non-realistically modular, that is modular *without* modules.

Why? Is the modularity of perception beyond objection? Can't we raise doubts about the claim that visual perception is cognitively impenetrable? Can't we produce cases where cognitive impenetrability is not absolute, cases where *thought* brings us to *see* a figure either as duck or as rabbit, either as an olive with a stick or as a Mexican riding a bicycle, to borrow an example from Ronald de Sousa (2004, 75)? Can't we claim that modularity is *never* more than functional individuation? And if modularity is never more that functional individuation or should only be defined in terms of functionally specialized mechanisms, is it not possible to assume that a module can be more or less "encapsulated," more or less open to cognitive appraisal, correction, education?

As Pinker puts it, modules as "encapsulated processors fed directly by sensory transducers are Fodor's obsession, not mine. *How the Mind Works* (...), proposes a number of criteria for specific social interaction (e.g. friendship, siblinghood, dominance). They are not rigidly encapsulated or directly translatable into psychophysical signals, but they do not encompass the totality of a person's beliefs either" (Pinker 2005b, 36).

I am very far from endorsing Pinker's views in general, but I do agree that if "module" means only "functionally specialized subsystem," then encapsulation should not be thought of as rigid.

Now I am in the position to present an answer to my first question: If shame involves beliefs, can it still be modular?

The possibility that shame might be modular seems to be ruled out within Fodor's theoretical framework. If it is true that shame requires the detection of specific social exchanges like avoidance or contempt relations, and if detection of social exchanges of this kind can't be modular because it involves beliefs, then shame can't be modular. But if our capacity to detect very specific forms of social exchanges, like avoidance or contempt relations, can be thought of as modular even if it involves beliefs, as Pinker would say, then shame can be thought of as modular.

I have tried to present a very short argument to the effect that we need not endorse Fodor's conception of modularity which rules out the possibility of shame being modular. After all, even the modular with modules in Fodor sense – the perceptual system – can be treated functionally.

Before leaving the subject, I would like to say a little more about why my argument departs from Pinker's and other evolutionary psychologists' as well. Fodor has objected to them on the grounds that if modules are just "functionally specialized subsystems," then we are left with no empirical explanation of their existence of the kind we would have if we were able to say something about their physical basis. Pinker argues in return that domain-specialization and its specific forms are *explained* by natural selection.

I believe, with many others, that when it comes to psychological or social features, explanations of this kind are too weak because we don't have any empirically grounded history of the process of selection. Pettit has called this objection "the missing-mechanism argument" and tried to answer it (Pettit 2002). I think that this argument holds good and is destined to stay with us.

In rejecting Fodor's narrow conception of modularity and Pinker's explanations, what I am left with is a description without explanation, something that could be called very generously a "theoretical device" – one that might help us explain empirical facts without itself having to be empirically explained.

IV. Could Shame Be Modular but Not Predictable?

Now, what about my second question? If shame does not display strict regularity or automaticity and strict predictability, as far as the relations between its cognitive antecedents and its action tendencies are concerned, does this rule out the possibility of it being modular?

Here again, I could have tried to answer with Pinker-style arguments. We can conceive of modules as functional subsystems limiting the range of possible responses without dictating them. As there is not one typical action tendency of shame but many, all that is needed for shame to be modular is that one of these many tendencies be implemented.

But I will present another argument to the same effect. I will borrow again from Jon Elster and his view about what he calls "explanation by mechanisms," that is, causal explanations which do not imply predictability, as opposed to ordinary causal explanations which imply predictability. I will even follow him in his general conclusion: when it comes to emotions, the best we can get is explanation by mechanisms and not predictable behaviour.

But let's first return to description. Contempt or derision or avoidance are supposed to be typical causes of shame, but they may trigger other emotions as well: hatred or anger or self-pity or sadness, etc. Shame is supposed to result in withdrawal behaviour, hiding, disappearing, or even suicide in the most depressing cases, but it may as well result in attempts to reconstruct or improve oneself or in aggression against others, etc. The scenario of complex emotions like shame is thus not totally predictable, according to Elster.

Within a standard causal frame, we could say that if we can't predict the behaviour from the mental or affective state, it is because we lack information about the mental or affective state and other related facts. The more information we get, the more accurate our prediction will be. Within the non-standard causal framework that Jon Elster proposes with his explanation by mechanisms, lack of predictability does not depend on lack of information. It is just a by-product of the commitment to a different, and non-lawlike, explanation. Let me try to put this in Elster's words.

Before any further comment, it should be said that the term "mechanism" has two different meanings in Elster's work.

In earlier writings, "mechanism" was the antonym of "*black box*" (Elster 1983). In more recent work, it is the antonym of "*scientific law.*" I am interested in this second sense. But something could be briefly said about the first.

Suppose somebody asserts that there is a strong correlation between unemployment and wars of aggression. According to Elster, "We would hardly accept this as a lawlike generalization that could be used in explaining specific wars unless we were provided with a glimpse inside the black box and told *how* unemployment causes wars. Is it because unemployment induces political leaders to seek for new markets through wars? Or because they believe that unemployment creates social unrest that must be directed toward an external enemy, to prevent revolutionary movements at home? Or because they believe that the armament industry can absorb unemployment? Although many such stories are conceivable, some kind of story must be told for the explanation to be convincing" (Elster 1999, 5). Elster called such kind of story a "mechanism" and opposed it to "black box explanations."

In *Alchemies of the Mind* (1999), Elster presents a new terminology. "Mechanism" is not the antonym of "black box" anymore but of "scientific law." What does this mean?

According to Elster, a scientific law asserts that, given certain initial conditions, an event of a given type (the cause) will *always* produce an event of some other type (the effect). Elster's example is the "law of demand": "if we keep consumer incomes constant, an increase in the price of a good will cause less of it to be sold." In more abstract terms, a law has the form "If conditions $C1, C2, \dots Cn$, obtain, then always E." By contrast, and at the same abstract level, a statement about mechanisms might be "If $C1, C2, \dots Cn$, obtain, then *sometimes* E" (Elster 1999, 5).

At first sight, explanations of this kind are not very promising. Actually, they can hardly be thought of as explanations. Elster puts forward the following as an example: "When there is an eclipse of the moon, it sometimes rains the next day." Who would suggest that the former fact explains the latter? But of course when Elster speaks of "explanation by mechanisms," he does not have in mind this sort of empty statement. He is rather thinking of a statement like the following: "When people would like a certain proposition to be true, they *sometimes* (but not *always*) end up believing it to be true. When it is the case, the fact that people would like a certain proposition to be true may explain the fact that they *sometimes* (but not *always*) end up believing it to be true, relying on the familiar mechanism of *wishful thinking*" (5–6).

According to Elster: "This is not a lawlike phenomenon. Most people entertain some beliefs that they would like to be false. Ex ante, we cannot predict when they will engage in wishful thinking – but when they do, we can recognize it after the fact" (5).

In order to understand exactly what Elster proposes, we should focus on what he says about predictability when he develops his analysis by distinguishing two types of mechanisms (6–10).

What he calls mechanisms of type *A* come in pairs of mutually exclusive behaviour: "When people would like the world to be different from what it is, wishful thinking is not the only mechanism of adjustment. Sometimes, as in the story of the fox and the sour grapes, people adjust by changing their desires rather than their beliefs" (6). We can't know in advance which strategy will be adopted; changing the beliefs or changing the desires. Other examples: "Some people prefer what they can have, while others tend to want what they do not or cannot have. Some people are conformists, some are anticonformists (they always do the opposite of what others do)" (7).

In short, in *type A mechanisms*, the triggering of the mechanism is not predictable.

In what Jon Elster calls *type B mechanisms*, the triggering of the mechanisms is sometimes predictable, but their net effect may not be.

His example here is the impact of taxes on the supply of labour: high tax rates encourage people to work less. But, on the other hand, it also lowers peoples' incomes, and thereby may induce them to work harder so as to maintain their standard of living. These two effects operate in opposite directions, and their net effect is impossible to predict from theory alone.

Elster's final point is that we cannot tell, in general, when a given mechanism, that is a type *A* mechanism, will be triggered or, in the case of several mechanisms that operate simultaneously or successively, that is type *B* mechanisms, what their net effect will be.

What Elster stresses throughout his reasoning is *predictability*. Explanations by mechanism are open to us when prediction does not seem promising. Explanation by mechanism can still help us make sense of some behavior *ex post*, when no better explanation is available.

What Elster calls "explanation by mechanisms" strongly resembles reason explanations, which help us make sense of some behaviour *ex post* without allowing us to predict it. But I will not go further into this comparison because, as I have said, my question is whether modularity is ruled out by lack of predictability. And within the framework of reason explanation, I am not sure that talk of modularity makes any sense.[6]

By contrast, the idea of "explanation by mechanisms" helps us see, or so I believe, how we may accommodate the fact that the relations of shame with its cognitive antecedents and its distinctive action tendencies are not strictly predictable, without giving up the causal framework that is indispensable to keeping alive the idea of modularity. Elster's plea for mechanisms is the opening chapter of his book about emotions. His main epistemological claim in this book is that, when it comes to emotions, the best we can get is explanation by mechanisms and not strictly predictable behaviour.[7] This claim does not imply that we are left with indeterminism when it comes to emotions. Or so it seems to me. After all, explanations by mechanisms, as Elster conceives of them, are just a subclass of ordinary causal explanations. What I would like to suggest is that Elster's views about mechanisms help sustain the idea that emotions like shame, pride, guilt, etc., can actually be modular, even if their triggering is not strictly predictable since explanations by mechanisms do not warrant prediction, while nevertheless being causal.

V. Conclusion

It is hard to deny that the question whether emotions like shame or pride can be both conceptual or partly conceptual and modular, both

---

6 It seems to me that it would have been a lot easier to explain what Elster seems so embarrassed to explain by referring to the specific features of *reasons explanation.* As Davidson put it, reason explanations are not lawlike. They give a rational frame that can help us make sense retrospectively of some behaviour (Davidson 2004). However, we should not confuse this rational frame of interpretation with a simple variable on the basis of which we could "predict" behaviour.

7 This should not lead us to the conclusion that these explanations are "un-scientific." As Luc Faucher and Christine Tappolet have made me notice, there is a trend now in philosophy of science of putting forward the idea that most of what biological and psychological sciences are doing is proposing models of mechanisms (see, for instance, Machamer et al. 2000). If such is the case, by considering emotion in terms of mechanisms, one is just being in continuity with what is done in some special sciences.

non-automatic and modular, admits of different answers depending on the theory of modularity to which one is committed.

For "Hard Fodorians," the answer is no. For "Soft Pinkerians," the answer is yes. And, of course, because, as philosophers, we want to add something to the debate, we will probably find all sorts of in-between positions. The risk is to end up with a Babel-like debate, where nobody speaks the same language.

This may explain why David Papineau has suggested to Peter Goldie he stop using the terms "modularity of emotional capacities" to express his ideas, on the grounds that "this notion can be more confusing than helpful to discussion in this area" (Goldie 2000, 98).

I am not that pessimistic. I believe that we can somehow clarify what we mean by "shame" or "pride" and by "modular" and express interesting conclusions within these frames.

Through philosophical analysis, at least we learn that when we ask whether emotions like shame or pride can be modular, the first interesting answers do not come at the empirical but at the conceptual level.

References

Aristotle. 1991. *Art of Rhetoric*, trans. J.H. Freese. Cambridge, Mass., Harvard University Press, Loeb Classical Library.

Atran, S. 2001. The case for modularity: Sin or salvation. *Evolution and Cognition* 7(1): 1–10.

Barrett, K. C., C. Zahn-Waxler, and P. M. Cole. 1993. Avoiders versus amenders: Implications for the investigation of guilt and shame during toddlerhood. *Cognition and Emotion* 7: 481–505.

Ben Ze'ev, A. 2000. *The Subtlety of Emotions*. Cambridge (Mass.): MIT Press.

Botterill, G., and P. Carruthers. 1999. *The Philosophy of Psychology*. Cambridge: Cambridge University Press.

Cosmides, L. 1989. The logic of social exchange. *Cognition* 31: 187–276.

Cosmides, L., and J. Tooby. 1992. Cognitive adaptation for social exchange. In *The Adapted Mind*, ed. L. Barkow, L. Cosmides, and J. Tooby, 163–228. Oxford: Oxford University Press.

D'Arms, J., and D. Jacobson. 1994. Expressivism, morality and the emotions. *Ethics* 104: 739–63.

D'Arms, J., and D. Jacobson. 2003. The significance of recalcitrant emotion (or quasi-judgmentalism). In *Philosophy and the Emotions*, ed. A. Hatzimoysis, 127–45. Cambridge: Cambridge University Press.

Davidson, D. 2004. *Problems of Rationality*. Oxford: Oxford University Press.

Deigh, J. 1992. Shame and self-esteem: A critique. In *Ethics and Personality*, ed. John Deigh, 133–53. Chicago: University of Chicago Press.

Deigh, J.1994. Cognitivism in the theory of emotions. *Ethics*, 104: 824–54.

de Sousa, R. 1987. *The Rationality of Emotion*. Cambridge (Mass.): MIT Press.

de Sousa, R. 2004. *Évolution et rationalité*. Paris: PUF.

Elster, J. 1983. *Explaining Technical Change*. Cambridge: Cambridge University Press.

Elster, J. 1999. *Alchemies of the Mind*. Cambridge: Cambridge University Press.

Faucher, L. 1999. Émotions fortes et constructionnisme faible. *Philosophiques* 25(1): 3–35.

Fodor, J. 1983. *The Modularity of Mind*. Cambridge (Mass.): MIT Press.

Fodor, J. 2000 *The Mind Doesn't Work That Way*. Cambridge (Mass.): MIT Press.

Fodor, J. 2005. Response to Pinker, 'So how does the mind work ?' *Mind and Language* 1: 24–32.

Garfield, J. 1994. Modularity. In *A Companion to the Philosophy of Mind*, ed. Samuel Guttenplan, 441-48. Oxford: Basil Blackwell.

Gibbard, A. 1990. *Wise Choices, Apt Feelings*. Cambridge (Mass.): Harvard University Press.

Goldie, P. 2000. *The Emotions. A Philosophical Exploration*. Oxford: Oxford University Press.

Griffiths, P. E. 2003. Basic emotions, complex emotions, Machiavelian emotions. In *Philosophy and the Emotions*, ed. A. Hatzimoysis, 39–67. Cambridge: Cambridge University Press.

Hirschfeld, L. A. 1994. Introduction. In *Mapping the Mind: Domain Specificity in Culture and Cognition*, ed. L. A. Hirschfeld and S. A. Gelman, 3–35. Cambridge: Cambridge University Press.

Machamer, P., L. Darden, and C. Carver. 2000. Thinking about mechanisms. *Philosophy of Science* 67: 1–25.

Morris, H. 1976. Guilt and shame. In *On Guilt and Innocence*, ed. H. Morris, 59–63. Berkeley: University of California Press.

Morris, H. 1987. Nonmoral guilt. In *Responsibility, Character, and the Emotions: New Essays in Moral Psychology*, ed. F . Schoeman, 220–41. Cambridge: Cambridge University Press.

Ogien, R. 2002. *La honte est-elle immorale ?* Paris: Bayard.

Pinker, S. 1997. *How the Mind Works*. New York: Norton.

Pinker, S. 2005a. So how *does* the mind work? *Mind and Language* 1: 16–17.

Pinker, S. 2005b. A reply to Jerry Fodor on 'So how the mind work.' *Mind and Language* 1: 36.

Pettit, P. 2002. Functional explanation and virtual selection. In *Rules, Reasons and Norms*, ed. P. Petit, 245-56. Oxford: Clarendon Press.

Prinz, J. 2003. Emotion, psychosemantics, and embodied appraisal. In *Philosophy and the Emotions*, ed. A. Hatzimoysis, 69–86. Cambridge: Cambridge University Press.

Rawls, J. 1990. *A Theory of Justice*. Cambridge (Mass.): Harvard University Press.

Sperber, D. 1996. *Explaining Culture: A Naturalistic Approach*. Oxford: Blackwell.

Sperber, D. 2002. Défense de la modularité massive. In *Les Langages du cerveau*, ed. E. Dupoux, 55–64. Paris: Odile Jacob.

Sperber, D., F. Cara, and V. Girotto. 1995. Relevance theory explains the selection task. *Cognition* 57: 31–95.

Tappolet, C. Unpublished. The Irrationality of Emotions.

Taylor, G. 1985. *Pride, Shame and Guilt*. Oxford: Clarendon Press.

Williams, B. 1993. *Necessity and Shame*. Berkeley: University of California Press.

Wollheim, R. 1999. *On the Emotions*. New Haven, CT: Yale University Press.

CANADIAN JOURNAL OF PHILOSOPHY
Supplementary Volume 32

An Unexpected Pleasure

TIMOTHY SCHROEDER

As topics in the philosophy of emotion, pleasure and displeasure get less than their fair share of attention. On the one hand, there is the fact that pleasure and displeasure are given no role at all in many theories of the emotions, and secondary roles in many others.[1] On the other, there is the centrality of pleasure and displeasure to being *emotional*. A woman who tears up because of a blustery wind, while an ill-advised burrito weighs heavily upon her digestive tract, feels an impressive number of the sensations felt by someone who is gut-wrenchingly sad. Yet, unless she feels *bad*, the way she feels is only a pale echo of the feeling of sadness. If she feels good in spite of the burrito and the wind, then she does not feel at all the way she would if she were sad. Likewise, a man falling asleep can hardly fail to feel his muscles relax, his heart rate fall, and so on, but unless he feels *good* his state is only a shadow of feeling content.

This paper will begin with a sketch of the nature of pleasure and displeasure, and the relation between them and the feelings that are characteristic of emotions. It will then argue that the capacity to feel pleased and displeased is, quite literally, a sense modality: one allowing us to perceive net change in the satisfaction of our intrinsic desires. As with any sense modality, the capacity to feel pleased and displeased displays substantial modularity. The paper concludes by considering the ways in which the modularity of pleasure and displeasure contributes to effects that might reasonably be called "the modularity of the emotions."

---

1 Quite a few books on emotions neglect pleasure and displeasure, for example, Green (1992); Griffiths (1997); and Goldie (2000), though there are exceptions (Prinz 2004).

I. Groundwork

From Plato through to John Stuart Mill or so, philosophers had a reasonably clear idea of the nature of pleasure and displeasure (jointly: hedonic tone). Hedonic tone, they held, is a distinctive state of consciousness, not unlike feelings of warmth and coldness.

In the twentieth century, this orthodoxy was frequently, if puzzlingly, rejected by a number of philosophers. Bertrand Russell and Gilbert Ryle argue that pleasure is merely a style of behaviour (Russell 1921; Ryle 1949; 1954). Michael Tye holds a very similar view (Tye 1995). Jesse Prinz joins neuroscientist Tony Damasio in the view that hedonic tone is a matter of a whole-body "landscape" of felt changes in breathing, heart rate, piloerection, and the like, rather than a distinct kind of feeling (Damasio 1994; Prinz 2004). And Elijah Millgram goes so far as to argue that pleasure is "the rock-bottom judgment of desirability of an object of present experience" (Millgram 1997).

I side with the older orthodoxy. Hedonic tone is a distinct type of feeling, not a judgment, not a composite feeling built out of the feelings of one's viscera, not a style of behaviour. The argument for this will be brief. (I refer those who are unconvinced to work published elsewhere.[2])

First, the phenomenology of intense pleasure and displeasure should be a sufficient refutation of the view that hedonic tone is a style of behaviour. There is something it is like to be elated off and on for the whole next day after one's first kiss, and something it is like to be profoundly saddened by the death of a parent, and a reduction of these feelings to behavioural styles is not credible. This would also seem sufficient evidence to answer Millgram, unless Millgram is willing to identify rock-bottom judgments of desirability with the distinctive phenomenology of pleasure.

The whole-body landscape view of hedonic tone survives this particular challenge. In elation and sorrow, one *does* experience global changes in one's viscera, musculature, and the like. The main challenge to the whole-body landscape view is that it fails to account for the grouping together of instances of pleasure under that heading, and likewise for the unity of instances of displeasure. What do pro-

---

2 See Schroeder (2004), 71–106; Aydede (2000).

found, lazy contentment and energized ecstasy have in common? At least this much: both are states of great pleasure. But what sort of felt bodily landscape do they share in common? Not the feelings of the viscera (heart beating lazily in the one, wildly in the other; breathing slower in one, faster in the other), not the feelings of muscle contraction and relaxation, not feelings of piloerection (ecstasy-causing news can make one's hairs stand on end, but contentment does not), not felt facial expression (compare the facial expressions induced by ecstatic sex and lazing in the sun). Perhaps a careful study would find certain bodily landscapes common to these two kinds of pleasure, but what is left after these differences are factored out will not be a reasonable candidate for the feeling of pleasure. One might object that profound contentment and ecstasy are really different feelings, and so should not be expected to share a bodily landscape, but the point is that, although the feelings are different, they are also alike in that both involve great pleasure, and it is this kinship that still needs explaining. Relatedly, one might ask how "feeling good" and "feeling bad" are terms easily learned by children, whereas the various species of these genuses are learned more slowly, if there is not some introspectable common quality shared by every way of feeling good, one that feels the opposite of every way of feeling bad.[3]

This could become a much larger discussion, but enough has been said for present purposes. This paper will proceed on the assumption that pleasure and displeasure are distinctive feelings.

What is the relation of these feelings to the emotions? The answer gestured at in the introduction is that every felt emotion involves some measure of pleasure or displeasure. A few distinctions will help make this clear. If a distinction is made between emotional states (being afraid of dogs, hoping that global warming is reversible), which generally persist over a long time, and emotional episodes (suddenly fearing a particular dog, or being filled with hope that global warm-

---

3 Jesse Prinz leaves open the possibility that what is felt is actually changes in one's neuromodulators – in dopamine or in endorphin, perhaps (Prinz 2004). This is harder to rule out, but also closer to the view I wish to endorse, since I suspect that the only feeling endorphin causes in people is pleasure itself: there is no distinctive feeling to endorphin that survives the above challenge, at any rate.

ing is reversible), which are generally short-lived, then emotional episodes are the ones on which this paper is focussed. One can be afraid of dogs even while profoundly unconscious, in the emotional state sense, but one cannot be *fearful*, in the emotional episode sense, and likewise one cannot be pleased or displeased either. The claim is that every emotional episode involves some non-zero degree of pleasure or displeasure.

"Involves" is deliberately vague. Perhaps some very cognitive theory of the emotions is correct. Then an emotional episode is an ontologically derivative event, involving feelings that are in no way ontologically necessary to the existence of the emotion in question. Or perhaps some Jamesian theory of the emotions is correct, and feelings are involved in emotions in that they are the ontological ground for the existence of the emotion. Or perhaps some hybrid theory is right, and feelings are part but not all of what makes something an emotion. There is no need to settle these issues here. The claim is that, whatever emotional episodes are, they always involve pleasure or displeasure.

The argument for this modest claim is straightforward: simply repeat the familiar Jamesian subtractive thought-experiment with pleasure and displeasure in the place of visceral feeling, and consider the result. In James's original thought experiment, we are asked to consider an emotional episode stripped of the feeling of a pounding heart, laboured breathing, knotted stomach, and so on, until all bodily feelings are eliminated (James 1890). What, James asks, is left of the emotional event? His answer, famously, is that nothing is left. To perform my version of the Jamesian thought-experiment, keep all of these visceral feelings, but subtract out all pleasure and displeasure, and ask what is left of the emotional event. The emotional event has been stripped of its core. Fear without displeasure is neutral arousal, a prickling sensation on one's arms, dampness on one's skin – a condition that, if observed with "scientific detachment," "dispassionately" (i.e., without pleasure or displeasure), is no more emotional than any other randomly selected conjunction of visceral states.

The above argument presupposes that pleasure and displeasure are something over and above felt bodily landscapes, and so will hardly convince everyone. A more broadly acceptable argument, making no particular assumption about the nature of pleasure, asks the reader to consider surprise. Normally, surprise is taken to be an emotion, possibly even a core basic emotion (Ekman 1972). But consider a person for whom life is a sequence of hedonically neutral surprises. The surprises are neither good nor bad, neither delightful nor shocking. They are simply sudden, visceral recognitions of the unexpected, perhaps accompanied, in the style of Mr. Spock, with a slight arching of one eyebrow. The life of such a person is, if anything, emotionally dull. It is certainly not a life full of intense emotion. Yet a person who battled depression – regularly slipping into sorrow, then finding calm, only to be dragged into sorrow again – would clearly be leading an emotionally charged life, as would a person who was often joyful, or often angry, or often fearful. So, too, would a person who was regularly shocked or delighted – i.e., subjected to a combination of displeasure and surprise, or pleasure and surprise. If having an emotionally charged life is having a life full of emotional episodes, then these considerations suggest that surprise that is not mixed with pleasure or displeasure cannot constitute an emotional episode, and that putative emotional episodes in general require pleasure or displeasure (whatever their nature) in order to count as truly emotional.

II. A Theory of Hedonic Tone

It is time to investigate hedonic tone in more detail.[4] Consider a few of the central facts about pleasure and displeasure.

1. They are opposites that come on a continuum with a neutral mid-point.

Although this much is straightforward, it leaves a few details unspecified. Perhaps there are upper and lower bounds to the continuum, or perhaps it simply becomes more and more difficult to ascend higher (or fall lower) on the continuum the further one goes along it. Nothing hangs on these details for present purposes, however.

2. They are not normally felt simultaneously, though they can be.

---

4 Similar ground is covered in my work elsewhere (Schroeder 2004, 71–106).

Normally pleasure cancels out antecedent displeasure, and vice versa, or at least ameliorates it. Cases of simultaneous pleasure and displeasure include the overwrought laughing/crying feeling one can have when suddenly relieved of some great stress, or the bittersweet feeling one can get from the needed yet regretted end of a romantic relationship.

3. They tend to be triggered by external events regarding which we have some desire.

Montreal's winning the Stanley Cup would cause pleasure in those who want Montreal to win the cup, displeasure in those wanting them to lose, and nothing in those not desiring one way or the other, for example. Likewise for the pleasures of the table, etc.: it is only when one desires water that one is caused pleasure by drinking it.[5]

4. They tend to be influenced by antecedent expectations.

If Theresa is accustomed to sleeping on a nice double bed, being forced to sleep on a plastic-coated single bed (say, in a student dorm) will be unpleasant; but if she lives in the dorm, she will become accustomed to the less-nice bed, and stop being caused displeasure by it. Similarly, if she is sure that Montreal will win the Stanley Cup, she will be more displeased by a loss than if that was what she was expecting all along, all else being equal.

5. They provide information about desires.

---

5 Two issues. First, one need only have a desire for something that one takes to be achieved by drinking water in order to be pleased by it, normally. There is no need to desire to drink a glass of water in order to be pleased by drinking one if one also desires to get to the bottom of the glass (say). This wrinkle is important but not particularly important for what follows. Second, one might wonder if the link between pleasure and desire really exists in cases such as getting pleasure from the smell of baking bread. Do people who get such pleasure get it *because* they desire to smell that smell (or any smell from a family that includes it)? In earlier work (Schroeder 2004), an extended argument is made that the answer is "yes," but the issue will be deferred here.

When a person is not sure what she wants, one simple strategy is to consider the possibilities as vividly as possible, and then note the resulting pleasure or displeasure that comes as one considers each. Whatever possibility evokes the most pleasure is likely to be the possibility one most desires.

6. They can be defective in some sense, when not triggered in the usual ways.

A person who drunkenly does something foolish may enjoy it at the time, only to bemoan the act in retrospect. Sober friends observing the drunken act are likely to speak of "clouded" judgment, remark on the "inappropriate" hilarity, and note that "he's not seeing things clearly right now." Similar remarks apply to those whose hedonic states are strongly influenced by mood disorders, major life events that infect every aspect of life (falling in love, losing a loved one), and so on.

7. They are associated in some way with goodness and badness.

When I was little, I first learned to talk about pleasure and displeasure through the locutions "feeling good" and "feeling bad," and of course many have thought that there is something inherently good in pleasure and bad in displeasure.

One would hope that a theory of hedonic tone would explain most of these facts, if not all of them. But consider what explanatory resources are available to standard theories of pleasure and displeasure.

A type-identity theory of hedonic tone identifies it with some particular state of the brain: activation in a region of perigenual anterior cingulate cortex, as it might be (Schroeder 2004, 76–83). Such a theory has no resources whatsoever for explaining why pleasure is the opposite of displeasure, since biologically the two states are (it seems) realized in adjacent, mutually inhibitory cortex, not "opposite" kinds of cortex, whatever that would be. There might be hope for explaining some of the other phenomena in causal/biological terms, but the "defectiveness" of some kinds of pleasure caused when there is no biological defect in a person is harder for an identity theorist to explain, and certainly the link to goodness and badness must be left a mystery.

A standard causal-role functionalist theory of hedonic tone identifies it with any state playing a certain role, such that it has two subdivisions (at least) that play off against one another, have their effects on a continuum, are not typically felt simultaneously, carry information about desires, tend to be influenced by expectations, etc. But by so identifying it, a standard causal-role functionalist theory leaves no room for explanation. Just as one can hardly explain why the glass broke by saying it was breakable, so one can hardly explain why pleasure and displeasure play off against one another by saying that they are any two states such that, among other things, they play off against one another. To be this sort of functionalist about hedonic tone is to give up explaining the core phenomenon (explaining them in psychological terms, at least) in favour of treating them as constitutive. "Pleasure is like that because, if it weren't, it wouldn't be pleasure" is about the best this sort of functionalism can do.

It would be nice to do better. Consider treating pleasure and displeasure as sense modalities that allow us to sense the thing that they tend to be triggered by: changes in desire satisfaction. Treating them in this way promises to provide an impressive array of genuine explanations for the phenomena in question.

First, desire satisfaction is the opposite of desire frustration, hence their representations will have opposite contents. Desire satisfaction and frustration also come on a continuum: on balance, one's desires can be more frustrated or less, depending on how many desires were just satisfied or frustrated, and how much one desired each thing. This continuum has a natural zero-point, at which desire satisfaction balances desire frustration (either by there being none of either, or by their cancelling out), just as hedonic tone does.

Second, desires are never, on balance, more satisfied *and* more frustrated, so any system representing them should not, as a matter of course, represent them as both. But any representational system can misrepresent.

Third, that pleasure and displeasure are triggered by desire-satisfying events is no surprise if desires represent change in desire satisfaction.

Fourth, the relation between hedonic tone and antecedent expectations makes sense if what desires represent is change in desire satisfaction, since change must be change relative to *something*.[6]

Fifth, hedonic tone is a natural source of information regarding one's desires if it is itself a sensory representation of changes in those desires' satisfaction.

Sixth, since any representation can misrepresent, there is nothing odd about the notion of error in one's hedonic tone.

Seventh, insofar as one accepts that what is good for an organism is defined by what the organism intrinsically desires, a measure of change in desire satisfaction is also a measure of whether things are going *better* or *worse*, so far as the organism is concerned.[7]

Treating hedonic tone as a sense modality, one representing change in desire satisfaction relative to expectations, is thus a more fruitful explanatory framework than other standard frameworks in the philosophy of mind. It is also a framework with implications for the modularity of the emotions.

III. The Modularity of Pleasure

It is a familiar idea about the sense modalities that they display some set of the various features of modules (Fodor 1983). That is, they tend to be domain-specific, to produce their output whether or not the organism desires it, to operate quickly, to be informationally sealed off from the rest of one's knowledge, to be subject to illusion, and so on. These features are readily seen to apply to hedonic tone. Hedonic tone is clearly domain-specific (it is designed for a limited, special purpose), it is obviously independent of a person's desires (as anyone who has ever suffered unwanted feelings knows), and it oper-

---

6 It should be admitted that there is nothing in representing desire satisfaction that requires that change relative to a baseline be represented, as opposed to raw current total of satisfaction (say), and so this fourth feature of hedonic tone is not really given a robust explanation by the current theory. But notice that some sense modalities focus at least as much on change from baseline as they do on absolute value. Compare hedonic tone to one's sense of warmth and cold, for instance.

7 As this is not a work of moral philosophy, I will leave it at this.

ates quickly (there is typically no perceptible time lag between being aware of some new fact and feeling its hedonic effect). If phenomenon (6) is to be trusted, then hedonic tone is also subject to illusions, another hallmark of modular systems. And phenomenon (6) *should* be trusted. Many people with mood disorders are quite capable of knowing, at some highly intellectual level, that things are not so bad, that their work is good, that they are loved, and so on, while also *feeling* that things are terrible, that their work is abysmal, and that they are not loved. These known-to-be-false feelings are best understood as hedonic illusions: a depressive disorder is a condition in which one's hedonic tone tells one that things are worse (that one's desires are worse satisfied) with respect to whatever part of one's life one considers, whether or not this is the case.

Most interesting for this paper is the idea that hedonic tone is, or is not, informationally encapsulated. On the one hand, it is clearly false. When Theresa is told that Montreal won the 2005 Stanley Cup, she does not feel pleasure, because she knows perfectly well that the NHL season was cancelled that year, and this high-level cognitive information blocks the power of the phrase "Montreal won the 2005 Stanley Cup" to induce pleasure in her. On the other hand, there is *something* to the idea of informational encapsulation. As an illustration, think of two people playing roulette, both of whom bet a small amount of money on black, both of whom win. Both have full knowledge of the objective probability of winning (17/36), which is transparent from the structure of the game. At the level of conscious deliberation, both agree about how likely the win was, but even so one may accept the win practically as a matter of course, being supremely confident in her luck, while the other may be quite surprised, having expected herself "at some level" to have bad luck. These differing expectations are not differences at the straightforward level of belief, and in fact appear to be insulated against the influence of conscious beliefs in a way that is characteristic of modular systems. Call these sorts of expectations "gut-level" expectations. Statements such as "Of course I knew she would be late, but somehow it still surprised me" are expressions of the effects of such gut-level expectations. The same sort of phenomenon is found in parents feeling sure that a missing child is alive even while accepting the rationality of holding that there is a great risk that the child is dead, and in people who "can't quite believe" they got the great new job, romantic partner, or piece of financial luck they did. Generally, one's gut-level confidence in a given proposition matches one's consciously held level of confidence, but the fact that these are separate cognitive states is shown by the ease with which they come apart under various conditions.

When considering cases, I think the reader will find that pleasure and displeasure tend to vary with confidence and resignation when the confidence and resignation are felt in the "gut" or "heart." Reasoned estimates of likelihood believed with one's "head" sometimes correspond to what is felt in one's gut or heart, but when the two come apart, tendencies to pleasure or displeasure follow the viscera.

To explain the way in which hedonic tone might be informationally encapsulated in some manner, while informationally open in some other, consider again what it means for hedonic tone to be a sense modality.

For most of the senses, input to sensory representations (in cortex) comes directly from non-representational (at least, non-psychological) structures: the eyes and optic nerve, ears and auditory nerve, and so on. So there is no opportunity for non-encapsulated cognition to play any role in the input side of sensory processing. However, there is no *need* for things to be this way in a sense modality. To calculate change in desire satisfaction, a sensory system needs information about what is happening in the world, and there is no reason inherent in being a sensory system that requires this information to come directly from transducers. And, in fact, there is no obvious way to directly transduce information about, say, whether or not Montreal has won the Stanley Cup. If this information is relevant to change in desire satisfaction, then any sense modality purveying information about such changes must get the information, not from transducers, but from sophisticated cognitive systems. So it is in organisms like ourselves. We feel pleasure or displeasure in a way that depends very much on how we cognize the world to be, using our fullest intellectual resources. In this way, hedonic tone is not informationally encapsulated.

Information about what obtains in the world is not the only input used to produce hedonic tone, however. Since hedonic tone represents change in desire satisfaction, three sorts of information are required: what obtains in the world, what was expected, and what is desired. The phenomenon of gut-level expectations suggests that information about what is expected to be the case is calculated in at least two ways, one that is informationally open and one that is informationally encapsulated. Even though two people know the objective probabilities in a game of chance, and so "at one level" expect the same thing, this knowledge need not influence their subjectively felt expectations; even though a woman knows "rationally" that while shopping for groceries her father is going to express surprise, yet again, at the high price of milk these days, she may still be capable of being astonished herself that he remains endlessly surprised; and so on. Furthermore, it appears that it is the encapsulated, special-purpose, gut-level calculation that is used to calculate hedonic tone. The two people with different gut-level expectations of winning at roulette will, all else being equal, take a win or a loss differently: the person expecting the win will enjoy a win, of course (unless playing with such supreme confidence that to win now is just boring), but the person not expecting it will be correspondingly more delighted to be proven wrong, all else being equal. Likewise, the person who has ceased to be surprised by her father's foibles is also the person who, all else being equal, is less exasperated by them.

There are complications in real cases. For instance, people with low confidence in the occurrence of good things are often people who are hurt worst by bad news, while people with high confidence in the occurrence of good things are often people who are most resilient to bad news. But this is because such people tend to be different in a large number of ways. People who tend to have low confidence that good things will happen to them are also people who tend to see each negative event as evidence that they are, more than ever, doomed to unhappiness, or as evidence that other bad things will soon happen, while people who tend to be confident that the future bodes well for them do not place such interpretations upon bad news. Naturally, this makes a difference to hedonic tone, but not one which conflicts with the present theory of hedonic tone. Likewise, people who have low confidence in the occurrence of good things often tend to depression, and depression is a condition in which one's hedonic tone is largely unresponsive to one's actual circumstances – a condition of systematic misrepresentation, in other words, akin to numbness in the skin or tinnitus. People who systematically misrepresent deviation from expected desire satisfaction, naturally enough, are not going to have displeasure which is readily predicted by the present theory. A certain amount of caution is therefore required in comparing everyday cases, looking for the effects of gut-level confidence and resignation. But when this caution is employed, the present theory fits the evidence of common sense well.

There is biological evidence for both of the most important claims just made: that there are two distinct systems, one encapsulated, one not, for forming expectations, and that it is the encapsulated system that contributes to feelings of pleasure and displeasure.

In a series of ground-breaking studies, Wolfram Schultz and colleagues have convincingly shown that the release of dopamine by key midbrain structures carries information about the difference between actual and expected reward (see, e.g., Romo and Schultz 1990; Schultz and Romo 1990; Schultz et al. 2000). Input to these dopamine-releasing structures comes, in the first instance, from sub-cortical structures thought to be involved in forming expectations about reward. The nucleus accumbens apparently features prominently here, perhaps along with parts of the caudate nucleus (Knutson et al. 2001; Pagnoni et al. 2002; Berns et al. 2001). These sub-cortical structures take input from cortical structures, but perform their own operations upon this input. As I argue elsewhere, information about the difference between expected and actual reward amounts to information about change in desire satisfaction (Schroeder 2004). Since output from midbrain dopamine-releasing structures appears to be an extremely important causal contribution to pleasure – their activity seems to be responsible for the pleasure induced by cocaine (Gawin 1991), ecstasy (Liechti and Vollenweider 2000), and other pleasure-causing drugs (Kandel et al. 2000) – the case that this pathway for determining reward-related expectations drives hedonic tone seems reasonably secure. But head- (as opposed to gut-) level expectations are the sorts of things one expects to be produced in cortex, especially in those regions of cortex involved in conscious reasoning, and stored in explicit memory. In short, one expects such expectations to be created in structures quite different from the sub-cortical structures connected to dopamine signalling. Hence there are two different routes to expectations, only one of which has a distinguished connection to pleasure.

IV. The Modularity of the Emotions

Having described a respect in which hedonic tone is modular, and having linked hedonic tone to emotional feelings, what is left is to draw the conclusions for the modularity of the emotions.

Talk of the modularity of the emotions brings to mind a number of phenomena. Without making an attempt to systematically survey them all, candidate phenomena include:

1. The cognitive impenetrability of phobias.
2. The power of fictions to excite episodic sadness.
3. The capacity people have to be shocked by what we knew would happen.
4. The tendency of anger to linger even after it has been undercut by new information.
5. The difficulty of ridding oneself of dispositions to episodic guilt and shame learned in childhood.
6. The power of fear to prime flight.
7. The fact that emotional feelings are organized into coherent clusters.
8. The fact that many emotional feelings are coordinated by evolutionarily old structures in the hypothalamus and amygdala.

For most of these phenomena (4–8), it is clear that understanding the modularity of hedonic tone contributes little or nothing to their own understanding. But we can gain insight into a few.

Consider the cognitive impenetrability of phobias. This might seem to be a prime example of the modularity of hedonic tone explaining something about the modularity of an emotional episode. When Justin is fearful of Alpha Helix, a manifestly harmless dog, that episodic fear involves a feeling of displeasure. Might it not be the case that the dysfunction, in a phobia, is in part a dysfunction in the gut-level calculation of expectations? This seems a reasonable speculation. If Justin's gut-level expectation of being bitten is much too high, then the dog will make him feel displeasure, which he certainly does. This sounds like the beginning of a promising inference to the best explanation.

Unfortunately, there are substantial complications. Research both conducted and reviewed by Joseph LeDoux (see, e.g., LeDoux 1996) strongly suggests that phobias are created by Pavlovian-style conditioning of the amygdala, a structure quite distinct from those involved in producing the midbrain dopamine signal, or from those instantiating hedonic tone. The amygdala mediates unlearned associations between stimuli and characteristically emotional bodily responses, and can learn to associate new stimuli with existing responses. And although the connections are not clear, it seems that one of the pathways leading out of the amygdala reaches the brain's centre of hedonic tone, exerting influence over it just as it influences heart rate or the activity of the gut. So it may be that the dysfunction in a phobia is located entirely in the amygdala and its too-strong association between certain stimuli (e.g., dogs) and characteristic fear responses, and that the displeasure that makes up part of the felt episodic fear is simply a causal consequence of dysfunction elsewhere. Even if hedonic tone were cognitively penetrable, it could well be that cognitive penetration wouldn't guarantee an absence of displeasure in the case of Justin facing Alpha Helix, given the causal action of the amygdala.

Likewise, insofar as other emotions such as sadness draw upon the amygdala for their production, they too will have their cognitive impenetrability best explained through appeal to the cognitive impenetrability of the operation of the amygdala, and not through appeal to the distinctive impenetrability of hedonic tone.

However, as one turns to somewhat different emotions, the significance of the informational encapsulation of hedonic tone increases. Consider the feelings of shock and delight, feelings that are predominantly made up of surprise and negative or positive (respectively) hedonic tone. These are phenomena that seem more promising candidates for explanation in terms of the hedonic system's modularity. Examples given above seem to suggest that the pleasure and displeasure involved in such feelings is strongly influenced by gut-level expectations, at least in many cases. (We might discount the shock of seeing a dog in the house when one is a dog-phobe, for instance, in light of the previous discussion.) One can know that one's hero has called a press conference to confess to misbehaviour, or to announce retirement, and yet still "at some level" not believe it will happen, and so feel a shock as the fateful words are pronounced. Likewise, it takes a certain length of time in a romantic relationship for one to cease to be delighted by the charming quirks of one's beloved, even once one has come to be intimately familiar with them at a cognitive level. (Eventually, of course, the actual episodic delight wears off. One's gut-level expectations clearly *do* learn, just less quickly in many cases than one's intellectual expectations.)

Hope and dread seem likewise very much influenced by gut-level expectations, and so present further cases in which the modularity of pleasure infects emotional episodes. It is easy to find oneself hoping for what one is intellectually convinced is a lost cause, dreading what one knows is quite unlikely, and so on.

These cases give us a puzzle, though. If dread is really a species of fear, then shouldn't its modularity be driven by the amygdala, and not by hedonic processing after all?

This is a deeper puzzle than contemporary neuroscience and contemporary philosophy are quite ready to solve. But there is a suggestion worth considering. As distinct structures, the amygdala and hedonic structures appear to have correspondingly distinct roles. The job of hedonic tone is to give us information about change in desire satisfaction; the job of the amygdala is to mediate innate fear responses and related emotional responses, and to support associative learning of new triggers for these responses. But as part of the ill-defined "limbic system," both receive signals, directly or indirectly, from the other, and send signals to the other. Perhaps it happens, then, that the amygdala can be triggered by cortical (and pre-cortical) representations, which is its primary role, but it can also be activated by gut-level expectations proper to the hedonic system. Perhaps, reciprocally, the hedonic system is designed to respond to gut-level expectations, but can also be activated by the amygdala. Then, in a given emotional episode, we would be justified in asking, not which system was responsible for the episode, but what role each system played in the episode: initiator or follower? The suggestion is one that warrants investigation, at least.

V. Conclusion

The path followed by this paper began as a straight highway of conceptual clarification and has ended up a track as convoluted as the surface of the brain itself. This is, I think, to be expected of work on the emotions, once it begins to ask not only "what is...?" but also "why is...?" questions, questions such as, "Why do the emotions display certain characteristic features of modularity?" Though I confess to a certain amount of frustration with the almost endless complications of explaining why things happen in our brains the way that they do, I cannot really say that I didn't expect it.

References

Aydede, M. 2000. An analysis of pleasure vis-à-vis pain. *Philosophy and Phenomenological Research* 61: 537–70.

Berns, G., S. M. McClure, G. Pagnoni, and P. Read Montague. 2001. Predictability modulates human brain response to reward. *Journal of Neuroscience* 21: 2793–98.

Damasio, A. 1994. *Descartes' Error: Emotion, Reason and the Human Brain*. New York: Putnam's.

Ekman, P. 1972. *Emotions in the Human Face*. New York: Pergamon.

Fodor, J. 1983. *The Modularity of Mind: An Essay in Faculty Psychology*. Cambridge (Mass.): MIT Press.

Gawin, F. 1991. Cocaine addiction: Psychology and neurophysiology. *Science* 268: 1580–86.

Goldie, P. 2000. *The Emotions: A Philosophical Exploration*. New York: Oxford University Press.

Green, O. H. 1992. *The Emotions*. Dordrecht: Kluwer.

Griffiths, P. E. 1997. *What Emotions Really Are: The Problem of Psychological Categories*. Chicago: University of Chicago Press.

James, W. 1890/1952. *The Principles of Psychology*. Toronto: Encyclopedia Britannica.

Kandel, E. R., J. H. Schwartz, and T. M. Jessell. 2000. *Principles of Neural Science*. 4th ed. New York: McGraw-Hill.

Knutson, B., C. M. Adams, G. W. Fong, and D. Hommer. 2001. Anticipation of increasing monetary reward selectively recruits nucleus accumbens. *Journal of Neuroscience* 21: 1–5.

LeDoux, J. 1996. *The Emotional Brain: The Mysterious Underpinnings of Emotional Life*. New York: Touchstone.

Liechti, M., and F. Vollenweider. 2000. Acute psychological and physiological effects of MDMA ("Ecstasy") after haloperidol pretreatment in healthy humans. *European Neuropsychopharmacology* 10: 289–95.

Millgram, E. 1997. *Practical Induction*. Cambridge (Mass.): Harvard University Press.

Pagnoni, G., C. F. Zink, P. R. Montague, and G. Berns. 2002. Activity in human ventral striatum locked to errors of reward prediction. *Nature Neuroscience* 5: 97–98.

Prinz, J. 2004. *Gut Reactions: A Perceptual Theory of Emotion*. New York: Oxford University Press.

Romo, R., and W. Schultz. 1990. Dopamine neurons of the monkey midbrain: Contingencies of response to active touch during self-initiated arm movements. *Journal of Neurophysiology* 63: 592–606.

Russell, B. 1921. *The Analysis of Mind*. London: George Allen and Unwin.

Ryle, G. 1949. *The Concept of Mind*. Chicago: Chicago University Press.

Ryle, G. 1954. Pleasure. *Proceedings of the Aristotelian Society*. Supplementary Volume 27.

Schroeder, T. 2004. *Three Faces of Desire*. New York: Oxford University Press.

Schultz, W., and R. Romo. 1990. Dopamine neurons of the monkey midbrain: Contingencies of response to stimuli eliciting immediate behavioral reactions. *Journal of Neurophysiology* 63: 607–24.

Schultz, W., L. Tremblay, and J. R. Hollerman. 2000. Reward processing in primate orbitofrontal cortex and basal ganglia. *Cerebral Cortex* 10: 272–83.

Tye, M. 1995. *Ten Problems of Consciousness*. Cambridge (Mass.): MIT Press.

Notes on Contributors

Vincent Bergeron is currently finishing his PhD in philosophy at the University of British Columbia. He works on the philosophy of cognitive science and aesthetics. His doctoral dissertation, which he is writing under the supervision of Mohan Matthen, is on cognitive architecture. He has an article on a new approach to the modularity of mind, which has just appeared in *Philosophical Psychology*, and one on the ontology of music (written in collaboration with Dominic Lopes), which will soon appear in *Philosophy and Phenomenological Research*.

Robyn Bluhm received her doctorate in philosophy from the University of Western Ontario. She is now a postdoctoral fellow in the Department of Psychiatry at Western, where her research focuses on using functional magnetic resonance imaging to examine alterations in the "default" network in psychiatric disorders. This research also informs her philosophical work on the epistemology of medicine and psychiatry.

Louis C. Charland is a philosopher who specializes in the study of affect and emotion and the history and philosophy of psychiatry. He is currently associate professor in the Department of Philosophy at the University of Western Ontario, in London, Canada, where he also has appointments in the Faculty of Health Sciences and the Department of Psychiatry in the Schulich School of Medicine and Dentistry. Previous appointments include various teaching, research, and policy positions at McGill University's Faculty of Medicine, the Toronto Hospital for Sick Children, and the Ontario Premier's Council on Health Strategy. Current research includes work on decisional capacity and anorexia and a book on the role of the passions in nineteenth-century moral treatment during the formative decades of modern psychiatry.

Ronald de Sousa is Professor Emeritus of Philosophy at the University of Toronto. He was educated in Switzerland, Oxford, and Princeton.

He is a Fellow of the Royal Society of Canada. He is the author of *The Rationality of Emotion* (MIT 1987) and *Évolution et rationalité* (PUF 2004), of which *Why Think?: Evolution and the Rational Mind* (OUP 2007) is an improved English version. He has published over a hundred articles, chapters, or reviews in a variety of periodicals and books. His current research interests focus on emotions, evolutionary theory, cognitive science, sex, and the puzzle of religious belief. His next book, also from OUP, will be *Emotional Truth*.

Paul Dumouchel is professor at the Graduate School of Core Ethics and Frontier Sciences of Ritsumeikan University, in Kyoto, Japan, where he teaches political philosophy. He is author of *Émotions: essai sur le corps et le social* as well as several articles on trust, moral sentiments, the strategic role and the biological dimension of emotions. He is presently working on a book on political violence and co-editing (with Reiko Gotoh) a collection on Amartya Sen and social justice, which is due to appear at Cambridge University Press.

Luc Faucher is an associate professor at the Université du Québec à Montréal. He published many papers on emotions, racial cognition and evolutionary psychology. Recently (2006), he has edited a volume of *Philosophiques* on philosophy and psychopathologies. He is also editing (with Pierre Poirier) a book on the philosophy of neuroscience.

Anne Jaap Jacobson is professor of philosophy and electrical and computer engineering at the University of Houston, where she is director of the Center for Neuro-Engineering and Cognitive Science. While her most recent research focuses on cognitive neuroscience and its implications for an externalist theory of the mind, she also works in feminist philosophy and in the history of philosophy.

Karen Jones is senior lecturer in philosophy at the University of Melbourne. She has written extensively on trust in both its epistemic and ethical dimensions. Her recent work focuses on emotion, rationality, and agency. Her work has appeared in *Ethics*, the *Journal of Philosophy*, and in the collections *Setting the Moral Compass: Essays by*

Women Philosophers and *A Mind of One's Own*. Much of her work is from a feminist perspective.

Mohan Matthen is Canada Research Chair in Philosophy, Perception, and Communication at the University of Toronto. He works on philosophical topics in perception and on philosophy of biology. His book *Seeing, Doing, and Knowing* was published by Oxford University Press in 2005, and he is currently working on a book on sensory phenomenology. An article arguing in favour of conceptual sensory content has just appeared in *Philosophical Topics*, and one on auditory objects will soon appear in the *European Review of Philosophy*.

Jesse J. Prinz is professor of philosophy at the University of North Carolina at Chapel Hill. His work focuses on the nature of the mind and the role of perception, emotion, and cultural experience in grounding human knowledge and values. His most recent book is *The Emotional Construction of Morals*, and he is also the author of *Furnishing the Mind: Concepts and Their Perception Basis* and *Gut Reactions: A Perceptual Theory of Emotion*, as well two forthcoming titles, *Beyond Human Nature* and *The Conscious Brain*.

Ruwen Ogien is research director at the Centre National de la Recherche Scientifique (CNRS, Paris). He has published several books on moral philosophy, the philosophy of action, and the philosophy of social sciences, including *Les causes et les raisons : Philosophie analytique et sciences humaines* (1995) *La honte est-elle immorale ?* (2002), *Le rasoir de Kant et autres essais de philosophie pratique* (2003), *La panique morale* (2004), *L'éthique aujourd'hui : Maximalistes et minimalistes* (2007).

James A. Russell spent twenty-five years at the University of British Columbia and then moved to Boston College, where he is chair of the Department of Psychology. His research has ranged from studies on the role of the amygdala in interpreting human facial expressions to a review of ethnographic and linguistic evidence on cultural variations in people's concepts of emotion to the psychometrics of the structure of emotion. A 2003 article entitled "Core affect and the psychological construction of emotion" is his attempt to integrate these strands.

Timothy Schroeder is associate professor of philosophy at Ohio State University. He works on the philosophy of mind and moral psychology. He has published a book on desire (*Three Faces of Desire*: OUP 2004) and papers on topics including concepts, consciousness, and Tourette syndrome.

Andrew Sneddon is associate professor of philosophy at the University of Ottawa. He specializes in moral philosophy and philosophical psychology. He is the author of *Action and Responsibility* (Springer 2006) and has published articles in such journals as *Philosophical Studies, Philosophical Psychology, Utilitas, Ethical Theory and Moral Practice, Journal of Applied Philosophy,* and *Metaphilosophy.* He is currently working on a book about externalism and moral psychology.

Christine Tappolet is Canada Research Chair in Ethics and Meta-ethics and associate professor at the Université de Montréal. She has written several articles on meta-ethics, moral psychology, and the philosophy of emotions, and is the author of *Émotions et Valeurs* (PUF 2000) and, with Ruwen Ogien, of *Les Concepts de l'éthique* (La Découverte 2008). She has also edited a number of volumes, including, with Sarah Stroud, a collection of articles entitled *Weakness of Will and Practical Irrationality* (OUP 2003).

Index